AN ORDINARY LIFE...?

AN ORDINARY LIFE...?

ANDREW MICHAEL DOIG

Matador
9 Priory Business Park,
Wistow Road, Kibworth Beauchamp,
Leicestershire. LE8 0RX
Tel: 0116 279 2299
Email: books@troubador.co.uk
Web: www.troubador.co.uk/matador
Twitter: @matadorbooks

ISBN 978 1788033 312

British Library Cataloguing in Publication Data.
A catalogue record for this book is available from the British Library.

Printed and bound by CPI Group (UK) Ltd, Croydon, CR0 4YY
Typeset in 12pt Aldine401 BT by Troubador Publishing Ltd, Leicester, UK

Matador is an imprint of Troubador Publishing Ltd

This book is dedicated to all in spirit who have encouraged me, taught me, inspired me, helped me and love me.

CONTENTS

PART 2
Interpretations

PURPOSE

Like very many others, I was not born a natural medium. I had no psychic gifts that I, or others, were aware of, though occasionally odd things did occur, but these were usually dismissed, as there was no explanation evident at the time. This situation continued until in my mid-forties. At that time I began to investigate with an open mind, and as a result many wonderful teachings, knowledge, happenings and gifts came my way. There was no guidebook; indeed, at the beginning I was reliant on others lending their precious books to me. So the purpose of this book, is to help, encourage, prompt and urge others in the same situation, to investigate for themselves.

We all have different talents, and psychic gifts can emerge in later life, just as they happen in those born with the wonderful gift of seeing, hearing and sensing spirit. Who knows, you may acquire the gift of healing, of clairvoyance, of psychic art, of being a speaker, of being a 'powerhouse', of being a scribe for higher philosophy, an organiser, a physical medium, a good listener, a helper, a teacher, a trance speaker, an inspirer. Apart from this what will emerge is a greater understanding of the real purpose of the material life, and the actual spiritual nature of humanity.

The events and details that are related in the following pages are my true experiences and recollections. Having kept notebooks since 1994, I have extensive material to refer to, but prior to that date I have to rely on memory, which, as we know, can sometimes dim with the passage of time. However, the fact that I can still today remember some events so long ago marks them out as special, and in my humble opinion often is an indication of the influence of our friends from the 'other side', or spirit.

The following is a condensed and abbreviated timeline of my 'spiritual' life so far. It has not been written because my life has been that interesting or that I think myself in any way important, but rather because it has been very ordinary – perhaps many would think it dull – yet incidents have happened that suggest the influence of others not living a purely material existence. So it is of these and other odd incidents that I write.

I truly believe that we all have spirit helpers, some for a brief time maybe, others for longer, and at least one who will be overseeing the whole of our life on Earth. This reflects the devoted service and love that is shown by what most term "the dead", who try to help and guide us – if we let them. Many of our triumphs and brilliant ideas were not 'ours' at all, but prompted by those unseen, unacknowledged and unknown.

INTRODUCTION

The book is divided into two separate sections. Part 1-'Experiences', is the straightforward record of the main psychic or spiritual events as I remember them, or how I recorded them at, or soon after they occurred. For the period prior to my note taking, which started in 1994, it is entirely reliant on memory, though I have tried to be as accurate and truthful as possible, as the circumstances allow. This has been set down as far as it is feasible in chronological order, though occasionally this has proved difficult, and then a rough estimate given.

I should explain a personal quirk of punctuation. During dialogue when person 'A' pauses and another speaks after a pause, 'A's sentence will end thus: ..." Where 'A' has been interrupted, his/her sentence will end thus: .." Also there may be sections where the 'Queen's English' may seem to be forgotten. However, it is important that I give a truthful account of what was actually said or written. Spirit have to use a human instrument and each medium will affect what they receive to a greater or lesser degree.

In the early Chapters I have given some brief explanations in relation to certain phenomena. Later on there may be given ideas that I had at that time, but these may not correspond to my opinions that I now hold. As we travel through life we are constantly exposed to new ideas and our thoughts, beliefs and viewpoints will be revised.

Part 2 is devoted to trying to give an explanation to some of my psychic and spiritual experiences. These are entirely my own opinions, based on limited knowledge, reading, experience, debate and philosophy. Each time that I have thought that I had arrived at some definitive 'truth', something would come along to demolish it, if only partly. So these ideas expressed here are the ones I had when this was written – I may have moved slightly on some of it, as it is an evolving process.

Included in this section are what I believe to be a few fundamental 'facts', though I realise that even some 'spiritualists' may disagree with what I have to say. At the end of the day, we all have to come to our own conclusions; it is better that the mistakes are ours rather than we follow the mistakes of others.

This leads me finally to the whole purpose of this work. I am not an intellectual, I am not special, I am only an ordinary person. If these things happen to me, then I am sure they happen to everyone. So I ask the reader to review their life and see if similar 'odd' occurrences can be found. All I wish is that they think about them, and then try to seek the truth for themselves. It is a journey that is most illuminating and most important.

PART 1

EXPERIENCES

CHAPTER 1

The Early Years

I was born one autumn evening during 1947 in the city of Belfast, Northern Ireland. Having read that a few people have extremely early memories, some even being in the uterus, I have to assure the reader that I have no such abilities, not even when I was apparently stung by a bee in my pram.

Roughly at the age of two, the family moved to live for a few years in Scotland, where my father had been born and raised. During this time it happened that I was nipped by a dog, appropriately a Scottie, which gave me an ingrained distrust of dogs for the rest of my life.

Conventional science informs us that we have five senses, with which we work and use to understand and live in this material world. They are the sense of sight, smell, hearing, taste and touch. With these we can experience great variation and sensitivity, even though there can be limitations in the extent of their range. We know that creatures like dogs can hear higher sound frequencies than humans; similarly our visible range is a fraction of the total spectrum. Yet we have enough to manage and survive on this planet; indeed our success has now reached a scale where our over population as well as our pollution has begun to pose serious risks for us, and for many other species.

Some of our earliest memories are related to our senses, so that when we encounter that sense again, the earlier memory will be triggered. My earliest memory goes back to roughly when I was two years old, but interestingly this did not come into my mind until I was about twenty years of age. I can remember how it occurred quite clearly. I was on a bus travelling along Sandy Row in Belfast, going to the main bus depot and train station in Great Victoria Street. Suddenly I smelt pipe tobacco, the variety that my paternal grandfather had smoked. At that point I had the memory of how I used to sit on his lap, and after he had lit his pipe he would allow me to blow the match out. Also I remembered being very fascinated by his pocket watch that he allowed me to look at and listen to.

The smell of the pipe tobacco was gone as quickly as it came. There were very few passengers and none were smoking a pipe, indeed no one was smoking at all. [This was long before the regulations on smoking were introduced.] I was completely baffled by the occurrence. However, that moment of that day is etched on my memory; I couldn't tell you anything else that I did that day. It would take over three decades to pass before I could find an answer as to how it had happened. I have the view that my grandfather, who had died many years earlier, came near to me at that moment. The clarity of the experience is typical of an encounter with spirit. Much the same as when one has a rare 'dream' that is unlike any other dream, the clearness and lucidity of it marks it out as 'special'. Almost without exception this attests to the work of spirit.

In this category is my next earliest memory, when I was about five years old, and the family was back in Northern Ireland. Playing on my own, suddenly I stopped what I had been doing: aware that I was not alone although there was nobody in sight. The material world became of no significance as I was surrounded by love, and in my mind I understood that I had a guardian, that I was always being looked after, that I was always loved. This was not a voice heard speaking, it was total awareness in my mind and heart.

The awareness came and went, and I got on with my childhood without another thought, I just accepted it as children do. Yet that awareness was so special that it was etched into my memory. Now this memory had nothing to do with sight, smell, hearing, taste or touch. It was nothing to do with the five senses of this material world, it was to do with the spirit, and I was aware because I also am of spirit. It was spirit connecting to spirit in love, and because it was so spiritual in nature the memory is lodged in the mind, not just the brain, because mind too is of the spirit. That is why the clarity is greater than material memories.

It is around this period that I begin to have many more memories, such as being awakened very suddenly after falling asleep in the back seat of a car. The car went on fire, but I was rescued quite quickly without coming to any harm, and the fire was quickly put out. I remember my maternal grandmother reading stories to me from a wonderful book full of lovely pictures, and the time when we slid down the stairs on our backsides when her arthritis was proving painful. She died not long after this time, and having left money in her will for the education of my elder brother and I, at the age of six I went to a boarding school.

My mother later said that she regretted agreeing to sending me at such a young age, but I enjoyed it, for there were lots of games and sports that I loved, as well as hobbies and other activities like clubs and theatre. The school would not be allowed to exist these days under Health & Safety regulations! Much of it could have been classed as a fire hazard – indeed part of it burnt down much later on – and there were the occasional outbreaks of illness due to bad food hygiene, which I think was less serious in those days rather than the modern varieties. At least the school instilled in each pupil a sense of right and wrong, manners, a moral compass and an attitude of social obligation that in this age seems to be old fashioned.

During my time there I had several close encounters with lightning. The first was when the school went to the beach for a swim, the pupils riding there on their bicycles. Our journey required us to cross over part of an old disused aerodrome. When I arrived at this section of the journey the weather seemed to change and be a little unsettled, though it had been hot and sunny earlier in the morning. Suddenly, there was a huge flash of forked lightning that struck the ground only about ten metres away. I hurried on trying to reassure myself and lessen my fear by repeating over and over, "you're fine, you're on rubber tyres"!

The second occasion was much more dramatic. I can understand if some find it unbelievable, but I saw and experienced it and assert that it is factual – unless it wasn't lightning, in which case I ask what could it have been? In a rectangular dormitory that contained two rows of cast iron beds, the head of each set against the long opposing walls, giving space between each bed and a passage in the centre to the door. On one side were three large windows that were half open, while I was in my bed opposite the windows. I saw a flash of lightning enter through one end window, travel along the centre passage and exit in less than a second through the other end window. The lightning must have been no more than one and a half metres from me at one point.

At around twelve years old, one episode at school is particularly notable, at a time when I avidly read Western novels and that genre was a staple of the film industry. During 'Prep' (a time given when pupils had to do set exercises for revision or prepare work for future classes) – that lasted for at least an hour – we were given a choice of writing an essay or poem for English. There may have been a range of subjects to choose from, but my memory has not been up to that detail. At the time I was reading a *really, really* interesting Western book, and so I decided that I would read for a while and then do the essay – I never was keen on poetry at that age.

Well, the book was *extremely* riveting, so much so that I lost my sense of time. When I finally looked at the clock I was horrified to see that only fifteen minutes remained to write my essay. There was no way that I could do it. But…then I thought…well, a poem doesn't have to be that long…so…surely I could write something that had a rhyme in the time remaining. The idea of a storm came to my mind, with waves crashing on the shore. The lines just 'popped' into my head and before I knew it the poem was finished – with time to spare! Gosh! I hadn't realised that writing poetry was so simple, what a fool I was to be writing an essay when it was so much quicker and easier to jot down a poem! Reading over my poem I was pleased and thought it really very good indeed. So did my English teacher, who praised me for it and decided to include it in the school magazine.

So, I was all set for the next English 'Prep', this time with a new cowboy novel to read. It too was exciting, but I made sure I didn't use up all the time reading, and when the last quarter of an hour approached I set it aside to compose my next rhyming masterpiece. However, try as I might, NOTHING popped into my head this time. Despair, and then desperation set in! But I then recalled that there was a poem near the beginning of the book. Even now I can remember the first couple of lines of it:

He was only a lavender cowboy
And the hairs on his chest were two…

[I have looked it up on the Internet and found that there are many versions, but Harold Hersey penned the original. It has been set to music and appeared in a 1930 Western film "Oklahoma Cyclone".] By now I was sweating and rushed to copy out the poem, but with some of the words used being outwith my full comprehension, I was not feeling good about it.

My English teacher decided to have a word with me. He said he found the poem really funny, but asked where the idea had come from, and did I really know what 'carbolic' was? Sweating profusely, I just about managed to wangle my way out of that interrogation. Never did I attempt to write another poem! My reading was confined to my own time or when I had completed all my set work. But that did not quite end the agony of it – my teacher also included this poem in the school magazine under *my* name. I was horrified when I saw it, imagining some of the parents writing to the headmaster to say that it had been 'pinched' from the same book that they had read, or that the author would be told about it and I would end up in prison. Luckily, as it turned out, nobody was that interested in it! Oh what a tangled web we weave!

When writing "The Storm", it had seemed so easy and clear, indeed, I had seen the storm visually into the bargain. It is only now looking back that I can realise that it had all been prompted by spirit, who kindly helped me out of a sticky situation – but very definitely were not going to make a habit of it! It had another purpose; it would remind me much later in my life just how close and how long spirit has been with me, even if I had no awareness at the time.

The only two other noteworthy incidents were an unearthly 'wailing' one dark night that could not be identified, though it made the hairs stand on end at the back of my neck. It was suggested by somebody that it was a 'banshee', who is according to Irish tradition a female spirit that warns of impending death. That seemed a very reasonable explanation at the time, and while now it would be easy to attribute it to an animal, I still keep an open mind on it. The other was seeing the tiny spot of light that was the Soviet 'Sputnik' zooming across the sky, and hearing its constant beep on a crystal set of another pupil.

CHAPTER 2

Secondary Education

Having tried a few wristwatches (my first had a picture of the singer and cowboy Gene Autry), I had to abandon them as they just stopped and refused to work! So when I went on to my next school, it was with a pocket watch, similar but maybe not as good as the one that my grandfather owned. However, within a few years I did manage to wear a wristwatch, though the first couple at the beginning tended to run either a bit fast or a bit slow.

By this time my reading material had changed to a much more varied diet, and I also found a new enthusiasm. While most of my fellow pupils studied their schoolbooks and gave attention to the teachers, I spent much of my time following my favourite interest – horse racing! Sitting at the back of the class I studied form, noting past efforts of the horses on that day's racing, seeing whether they ran best on soft or hard ground, what distance was their best, and so on. It became my major preoccupation, for not only did I like to bet on the horses, but in addition I was the school 'bookie', from whence I derived my main source of income.

There are lots of gamblers who freely like to give advice to others on what horse to put their money on. "It's a dead cert", they will say, "sure to win". Yet these people seldom seem to make any money and keep chasing that elusive run of luck that will make their fortune. Most of us know that it is a very difficult task to pick a winner even when there are only a few horses in the race, as there are so many imponderable factors involved. With much studying of form I could usually make a good educated guess at which horses were likely to be there near the finish, and sometimes I won money but often I lost it.

Twice however, I *knew* what horse would win. This is not to be confused with premonition; it was much, much more than that. I knew it not only in my head, but also in my heart, in my bones, in the very depth of my being. I have never been able to explain adequately this total awareness and feeling, to get across the utter certainty, the *absolute knowledge* of these two moments. That it happened once is amazing in itself, but to happen twice is a double miracle, a blessing that could only be truly appreciated much later on in life. I now think that both these experiences were only possible because *I was unable* to back either of the horses at the time. It was yet another 'marker', repeated a second time to really ensure that I would never forget them. These signs and markers were placed before me, some to get me to think, but most merely to occur and stay in my memory, their significance and relevance only becoming apparent when I eventually 'awoke' many decades later. I believe most people experience similar occurrences, though fitted to their particular circumstances, interests and life. Sadly, many just simply dismiss them.

The only other significant area at this time was religion. While I was quite interested in getting an understanding of God, I couldn't believe much that was told to me. Refusing to undergo confirmation, I opted to take 'Religious Study', thinking that I might be given deeper and more meaningful information. However, when realising that this was not going to occur, the subject was dropped very quickly. I toyed with the idea of being a monk, having the time to contemplate and study – until I latched on to the fact that gardening would play a big part of that life!

At that stage in my life God was never that far from my mind, and this was reinforced by the headmaster being a minister, as was another teacher, and yet another was a lay preacher. Into the bargain we all had to attend both a morning and evening service, seven days a week, in the school chapel. Pupils would line up in the cloister area and then there would be a procession, in a double line, of all into the chapel. I got very concerned near the end of my time at school, that I could never remember what had occurred during the service! Try as I might before going in and as determined as I could be to pay the utmost attention to what would transpire, whenever I filed out with the others it was only then that I 'awoke', to discover that my mind was a complete blank – I couldn't remember a thing! This continued day after day for quite some time until

I just gave up trying. Perhaps as I was becoming an agnostic – and even thinking about being an atheist – my subconscious was blocking it all. I now think that spirit had a part to play, turning me away from any thoughts of a close religious life, as that was not the pathway that had been planned for me.

CHAPTER 3

Treading Water

My examination results were neither 'good' nor 'bad', although if I had studied less horse racing they might have been the former! Geography had been my best subject and I had a vague thought that I might follow a geology course at Trinity College, Dublin, but now that did not seem likely. In the end I opted to take Business Studies at Magee University in Derry. This choice was prompted by trying to please my father; rather silly really, as I was not at all interested in business!

The first event happened very early on. Still with some interest in horse racing, I looked into a local bookmaker during the first couple of weeks. Here I saw a fellow student betting quite heavily, seeming to be interested in nearly every race. It was not long before he dropped out of the university and I learnt that he had lost his entire grant for the year to the 'bookie'. It is very doubtful that I would have followed such a course of action, but it did bring home to me the dangers of addiction. It is a lesson that stood me in good stead in the following years, when I met the widespread interest in various kinds of drugs by the 'swinging' generation.

My lack of interest in business showed when I failed a few of my exams, although as I had nothing positive to replace it, I decided to do the resits. In the meantime it was the summer holidays, and I went over to England to earn some money being a waiter in a hotel in Skegness. Here I was given another sign or marker, and while many may merely dismiss this as pure coincidence, I believe such occurrences are more profound in their nature and have happened many times to me throughout my life.

I was cleaning out a room used by the hotel for late night diners and found lots of aniseed balls on the floor. After this, while having breakfast with the rest of the staff, the headwaiter, out of the blue, asked my opinion on a particular horse race. This person was a gambler and always studied the day's racing in his paper. Though I still had the odd 'flutter' on the horses now and again I didn't talk about it, so was taken by surprise at his request. I looked down the list of horses and saw one called 'Aniseed'! I told him that it would win, but he just laughed, it was a rank outsider and he thought that it hadn't any chance at all. Needless to say the horse came romping home to his complete amazement. He continued to seek my advice until realising that I could not repeat the phenomenon.

Having carried my business books over with me, I returned home without any revision having been done; therefore as expected I duly failed the resits. So now I was on the dole and on the lookout for a job. Applying to join the Civil Service, at the interview I was given the option of getting a job locally, or moving up a grade and working in London. Well, it was with no hesitation that I naturally chose to go to the 'Big Smoke'.

The main incident that I wish to relate happened shortly after I arrived in London. Although in work, circumstances were such that I found things quite tight financially. During this period I experienced facing a bleak weekend with only two shillings (10p) in my pocket. Looking at a weekend in the capital, unable to do or buy anything, put me in a very miserable frame of mind: two shillings – what could I do with that? I might as well stick it on a horse! So that is precisely what I did. Going to the bookmakers nearby, I realised that getting one winner would not be enough, so I decided to do a 'double', choosing two horses to win. Looking over the board of runners my eyes were drawn to two horses, both being outsiders and therefore had long odds. I placed my bet, but didn't have to wait long before they both won! I collected my pound notes and had a great weekend eating, drinking and going to the cinema, forgetting for the moment how incredible it really was.

London was an eye-opener for me, and I learnt much about people, prejudice, poverty, race, culture and food etc. I had a great time going to the cinema, as well as seeing many of the pop music groups, most of them in the free concerts that were held in Hyde Park, including Pink Floyd and the Rolling Stones. During this time I also took evening classes to pass my Art 'O' Level; a subject that I had always been interested in from an early age, but it had not been included in my secondary school curriculum. The many galleries were a great stimulus, as I was introduced to the very new as well as to the styles of the past. However, I became aware that I didn't want a career in the Civil Service, and decided that I should follow my life long passion and head back home after two and a half years in 'Swinging London'.

Starting with an Art Foundation course in Belfast, I ended up getting my honours degree in England, before travelling back for a post-graduate course in the Belfast Art College. During this time I thought long and hard over what I should do next. Despite my father generously offering to convert a barn into a studio for me, if I wished to follow a career as an artist, I thought that teaching was the direction that I should go, and so completed my Art Teachers Diploma. Not long after this I got a post in a secondary school in the lowlands of Scotland. Interestingly, during all this time since leaving London I cannot recall any unusual happenings of a psychic or spiritual nature.

CHAPTER 4

Back to School

Initially, I had thought that my time at this school would be fairly short, and that after getting through my probationary period I would probably head to a bigger town or even a city. However, with each passing year this desire lessened, finding some excuse to stay and put off any possible move. In the end I remained at the school for thirty-four years before I retired, and still live in the town, so you could say that I kind of like both the people and the area!

At this point I'm going to break with the time line that has been followed so far, as most of the events that I will be detailing will have occurred outside the domain of formal education. Yet some incidents have been noteworthy and will be described shortly. First I wish to give a more general view of what I consider has been help in my teaching from those friends in spirit. The guidance given to me has necessarily been discreet, and probably more often for the pupils' benefit rather than mine. Ideas have 'popped' into my head to do certain things, or watch certain individuals, or to stop what I was about to do and make me change tack.

One particular day early in my career, I had set out individual objects in front of each pupil so that they could do a pencil study. After giving them a few minutes to get started, I had intended to go around the class and help any who may be struggling, but suddenly I felt that I should sit down and just 'watch'. What a revelation that was! Watching carefully, I soon discovered for how little time some of the pupils actually looked at the object in front of them, and how they approached the task and what level of concentration was brought to bear! It was something that I did more often and changed the way I approached particular aspects of my teaching.

This direction from spirit also happened just a few years before I retired. Instead of admonishing a certain boy, who was often disruptive, again I was given the feeling to just watch and not say anything for the moment. I let the banter with his friends continue, and then realised that he seemed a bit deaf, especially in one ear. I duly wrote a note concerning this fact to the Guidance Department, but got a very frosty reply, to the effect that I was not a doctor and should mind my own business and there was nothing wrong with him. All I could do was shrug my shoulders and say to myself that at least I had done what I thought was right. However, a few months later one of the Deputy Headmasters came to see me, and related that the mother of that boy had just informed the school that her son had hearing problems!

Nevertheless, this counsel from spirit didn't always work one way. One particular pupil seemed to receive rebukes and sharp responses from me, until one day the word 'why?' popped into my head. When I thought about it, there seemed to be no reason at all, he was a perfectly normal boy and his manner and behaviour didn't justify my reaction. So I made sure that I changed my attitude towards him. [I will come back to this again in Part Two]

Occasionally, pupils would confide in me about 'psychic stuff'. I remember one girl who related that she experienced disturbing things in her bedroom and was a bit scared about it. It seems that she had sensed a presence in the room, and was sure that it had actually sat on her bed. My first reaction was to try and calm her fears, and gave the 'ghost' the name of Fred. I told her that she should take command of her room, and talk nicely to Fred, telling him that he was in the wrong place, that he should just go to the light, where people he knew were waiting for him. This she did, though it took a month or so before she reported that Fred had gone. One of the adverse consequences of some television 'shows' concerning this area is the building up of the sense of fear, more to do with inserting drama and keeping ratings up than informing the public.

The last episode that I wish to refer to didn't happen in school, but rather on a school trip. Every so often, when there were some big exhibitions in London, we would take a group of senior pupils down to see them over a weekend, going down on the Friday night and returning on the Sunday. In 1985 there was a major exhibition of Chagall at the Royal Academy and also a Renoir exhibition at the Hayward Gallery. Not having enough numbers to make it viable, we teamed up with another school nearby, and we all, plus my girlfriend, duly went down to London, arriving in the early morning. Naturally, at the end of that day we were all quite tired, and glad to go to our rooms for much needed sleep.

I was awoken in the small hours of the morning by loud screams from my girlfriend! Trying to calm her down, I asked her if she had just had a bad nightmare. But she was adamant that this was not the case, she had seen a figure at the end of my bed. When I questioned further she related that it had been naked and had looked just like me! [Again I will refer to this in Part Two]

That didn't give a great start to the day, and at breakfast one of the pupils from the other school had an epileptic fit, and he was rushed to hospital with his teacher beside him. I had to take the whole group to the Renoir Exhibition, but the pupils were not really interested, they had got a fright too at breakfast and their thoughts were naturally with their friend, concerned for his welfare. I did my best to reassure them, saying he was in the best place for a good recovery, but it was an anxious group that I accompanied. We did in fact leave on the Sunday without him, but he made a good recovery and arrived home a day or two later.

My girlfriend wouldn't talk any further about her experience, despite my attempts to do so, therefore I never got to allay her fears or even give an explanation – she just wanted it to go away, and dealt with it by refusing to think about it!

CHAPTER 5

The Slow Awakening

For most of the time since my own schooldays, I had thought little about religion and had become a normal everyday materialist. So it was a shock when, around the mid 1980s, one pupil put up their hand in class and said, "Please sir, can I ask you a question?" I indicated for her to go on, and then she said, "Do you believe in God?" Well, it was so unexpected that I didn't know what to say! I had no idea what I believed! In the event I really don't know what I exactly said.

That didn't really jerk me out of my materialistic lifestyle, but when another pupil a year later asked *exactly the same two questions*, I had to sit up and take notice. Now I began my 'search', which started with joining a night class on astrology, which I took further by attending a weeklong course in Glasgow, and then doing a correspondence course. I even introduced a lunchtime astrology club at school for a while, and started writing an astrology manual that could be used by them. However, lots of changes were happening and I never managed to finish the manual before the club closed. The symbolism of the subject interested me and about that time I bought my first pack of tarot cards.

Deciding to try a little experiment, I got a colleague's mother to choose a number of cards, and then later I consulted the accompanying book to give her a 'reading'. Well, I was a bit worried and perplexed, for in her past all I seemed to get was death. I confided to my colleague about this, and after talking with her mother, it transpired that she did have quite a few miscarriages at the start of her marriage. This spooked me, and I then perceived that this was no game or simply fun, as it could have serious consequences in the wrong hands. I never tried to do that again, although

I've bought a few more tarot packs through the years, but only for their imagery.

Other changes were happening; after a few disappointing efforts I finally stopped smoking; my girlfriend and I broke up; I decided to take up hill walking; later went to Buddhist meditation meetings. Then one day I saw in the local paper that there was an evening of clairvoyance at the Community Centre. Intrigued, I decided to see what it was all about. On entering the room I was greeted by this smiling lady, who suddenly asked me if I would be interested in going along to a healing group that met every Monday. Taken by surprise, I said yes, and then wondered what on earth I had got myself into! I remember nothing else about the clairvoyant evening.

The first meeting arrived and I was introduced to the seven or eight people there by that same smiling lady, who was called Audrey Peachey. Her husband Mike was the representative for southwest Scotland for the National Federation of Spiritual Healers. There followed a talk on the energy system around the body, talk of an aura and the series of chakras, which were spinning wheels of energy. It all seemed a bit complicated and eastern in influence. When asked if I wanted some healing, I very firmly, but politely, declined, saying I really felt fine. Asked if I would come again, I again said yes, not quite sure why but at least it didn't look like a dangerous cult!

At the second meeting Audrey changed her tack, and asked me to give healing to somebody else. I started to protest that I knew nothing about how to do it, but she calmly asked me to just see if I could feel any of the energies. So I did as instructed and…I was astounded! Yes, I could indeed feel energy, but not only that; I could feel the energy at the chakra points spinning! This was not a load of nonsense; all that they had been telling me was true, and it had incredible possibilities. Even I may in time be able to help others through this method. In that instant I was on a firm course, and joined the NFSH as a probationer in 1994. I went down to Camberley in England both in 1995 and 1996 to take the required healing courses, and continuing with the healing group got my full healer membership in 1998.

The meetings were not just confined to techniques and education on healing alone, there was usually a time set-aside for meditation. Basically, we tried to relax the brain as well as the body, sometimes in silence, though usually with quiet music; at other times there would be a visualisation, where somebody would talk us through an imagined walk in the forest, or by the sea, or some other picture in the mind's eye. During these meditations, often various images would form, some totally different to what one would expect, and others could be odd and baffling. It took me almost six months even to learn to relax my body, and I had (and still have) great difficulty in relaxing my mind, although it is easier to do when there are several people joining in.

To give an idea of some of the images that came to me, I have copied some early extracts from my notes; whenever I do this I shall use another typeface to make that clear.

31/01/94 Very relaxed. Started with a vague face, then a pinkish purple colour came into another face that was looking right - it came in 'pulses', going slightly fuzzy each time until it disappeared. Next a young man's face, late 20s, which changed into a young girl. Later a line drawing of a head in bright yellow. Then a young person, small image of a head, which turned into an old man. At the end there came a head and shoulders straight on - but no face, like a surreal image - a mirror behind with the same image on it.

21/02/94 Very relaxed. Little in the way of faces - which were very brief - but a fantastic light display. Similar to a fireworks display in that it was spectacular and with vivid colours - but really organised, changing patterns, sudden switches of colour, and again gradual changes at other times. At the very end saw a small light spot that focused into a crystal, cut like a diamond.

2/05/94 Very relaxed. Had a soft chair tonight. Asked to visualise a many faceted crystal - but I failed to do that. Got flashes of faces and lips, all the latter in profile. Just for a split second "saw" a black robed figure behind me -

but no head. Felt that if I had longer time I would have "known" the person. At any rate I felt that the figure was there to help me, as if 'it' was going to place 'its' hands on my shoulders. My neck tingled and this sensation went round my left side of the neck to my throat. A little later I saw a window - just by itself and not attached to any house etc. It was open, but something was not quite right. There was a slant in the glass area, but I couldn't understand what was not right or if it was just a reflection. Then a door appeared - wooden, closed, and again just on its own. Felt that this was probably symbolic and that I should really open it, but it faded away. Again flashes of faces appeared and also eyes which I understood to be all female and either Egyptian or Arabic. Got a few colours after this.

For those with little knowledge about spiritual healing, I have given a chapter in Part 2 on the subject, with some accounts from experiences that occurred during the healing sessions. However, due to the confidentiality due to all those who were involved in this, no names can be given, nor any clues that might identify them.

CHAPTER 6

Laying the Foundations

The healing opened up a totally new territory for me, but I did not remain just in that narrow focus. I was now interested in a diverse range of subjects. I continued to go to meetings of the local Spiritualist Group (CDSG, founded in 1992) as well as attending an open circle in another town. One lady – Doris Lowe, who gave her time and advice to the Spiritualist Group in the early years, ran a Between Friends Trust (BFT), which put on occasional events and helped people financially. This BFT put on a day workshop in a hotel near Lockerbie in June 1994, with the renowned medium Ursula Roberts. It had a very good attendance and I thoroughly enjoyed it, but sad to say I didn't take down any notes! Doris stepped in to help the Spiritualist Group in August of that year when a medium had to cancel at the last minute. She gave an evening talk and workshop on 'psychometry', my first introduction to that subject. The local Town Hall was even filled with 'An Evening of Clairvoyants', the mediums being Alastair Forbes, Clemmie Harvey and Mary Duffy.

In November I attended a talk on Past Life Therapy, followed the next morning by an all day workshop on the subject. Though I found it interesting, I also realised some of the dangers that might be inherent in its procedure, and never felt the urge to undergo it myself. However, I know that many people have been helped to overcome some difficulties in this life by going through what is called a regression to a past life, which may help to explain why they may have an inborn fear or phobia.

Then the BFT, from 18th to 20th November, put on 'Experimental Pathways to Mediumship', again in the hotel near Lockerbie, with Eileen Roberts, who was the President of the Institute of Spiritualist Mediums, and an assistant. I was given some financial assistance for this, which was much appreciated. This time I made notes of the proceedings and can refer to some of the programme. To those who may not know what kind of activity this sort of seminar involves, I give below a brief outline of the range of events, and will also quote some of my notes concerning one particular incident that did not make me – or Eileen – at all happy! Friday:

4.00pm. Registration, settling in.

6.00pm. Dinner.

8.00pm. "Energy Re-actions". Sensing energy between your hands, then the same between you and others, after which using just one hand sense things about another person. Brief talk on dowsing, using rods and pendulums, finding personal compass orientation. Ended with instruction to get 'greenery' in the morning and put it on one of two sets of numbered grids – remember your number! Saturday:

9.30am. "Telling Tales, with Bits and Pieces". Working in two groups, select 'greenery' and give a 'reading' – how we felt about that person and their character. Followed by tea break.

11.10am. "People, Places and Perception". Next in smaller groups, given three minutes to sense a covered portrait photograph, sex, alive or dead, nationality and character.

12.30pm. Lunch.

2.00pm. "Every Picture Tells a Story". Given a sheet with a circle. Put initials at top, dampen paper and paint pattern or marks using black, white, red, yellow, green and blue, fold and press lightly, allow to dry. Then choose one and pair up and give a 'reading'. Given a guide, that early life was represented at the bottom and the further up the circle, the greater the age that it represented. Followed by tea break.

4.00pm. Group work in "The Old Clothes Shop". Put into about 5 or 6 groups; visualisation: going across a cobbled street into an old clothes shop that was full of old Victorian costumes, etc., dress up in some of the clothes, and at the end as we came out of it, think who we were connected to in the group.

6.00pm. Dinner.

8.00pm. "The Manifestation of Spirit Co-operation". An experiment at table turning. We all formed a huge oval 'circle' of about fifty to sixty people, with two tables within it, one small and light, the other bigger and heavier. Selected people from the circle were assigned to sit at each table, the four around the small one included Eileen's assistant – let me call her Mrs. X. Eileen then explained in great detail how the sitters were to position their hands, and we were asked to sing to help raise the vibrations. I now quote from my notes. *The leg on the small table came of the floor…the table twisted slightly to begin with. This went on for some time and then occasionally two legs went up. The legs on the floor were on Mrs. X's end. At first I was quite excited, and then my sceptical nature made me look closely. It ALWAYS tipped up away from Mrs. X, and she was THE ONLY ONE WITH HER HANDS FIRMLY ON THE TABLE. I WATCHED HER ARM (she had on a short sleeved blouse) AND WAS SURE I DETECTED HER MUSCLES MOVING - EXERTING PRESSURE. WHEN THE TABLE STARTED SLIDING AROUND THE FLOOR - SHE WAS THE ONLY ONE WITH THE HEEL OF HER HAND OVER THE EDGE OF THE TABLE.*

I felt really sick in the pit of my stomach and outraged. I WAS SURE SHE WAS DELIBERATELY PHYSICALLY MOVING THAT TABLE. I shook, and felt utterly betrayed. I considered leaving the circle and going out of the room, but was afraid that my breaking it would upset things at the other table, which trembled but never quite moved. The small table "spoke" to several people and stopped in front of me twice – but I pointedly refused to put my hands on it or have anything to do with it while Mrs. X was part of the four round the table. …Later, when Eileen Roberts was speaking, she asked if there was anybody who didn't think the evenings event had been a manifestation of spirit co-operation – AND I HAD TO PUT UP MY HAND (I saw one other person on the opposite side also put up their hand) – SHE LATCHED ONTO ME AND WENT INTO A

LONG 'TIRADE' ABOUT NOT BEING A CHEAT etc., etc. Afterwards I explained everything to Doris, but it left a sour taste in my stomach.

Sunday.

9.30am. "Popping the Question". A question and answer session that was followed by a tea break.

11.15am. "Participation Problems & Methods". Talk on group work, with suggestions regarding books and information on tapes, etc. *Felt again that there was a wee dig at me! But at the very end I went up and said that I did not consider her a cheat and that I should have put my hands on the table: she looked me in the eye and then stuck out her hand - and we shook! ...I saw Mrs. X - but could not bring myself to go over to her - what could I say? YOU ARE A CHEAT! She didn't make any approach to me, though Doris had informed both her and Eileen of my feelings almost immediately after I had told her. So, I don't think I could work with her feeling the way I do. There was another short session after lunch ["A Surprise Between Friends"] - but felt I had so much to do to get ready for tomorrow that I left before it started.*

This was also part of the learning process; there is never anything 'pure' where human beings are concerned. Why some people feel the need to cheat in this particular sphere of life I'll never know, especially as the damage that can be done could be considerable. Do they get some sort of 'kick' out of duping people? Do they get a sense of power when manipulating people? Do they lack or have failing ability themselves, and try to cover that up? Do they not really believe in the power of spirit? Do they just want to be the centre of attention? Are they so eager to make a 'good show' that they will do anything? If I had not been so sure of my understanding of spirit, then that event could have turned me away from it for life. To this day I can still remember my feelings when I realised that fraud: intense emotions of horror, disgust, anger, sacrilege, nausea, revulsion and contempt. It is no wonder that my whole body actually shook uncontrollably. However, one comes to understand that it does and will happen again and again, the only hope being that it will remain a small minority. In this area one must be ever vigilant.

One consequence of that course was to be invited to a closed circle, subsequently named the "Willow Circle". I joined in December of 1994 and it ran until April of 1996. Here I learnt more about the workings of circles and the philosophy that can be given by spirit through their human instruments. Little by little I was being given knowledge and a better understanding of what this life is all about, though I had a long way to go yet. But this was the time of laying foundations on which I could build in later years. The icing on the cake came in October 1995 with another BFT event: "The Physical Phenomena of Spiritualism" in association with the Noah's Ark Society, with Stewart Alexander, Alf Winchester, Ray Lister and Bill Anderson.

This was a whole day event, starting at 9.00am with an introduction by Alf explaining the Noah's Ark Society and its aims, plus saying what physical mediumship was. Then Stewart gave the brief history of this form of mediumship with the aid of slides. After lunch Bill explained the mechanics and safe practice of physical mediumship, followed by Ray outlining his life in Spiritualism. Following the tea break, there was a question and answer session that led to Alf giving us the instructions for the séance that would take place after dinner.

We were then called to our seats individually for the séance. We were asked to leave keys, watches etc., outside and everybody was searched as they went in. The room consisted of essentially three circles [horseshoe shapes really] with me on the outside where I couldn't see the medium! The room was totally blacked out so no daylight or any light could get in, and the lights put off - after the medium had been tied to his chair.

Some time later a voice came through, White Feather, saying that we would see proof tonight. Then a child came through - sounding a little, and acting like him as well, like 'Jimmy Clithero'! He was there to relax us and prepare things. Then another person with a 'put on' kind of American drawl came through, who apparently chose a girl to come forward and be touched with an ectoplasmic hand - she confirmed this as feeling real. [Later I found out that the accent wasn't 'put on' at all – he was Canadian!]

Then 'wee Jimmy' (can't remember names) got the trumpets moving and I saw these! Flying around the room, sometimes at great speed, stopping suddenly, moving gracefully, going up and down, tumbling etc. No doubt of any trickery being involved. Quite fantastic! Then voices of relatives came through for a few. ...Remember that the young spirit ...was called Christopher; the other was Walter Stinson. Also the medium's jumper was found on the floor when the lights came on <u>before</u> he was untied!

These notes don't do justice to describe the amazing spectacle that about forty others and I witnessed that evening. My eyes must have been like gobstoppers! It was just thrilling, I was in ecstasy at not just the display, but also the utter confirmation that it broadcast: here was the proof of the existence of the spirit world and those in it. Once you have actually experienced an event like that, then *everything* changes. No more ifs and maybes, now I had sure knowledge and my pathway was clear. There could be no retreat from the direction that I was on, I would continue my searching for the 'truth', but that search was founded on an unshakeable and unwavering veracity – *no one* could change that.

Just how much that experience meant to me showed eighteen years later, when I got a chance to say thank you to Stewart Alexander personally. I was so overcome with emotion I could hardly speak, and nearly broke down. How can you tell somebody who has dedicated his life to serving spirit, how much that particular event changed your life forever? A simple thank you seems so inadequate. Even now writing this I can feel the emotion come over me. How many people he must have helped, a truly remarkable achievement. *This* is what's really important; this is what service can do; yet silly and dangerous people like Mrs. X put such knowledge in jeopardy. What a crime!

Anyway, the day after that visit to the Noah's Ark Society, it was still with a sense of euphoria that I attended a single day workshop on Kirlian Photography. However, apart from the actual physical photographs, I can remember little of it, and my very brief notes conclude: *Am really no wiser about Kirlian photography!!*

So those few short years gave me a chance to see some of the best – and the worst – examples of Spiritualism and other related subjects.

CHAPTER 7

Full Steam Ahead

By the start of 1996 I was beginning to feel the effects of my constant thirst for more knowledge. Attending the 'Willow Circle' and the Healing Circle on different nights every week, I was also present for many of the CDSG meetings, this on top of all the other extra time that needs to be put in by any teacher. Into the bargain, I was still suffering recurring and occasionally debilitating pains in my stomach area, a bit of acid reflux, and sometimes experiencing excessive wind that was embarrassing, as I could not control it. Several trips to the doctors since 1993 brought no relief – on my first visit I was told to eat more roughage! Eventually I was diagnosed – when I was severely ill in Merseyside in 1995 – with gall bladder trouble. On my return to Scotland I was put on the surgical waiting list. In the meantime I just had to soldier on.

Nonetheless, my time with the Willow Circle, which I tried never to miss, was about to come to an end. In order to give a little flavour of it, I will show just a few extracts from my notes:

1/02/96 ...Chi came through. ... "I would just like to say a very quick word of what my lady [Audrey] says to herself - well, not always to herself! As she does not always say it every day - she forgets sometimes, but I think it is rather nice... She says - and I will speak for her - "you are part of everything that ever was, that ever is, and that that ever shall be". We are a part of everything that ever was. There is no beginning and no end - it is eternal. So the beginning is now and the future is now. Can you understand that?"...

15/02/96 ...Chi came through. ... "It is difficult you know, to come back through the heaviness of your material world and not realise that you do not have to carry this burden of the material as you come back down. It is a lesson that we have to learn when we become guides, and when we wish to get in contact with you on this plane. But, she receives the messages through the ethers, as we all do. And of course you know that she is with you - don't you? [Bernard: "yes I do".]

"It is very easy for us over here, and also for you people on earth, to say 'do not be lonely'. We understand, when you love a soul and you materially loose the sight of that person, that you think that they are not with you. But they are only in the next room. There is only a very thin door between your world and the one that the souls go to, to start with. I hope this does not make you feel even sadder!"

... "Do be like your tree! Give love to all that you meet, even if it is difficult at times! You know, plants will not grow without nourishment. So you must be as the nourishment and feed the poor souls, feed their roots, as the tree feeds through its roots and becomes a magnificent sight to see. God bless you all." Then after the rest of the notes on the evening, I wrote this last sentence: *In the car on my way home, felt a presence with me - 'touched' my left hand and my face.*

22/02/96 ... Chi came through. ... "We observe you all, and we would like to help you, but we have to let you find your own way. We try very hard to open peoples' eyes, to open their minds, but we are not allowed to show you. As you know you have got free wills, and if you don't want to go along that path there is nothing we can do about it."

... "What do you think my name is?" (Chi?)

"Yes, I will set you that question" (Life-force)

"And yourselves?" (Singing bird!)

"Oh, that is very nice, I like that one." (I thought I read it recently - but I've forgotten!)

"You've forgotten. Well you see, it has two meanings. You are correct in saying it is energy, life force, but it also means service." (Which we all must do.)

"Yes, in your different ways. Chi is energy and as I say service. I thought I would just put that one in!"

29/02/96 …Chi came through. "Good evening. I see that you brought your pads and your colours. This is very good, I am pleased about this, because I wish that you will use these pads to open up your emotional minds - not your mental, logical minds but your emotional being. I do not wish you to write but to put on paper the things that you feel within the circle here. The things that may come to you - perhaps it is a cold draught. Think how you would describe that around whatever area of your body that you feel it, and what colour you would put in. Also it may be heat; pictures that may be shown to you; I wish you to draw them and not write them so you will gradually open up your potential for seeing things. For I feel that you are very closed and by just using your logical mind and writing things does not help open up that emotional side, as it does when you have to do it in picture form. Do you understand?" (Yes)

The circle continued shortly after that with a meditation, and then another spirit talked to us for about five minutes before we closed.

Due to illness I missed the circle on the 14th March, but was told that it was almost completely taken up with the sad events that happened in Dunblane the day before. We were asked to send our healing prayers to both to the dead and the living, especially the latter, and to continue them

"…not just for a week or a month, but for a long time."

Bernard had been through a tough time that winter, including being snowed in and isolated for over a week. With the rest of his family down in the south of England, he decided that it would be best if he sold the house and moved back to Kent, the county where he was born. So with Mike and Audrey deciding to concentrate just on healing, we soon came to the last meeting of the Willow Circle:

25/04/96 ...Chi came through. "Good evening friends. The last day of term has arrived! Over the last few years you have learnt many things. Your eyes, that were once closed, are now open, and it is time to spread the knowledge you now have in other directions. This is meant to be. When you are at school you do not stay in the same class year upon year upon year. Is this not so?" (True)

"You have passed the first stage, now you have got to go and help other people to reach the stage that you are now at. ...And there is work also for the rest of you to do, a great deal of work. You may think at times that it is not appreciated, but this is looking inward on yourselves. We need all the people that we can muster, to enlighten, even if it is only a glimmer, to those who are seeking. Once the crack has been opened then it may be for others to open it further - but that crack has to be made first of all. Ways are always found to go round. We do not use force - that is not our way. But if there are obstacles ways are found around. The light and the knowledge has to be spread in all directions.

... "I will go now. ... God bless, go in love into light. We will meet again."

Meanwhile, having been dropped from the surgical waiting list when they split the patients into two groups, I was offered the first available place. So while waiting for that I continued my diet of fat free salads and got on with life. Now I was given experience in dealing with the public, when I went to work with others on the NFSH stand in the Assembly Rooms, George Street, Edinburgh, where the Scottish Health Exhibition was held in March 1996. This was added to with the Dumfries Festival of Body, Mind and Spirit, where the NFSH had a stand for spiritual healing over two days at the end of April. The next month I finally got my gall bladder removed, and receiving healing from others in the Healing Circle I was soon back to practising as usual by June. Then having completed both parts 3 & 4 of the NFSH Healing Development Course in August, I started to work on individuals, to build up case studies towards getting full healer status.

CHAPTER 8

The Learning Continues

While concentrating on the healing, I also attended workshops with the mediums Mary Duffy and Paul Jacobs both in 1996 and 1997, as well as a couple on NLP (neurolinguistic programming). However, most importantly, I was invited to attend a day workshop once a month run by Doris Lowe. This started in February 1997 and continued until ill health forced Doris to stop them in October 2000. Here I was given excellent teaching (totally free with lunch etc., provided into the bargain) on all sorts of subjects connected to both the psychic area and Spiritualism. All the other participants were clairaudient and/or clairvoyant and clairsentient, so as just a healing medium I did feel quite out of my depth. Despite several changes in personnel I was always invited to take part; so I greatly appreciated both the support given to me, and the willingness of Doris to pass on her wealth of knowledge.

Thankfully, Doris decided to start with the basics and gradually built on them. The very first meeting on 23rd February 1997 started with breathing exercises, followed by talks and discussions on 'Guardian Angels', 'Doorkeepers', and other spirit teachers and helpers; ending with a visualisation. There is no way I intend to catalogue all that happened there, but it did range from séances, psychic exercises, healing, karma, reincarnation, trance, energies, 'rescue' work, chakras, auras, discipline and meditation. After each meeting I would write up my notes as soon as possible, but finally I started recording the workshops on cassette tapes as from August 1998, though even then some of them were subject to interference from the energies that were around us. I propose to include excerpts that were of interest to me, and conceivably might be of similar interest to the reader.

25/05/97 … After lunch we had another visualisation: with flowers… choose one, pick it up and then think for whom in the circle it is for and why. 'M' got a tiger lily (orange) to give to me. It has a connection with a lady that had passed on - a memory. Also thought that I would draw it.

I could not connect any memory of a lady with a tiger lily, however, it actually did come about that I drew a tiger lily a few months later when I visited Bernard in his new home in the south of England!

22/06/97 … We started with Doris talking about various aspects of mediumship and reactions of people to trance etc. Doris then said that she was being told that her doorkeeper 'Zen' wanted to talk through her. So she went into trance: 'Zen' then said that this was difficult for him so we had to excuse him (but it was quite ok). He opened Doris' eyes and looked at 'A' the whole time that he talked. Apparently 'A' had a question about his doorkeeper and 'Zen' was answering him (but as usual it was a lesson to others as well). He told 'A' to watch his thoughts and to remember that like attracts like. He also said that souls (not "entities") in the lowest spheres were too evil to see the light, but those in the upper levels who were ready to be helped would see and be attracted to light. So that the person that had come through to 'A' had been allowed to do so by his doorkeeper because he was ready to be helped. …

… When she 'came back' Doris said that she had tried to know her doorkeeper and what he was called for years. Eventually she had got the name 'Zen'. She had thought that perhaps he was an Eastern, Chinese or Japanese, person - but had been given a brief glimpse and noted a Nordic individual with blue eyes and blond hair. We suggested it may have been 'Sven' rather than 'Zen'. …

After lunch we sat in circle … Then Doris went to 'A' and he had a 'David' come through, but A's head and arm flapped about - and he began to hit his chest. Doris forcefully told David to go and when this had little effect immediately stopped the session and brought us all back to awareness at once! Apparently this soul had approached 'A' before - he had been in a wheelchair on this side and had been very frustrated in not being able to communicate. Doris told him not to bring his condition to 'A', that he was not welcome here if he did, but if he respected his instrument he would be welcome to the circle another time.

This brought home to us all the value of Doris's early teaching on being able to be called back to awareness at a moments notice. It also informed us about the physical wellbeing of the medium - 'A' was quite ok but needed lots of water to drink. We had quite a discussion on how others might have viewed the situation, etc. Sometimes the medium is not really in a distressed state at all, but merely showing the earthly conditions of the soul's life or passing. However, we should be aware of the dangers and be ready to give immediate help ... or to stop the sitting with robust voice and language!

9/11/97 ... Doris ... went on to talk about one particular circle in Exeter, which was a rescue circle that met together once a month, and that was all the work they did. Any other work was referred to other mediums. They had been formed initially to send 'peace' thoughts at the time of the Gulf crisis with Iraq, and had been asked by spirit if they would be willing to be a rescue circle when the war started - this they did. Doris then read out part of a report by one of the group into the work they had done [with] American and British service personnel plus English speaking Iraqis. Some were easy as they knew they were dead, others were harder and had to be convinced that they were actually dead before they could be told to ask for help and seek the light, when they would be assisted by spirit helpers. There were 3 or 4 mediums in the circle - so a lot of work was able to be achieved. For those who had passed over and were 'trapped', spirit helpers would put a cocoon of thought around that spirit and transport him or her to a rescue circle or to a spirit "healing station"…

7/12/97 … However a lot of points were raised - including that we seemed to differ on the cocoon idea, although I didn't really get to the bottom of my reason for bringing this up… However, spirit (thank goodness) were listening and after 20-30 minutes, Doris dropped out of the discussion and Ho-Lin came through not long after. He said he had been listening and proceeded to give lots of advice etc. … He said he would give us the opportunity to ask 3 questions.

'A' asked about the cocoon we had been discussing earlier. Ho-Lin said that it was the love and kind thoughts from the material side that made the cocoon of love that shielded the one who had passed over from any harm from malignant spirits (who might try to entice the person into the lower spheres) and eased their passage into the spiritual spheres. It was so important that we give out our love and also try to educate, educate, educate others on what really happens at 'death'. …

Lastly 'E' asked about those on this side who had such strong religious convictions about the next life, such as being raised again in the flesh at the 'last trump', that when they passed over did they wait in their coffins? Ho-Lin said yes, there were many who were caught in what we might call a 'time warp', and some may wait forever to hear that last trump! … Some religions were worse than others, perhaps the hardest being Presbyterians.

24/05/98 … Then got all to send out thoughts and energy to Doris. … But shortly after that somebody eventually came through. Later he gave his name as Aaron Whitelaw, an engineer when on the earth plane. He said that the vessel (Doris) had a very dry throat, and that they had to be careful to not overtax her. He suggested music at the start to help relax everyone. ... They were trying on their side to set up an independent voice box, but it was very difficult. The energies each time were different. ... He said that engineering was just as hard in spirit as on the earth plane! He also said that they wanted to do some experimental work with two others - but they would indicate whom at a later date. He then went - but Doris didn't come back to normal awareness! She said there was a heavy weight in her hands, so that she couldn't move them. Later Doris said that the weight was heaviest on her left hand and drew a kind of knobbly box affair. She said it was strange that she could speak and hear what she said and think about it, all at the same time!

... I asked her if anybody was there - and a voice said, "I was wondering how long it would take you to ask me!" A woman who was called 'Plain Jane', though the name was a mocking one given to her. She had been physically handicapped - spine, neck, hands, and maybe face. 'E' said that she felt 'shrunken'. However, although handicapped, this woman had people come to look at her - but she had time to speak to spirit, and so could tell her visitors a few amazing things! She came from "the south-west". Although physically handicapped - she was alright mentally. She turned to me and said, "you like to work with colour and designs", then "you all create a lovely pattern - but watch those thoughts". Spiteful thoughts could wreck the lovely canvas we had painstakingly built up. She had listened to our talk on death - it was nothing if you had lived a good life. She has such freedom - especially appreciated as she didn't have that in her material life. Spirit is beyond our imagination. "I see the light of your sun, but it bears no comparison to the light of the spirit world."

Two days later I visited Doris, and our discussion on the circle was interrupted by telephone calls. After one, where the caller had mentioned a camera, it clicked with Doris, and she told me that she was sure that the heavy object on her hands had been an old-fashioned camera, the heavy type with bellows. I thought that maybe we should experiment with taking photographs.

19/07/98 … After lunch we started to talk about different things. Doris started with how spirits influence us - influencing our hands and arms, especially with healing - to tie in with the spirit healers. To promote understanding or love in the minds or hearts of healers. They connect strands of colour, fine spider threads of colour linking healer and patient. There are circles of attending spirits with each healer, doctor and nurse.

We then talked a bit on exorcism and rescue circles. It was better to encourage the householder to talk and put the spirit to the light and so 'exorcise' the house. These spirits are near the earth plane and often 'play' with people, pretending to go away and then come back, frightening people etc., sometimes they themselves are influenced by 'lower' spirit beings.

… Had a 'sitting' then. … I thought I heard Doris move about the room at one point. Later Doris said that a spirit had appeared and had stood close to each of us in turn. 'X' had also thought that Doris was moving - but Doris had remained seated throughout. She was not sure if this new energy was for physical or development.

16/08/98 [At this session I started using my tape recorder] … Doris told us some details of a long talk she had with her spirit helper Hemron … *that's important. We've got to keep stressing the proper need for relaxation, proper grounding, proper quieting of mind. And then, if they are attuned that way through the mind, well, then spirit can use their vibrations for making contact, communication, by way of tape recorders, sound equipment, video recorders, and this will be the new kind of mediumship. ...*

That explains all the different energies we have been experiencing. We have got to understand different energies and how at one time a spirit communicator had to find a medium who was on the same level so far as the level of vibrations or energies were concerned. With the mediumship of the New Age (and he said he didn't like the term 'New Age') they will be able to communicate with people a lot easier, or use the energies of mediums that at one time they wouldn't have been able to draw close to, unless they were on the same wavelength. If it's a medium who is aware of energies / vibrations and are geared up for anything to happen - they can use them. So plod on...

11/10/98 It was on this occasion that I experimented taking photographs with a very fast film in the hope that something would show up in one of them. However, there were no positive results.

31/01/99 ... Then we had a visualisation ... At the very start when Doris came over near me to fix the music - I sensed and heard the noise of a cat scampering over the back of my chair onto 'E's.

28/02/99 Doris away in Malta. (I was 'in charge'!) [Only three of us altogether] *'E', 'X' and myself.* [We each in turn read out a Ramadahn lecture, and after each one we all discussed it fully, and I also gave several visualizations.]

We then had a short session where we opened up to spirit. Soon 'E' seemed to have something, so I asked. 'E': "yes, my Chinaman. He has been in the spirit world for a long time. He has been told to abide by the rules of behavior today! He has been around for many lifetimes. May I stand? " (Yes certainly) And 'E' stood up.

"Greetings friends. Greetings. I have waited a long time for the opportunity to speak once more through this, my friend. Opportunities have not really been given, not in the right circumstances, for quite some time, but I have waited. I am a very old Chinaman, from long, long ago, when I lived in that country. I was quite - as you would say these days - I was quite well off, I was quite well up the ladder of the people of the time. I was very lucky, I was very lucky. I was given much opportunity to study and to learn. I did not go hungry, I did not have to toil in the fields, so I count myself most fortunate. I had good clothing, I had good parents. I was lucky for the family I was born into. But as you know, we come back into these different families to learn lessons. I had other lifetimes before, not as good as this one. I learnt much. I was considered to be a man of learning, and that is my purpose now, to bring that knowledge to other people. I wish to work with this one more often."

(Me: "In what circumstances can this be done?")
"It must be in a group. It must be where people are of like mind. We do not want jealousies - that is not why we come. We come to help all those who wish to learn. We want to spread this knowledge, we want it passed on. What is the good of knowledge if you keep it to yourself? It is wasted. It is of no use. The person may learn - one person may learn, but when they pass over, that learning has been wasted.

"I have been listening to your discussions, and you see what you learn here, and how you must give it out, how you must give of charity, how you must give of yourself to persevere. That is the only way you give of yourself, when you persevere. That what you have - you must share. Again that comes back to your charity. You must share of yourself, not just your material wealth; you share of yourself, of your love for your fellow man. You give from here (heart), not just from there (head). Everything must

40

start from there (head), but it must come through the heart, and the feeling of love for your fellow man. We want this knowledge spread. We want it to go forth from one to another. That this is how you have - not you have to! I beg your pardon - not you have to - this is how we would like you to work. This - it is your choice! It is your choice. But this is what we would like to see, that you give in this manner, that you think in this way, that you work in this way. To pass on your knowledge and not keep it all inside - 'that's mine' - that is no good, no good at all. We want knowledge spread."

(Me: "Is there any advice you wish us to convey to your person you use?")

"She can hear what I say - she can hear. She may forget, but she can hear."

(Me: "Thank you for that.")

"I haven't finished yet! I have shown her before my outfit, my tunic. I have shown her my autumn season, all the colours on my tunic. I showed her the winter season, I opened my tunic and all was black - no colour. I promised her I would show her the seasons, but that opportunity has not arisen, but I will.

"You have spoken today of the new growth, the new beginning. We are almost in the spring season - not quite but almost. Things are beginning to come to life. Things are beginning to grow. This is your spring season which is so important. It is the beginning of the year of the earth, of the growth. But take that also as the beginning of the year of the spirit. You may have lived many years, but you have a new beginning - now. And the growth of your soul is what we are interested in. And we are so pleased that you do meet together and that you discuss these things, that you think about them.

"You have had three directives today, which you have talked about. I have been listening! And you talk about these papers and what is contained therein. And

we listen to you, and we listen to the thoughts that you bring forth, and we are pleased. We are very pleased that you come forth with these things, that you think, that you try to work things out and you try to understand. We know in the spirit world that your understanding is necessarily limited. We know that. You could not begin to understand all that these papers imply. You could not, you are not capable at this moment of understanding, and that is not being rude to you. Because we appreciate how far you have developed. And we are very pleased to see your lights burning brightly. Because although you may not see them - we do, and we see how they are getting bigger and brighter because of your thinking and your actions. We know that the actions are so important, as in your paper on charity. Your actions of giving, of giving of yourself to other people. It matters not whether you were - what they say - 'taken for a ride'. It matters not. What matters is what was within you. You understand this?"

('X': "Yes.")

"Thank you, I have your voice at last.'

('X': "Sorry about that.")

"It is quite alright, I understand. I know the feeling that is coming from you, and that is what matters. But we watch and we see what you do. We know what you do, but we also know what goes on within, the thoughts and the feelings, and the love for your fellow man. Do not worry about your son - with the other coloured people. Do not worry! Don't worry about that. That is his lesson and he will learn it. Something will be brought to him, to bring the lesson home. But don't worry, don't worry about it, he will be alright - and so will the one with the thumb."

('X': "It is the same one.")

"The same one. That will be better than you think. Put your healing power on it - I know you do healing. But put your healing power on it and leave it in the hands of

42

God. He will learn a little lesson, to do with our brethren. He will learn a little lesson. It will not be a painful one, but he will learn it."

('X': "I don't think he really means it.")

"No, it is not deep rooted. No. It is more on a superficial, yes, level. And he does not really think what he says or mean what he says. Does that make sense?"

('X': "Yes.")

"We know him! You have also talked about your homes in the spirit world. There is such a variety. But when you have learnt what you are learning here, it will not matter to you the same, when you come over to our side of life. It will not matter. Because you will have that knowledge, which so many others haven't, maybe haven't even had the opportunity to learn. So many have no idea at all. They will be provided with the homes they wish. But you are progressing beyond that level. You may not - you will go to the beginning, but you will not stay there for long. Because you have already acquired some knowledge and you will go on to higher levels. Not immediately, but rather quicker than a lot of other people.

"You have the open minds. And with the open minds so much is possible, so much more than people realise. That you can achieve so much more with an open mind. And that is what we like to find, because then we can work, we can work with that soul. People with closed minds - it is like coming up against, not even a brick wall, it is a huge, what appears insurmountable object - and it is so hard for us to work with people like that. But we have to keep persevering, persevering to get through to them. So that we can make a little chink in the barrier, to get that little bit of light through. But it takes a terrible amount of work and a terrible amount of perseverance to do that. But that is our work and our objective. We have to do this in the spirit world.

"Some people have the funny idea that you die and you just lay there - and do nothing! Believe you me - you work in spirit! Work does not cease. You work in spirit. So if you think you are coming to our side of life for an easy time - you can forget it. For you will not, you will work very hard. That is when you are prepared to work and you will want to work. It will not be easy, but it is very, very worthwhile.

"I hope what I have said may have put another little chink of light somewhere, and I would like to meet you once more if you would have me?"

(Me: "That would be very nice.")

"I have so much more that I would like to say, but I am aware of you both, you are within my little radius of people that I meet with this one. She does not always know I am there - but I watch. I watch and I take notice. And I have been here before. I have been here. And I am very pleased to meet you and to converse with you. But now I will say goodbye, and I will meet you once more. Not just once more, but many times. So blessings on you both."

('X' and Me: "Thank you.")

'E' then sat down, "I've not had him for a long time." We closed - 'E' did the honours, and mentioned "Mr Chang".

12/09/99 ... Doris had asked for advice and been told to do a 'contemplation' rather than a meditation. ... 'I wept because I had no shoes, until I met the man that had no feet'. We had to think about that for a moment or two, and then 'When life lies out before you like a field of untrodden snow, be careful how you tread it, because every step will show'. We had to think about the connection. We had to visualise a wide expanse of snow, a field; how were your footsteps? Look at the pattern your footsteps have made, what are they like? What is the connection with the man who had no feet?

I saw myself at a gate (I sat on the top to look back),

and looking back at my steps up a country lane I noticed that they went straight for a bit, but then over to the ditch and 'shuffled' around a bit, before going back to the middle of the path. The field ahead was pure virgin snow, and I thought about how I should cross it - around the edge, or straight over the middle to the gate on the other side? I chose the latter, carrying the man with no feet on my back. We fell over, but just laughed and got up and on again.

Earlier I had thought that the first saying was about our own little world - we are too self-centred and think only of ourselves and our little troubles, until we come up against somebody who is obviously much worse off than ourselves. After falling in the snow with the man on my back and laughing, the thought came to me of children playing in the snow. How much they enjoy the experience together, that playing in the snow by oneself is very limited. We must experience life with others - no matter what limitations they may have, or that we may have.

We all related our thoughts on this. ...

[Later in the day there were several instances of 'rescue work'. The first took a long time, as the person did not really believe that anyone would want to help him; he had died alone of a gangrenous leg. Below are my notes regarding the second one.]

After a bit I asked 'E' again.
'E': "I've got a man. Who was hung. He was hanged for sheep stealing. And he took a sheep to feed his family, and he was hung. I can see the gibbet and him hanging."
Me: "Does he have a name?"
'E': "It must be a surname because I'm getting Arbuthnot, but he is saying "Arbuthdid"."
Me: "What drew him to us?"
'E': "He was listening. They are saying he wasn't all that

bad. He wasn't a wicked man, but he did take that sheep."

Me: "Did he blame himself? Somehow.."

'E': "Yes. He took it. He took it."

Me: "But what is past is past. Does he wish help?"

'E': "He is saying he thought that was all there was, the condition he was in, that was all he was entitled to, because of what he'd done."

Me: "But he now knows different?"

'E': "Yes."

Me: "And he can see the light?"

'E': "Yes, and he now realises that he wasn't so bad really. He had a good reason for doing it. He was told how bad he was, how wicked he was for what he had done."

Doris: "Spirit world judge on the thought behind the action and not the action; does he understand?"

'E': "Beginning to understand. He was resigned to being where he was, because he thought that was what he deserved."

Me: "But he realises now that that is not really the case?"

'E': "Hmmm."

Me: "That there's something better."

'E' "He's... he said being hung is a terrible punishment for what he did."

Me: "Yes it was."

'E': "And then his children had no one to look after them."

Me: "So maybe he blames himself, more than anybody else would blame him. He needs to let go of that."

'E': "Yes."

Doris: " Did he kill the sheep and then.."

'E': "Yes. Yes. He's not terribly emotional like the last one. He.."

Doris: "He has to move on over the bridge to the next plane."

'E': "Yes."

Doris: "They're waiting for him to do that I think."

'E': "And he's ready, he's saying he is ready."

Me: "Good."

'E': "He's ready to go."

Me: "What can he see now?"

'E': "He's on his way."

Doris: "They can only come so far, he will have to cross himself the biggest part of the divide."

'E': "He's tried and out, he's on his way."

Doris: "And they will take him across the last part. We wish him well."

Me: "Yes. We wish him God speed."

'E': "He's running now. He's running! And arms outstretched." ('E' then broke off and drank water, etc.)

10/10/99 ... Doris talked about groups. Some groups, or circles, didn't encourage people to ask questions, in fact one or two positively discourage it. This is against what spirit have repeatedly said - question everything! ... We must always progress, be open to change, how spirit can change their use of us, we must keep thinking and questioning, keep an open mind. ...

We then had a talk. We should learn more, think more. The spirit world have to continually remind us of the true nature of life. ...

... a little break, before going in to what Doris called 'Rescue Healing'. ...

[After failure with the first soul, but success with the next two.]

Doris said, "I'm being told now that we have to use a different candle. And the words that are being used are attempted, attempted rescue. And that whilst it is healing work, it is of a different nature. Got to keep the candle lit while attempting rescue work. And we have to get rid of the words 'rescue work' - we are helping lost souls." ...

Doris then explained that once they have started to

go we can break the link, drink water and then we are ready to receive anybody else. Then it was repeated for Doris - helping lost souls. … Doris thought it was not really 'rescue' work, more like "getting something off your chest" to move forward.

7/11/99 …

Doris then opened, "We are here to help anyone in the spirit world … or to assist them in any way. Anyone who wishes to speak to us … may use us, but not abuse us … We are here to help lost souls …

… 'E' then got a picture of a dark haired girl sitting in front of the fire, she had a fringe cut down at the sides, and she was just sitting there, she was taking something out of a parcel. "At first I thought it was a skateboard, but she would have been too young for it."

Doris: "How old is she?"

'E': "I would say about two and a half to three."

Doris: "What is she here for?"

'E': "Because she wants to see Christmas, and all the things for Christmas."

Doris: "Did somebody bring her?"

'E': "I didn't see anybody with her, but I will ask. She's just saying the nice lady brought her."

Doris: "We've nothing Christmassy, but we could show her…"

'E': "She's been to the shops she says. She's been to see the shops, with all the decorations and all the toys. She died before she could open her Christmas presents."

Doris: "Right. Well hold her with you, keep her here, and we'll see if we can find her something for Christmas" (Doris then left to rummage in a box - got a glass night light thing with nice colours).

'E': "She likes the candle and the fire."

Doris: "Still holding her 'E'?"

'E': "She's sitting on my knee now."

Doris: "Have you got a name for her?"

'E': "I asked, but she says she couldn't remember if she was a Mary or Margaret, and it was a long time ago."

Doris: "Right, here's a little Christmas light especially for her, and we'll play a tune for her and she can watch the lady go round." (A wind-up rotating lady that played a tune)

'E': "She's tearful now."

Doris: "I wish her a happy Christmas and ask her to accept the tune and the candle as a gift from us with love."

'E': "She's saying she went on the fire."

Doris: "She's alright now though. Thank her for coming to us as she was when she passed over, and we hope that she can go on now, to grow up and progress well in the spirit world."

'E': "She looks a well-cared for child. She's saying I'm fifteen really."

Doris: "Is she?"

'E': "I missed all those birthdays."

Doris: "We will treat her visit today as a birthday as well as Christmas, and she can celebrate all the birthdays that she's missed. We'll let her go on now with the lady that brought her, so she can now move on and progress. And is able to come again, we will welcome her in a month's time, and we can get a little news from her then."

'E': "Thank you."

Doris then asked 'Y' if anybody was there with her; 'Y' didn't know - but felt there was some sort of contraption in her hands - like a double rolling pin.

Doris: "Why do you think they have placed that in your hands?"

'Y': "Something I used to work with."

Doris: "Were you a cook? A baker?"

'Y': "Yeah! A kitchen."

Doris: " What do you feel like in stature?"

'Y': "Larger than what I am, but I'm not aware of any sex,

either male or female. Quite big hands. Possibly a heavy woman I think."

Doris: "Now, how do you feel you are dressed? Start with your feet, your shoes."

'Y' "My feet feel quite heavy. I don't know about shoes, but I feel the clothing is down to my feet. That's quite heavy. Don't know about colour. Just sort of negative image."

Doris: "What about round the neck.."

'Y': "I feel there's something on my head, possibly tied at the back as it feels quite tight."

Doris: "A scarf of some sort or a hat with a tie. Is this to keep your hair in?"

'Y': "I think so, because it's quite long."

Doris: "Have you got long sleeves, short sleeves?"

'Y': "I feel quite covered up all over."

Doris: "Now take a look at what's about you. Or do you feel you are in this room, dressed as you were in this life? Just think about it."

'Y': "I'm getting a vision of a kitchen. There's a fireplace, looks like a working fireplace."

Doris: "A range?"

'Y': "Ahha…there's a window, sink, a small house, a home."

Doris: "What happened in this home? Ask her, because she's showing you that for a reason."

'Y': "It's very bare."

Doris: "Ask her why she's showing you this."

'Y': "There's no children."

Doris: "Husband, parents?"

'Y': "No, she's…it's her home."

Doris: "So she's on her own. Why is she on her own? Is she a widow or a spinster?"

'Y': "Husband's not there."

Doris: "Temporarily, or has he left her?"

'Y': "I think it's temporary, for it's as if she's waiting. I'm getting sensations in my legs - bad circulation, swelling. Isolated, it's not in a village or a town. It's not a farm."

Doris: "The condition of the legs - is that an ongoing thing, has she been troubled long?"

'Y': "I get the feeling it's ongoing. It has to do with weight."

Doris: "Try to find out how she passed over. This is what she is trying to tell you."

'Y': "The letter 'T'."

Doris: "What is it then?"

'Y': "It's a nail."

Doris: "A nail?"

'Y': "Ahha!"

Doris: "Ask why a nail."

'Y': "It's a blacksmith."

Doris: "Now I'm going to speak to her direct 'Y', and I want you to answer what comes into your mind. I'm hoping she will answer using your voice."

'Y': "It was quick."

Doris: "Was it a normal illness? Was the ongoing complaint with your legs the cause of your death?"

'Y': "I think so."

Doris: "Can you give me an approximate time, year?"

'Y': "17…"

Doris: "Yes, the 18th century, that's near enough. Did a doctor attend you?"

'Y': "No."

Doris: "What are you doing now in the spirit world? Or are you just staying close to your old home, or the image of your old home?"

'Y': "Just waiting."

Doris: "Waiting for what?"

'Y': "Waiting for someone."

Doris: "Who are you waiting for - someone you knew or someone to help you?"

'Y': "Someone to come near."

Doris: "You do know that you have passed on - no doubt about that? You do accept that? Do you?"

'Y': "Yeah."

Doris: "Yes? In that case now you have to leave behind the images of your life at the home where you lived, and your illness, and ask for someone to take you onto another level. Someone will come. You may see only a small speck of light. Move towards it if you can, or ask them to help you to move towards it, and you will go on from there. If you want to that is. How do you feel about that?"

'Y': "They've gone! I felt very lightheaded."

Doris: "At what point did they move?"

'Y': "Realisation, about talking about how she passed over, she realised she passed and…physically I felt very lightheaded and then very light, and then just back here!"

5/12/99 …

… Doris brought up about our 'spirit groups', with some incarnating, some not. We talked about some spirits who came through always say "we", which suggests a group, and people like Ramadahn even gave a number to his one.

Different spirits for different things, i.e. healing, mediumship, etc., plus certain times - like regular meetings - will be a certain group or guide, but at other times a different spirit, or a different member of the spirit group will come through.

…

Then Doris said we would sit for me! I was to totally relax and just see what happened, but be aware of any changes etc. I felt that there was a lot of energy around my forehead - my whole head, and also felt it on the backs of my hands. Doris said she felt energy 'pulling' from her hands, and 'M' also, who said it was very strong.

As I was relating my story, I started by saying that as soon as Doris had invited spirit to come, I had seen a tiny wee bright blue dot of light, slightly to the left. It went, but came back briefly again later, but didn't grow in size. Didn't feel any change of temperature or hear anything. I did get a sense of something 'rotating' in front of me (at one point it was gold - like a satellite - but I forgot to mention this). I also later on got a sense of a light shining by my left side - I couldn't remember if light had been actually on (it hadn't) but it was like that.

Doris said that somebody was by my left - he was wearing a dark blue robe, an Egyptian, blind, and had a wooden bowl. The blue robe had sleeves and stopped below the knee at the calf - like a dressing gown. Doris assumed he was a beggar. 'M' 'got' a piece out of the Bible of a man with a begging bowl as Doris was talking. [Mark 10.46; Luke 18.35] 'E' got a peach colour going towards me. She also got like I was a 'mummy' and they were unwrapping the bandages from my head. ... 'E' also said she wanted to get inside my head! She also thought it was preparatory.

...

Then we all opened to spirit. ... I felt as if someone had touched my knee lightly - maybe just energy. 'J' felt a man hit her chair, as he seemed unable to make up his mind to which person to go to. ...

...

I had an odd image, lots of tight circles outside each other, with a little square or rectangle in the middle. I felt that I was 'away' at times - couldn't place what was being said or remember some of the details that others talked about.

...

Doris then talked about our 'drifting' and about my circles - maybe they are trying to tell us something. I said I thought that we are now required to 'think' more. Earlier the lessons we got were more straightforward. ...

The above is a drawing of the image that I received, and I included it in a letter to Doris that I wrote three days after the workshop. In the letter I put: "I know you don't like symbolism, but I think this is symbolic. The wee square in the centre is us – on the earth plane, and around us is the circle of spirit – but what we don't think about is that there are other circles, each one bigger and bigger. Rather like we have our circle of family, circle of friends, circle of community, circle of country, etc. A symbol of reassurance?"

Since then that symbol occasionally comes back to my memory, and I think that there is greater significance and greater teaching to be found in it.

Doris' health had never been that robust, but after this date she began to gradually deteriorate. At the beginning of 2000 she had a fall and three successive meetings were cancelled. While she rallied during the summer, there was only one meeting in October during the rest of that year. Then she moved house, at which the last meeting was held in April 2001.

I did keep in touch, occasionally visiting, but on the 7 January 2002, one of her daughters telephoned to inform me that she was now very seriously ill, and had been admitted to the Alexandra Unit in the Royal Infirmary, Dumfries. I visited her two days later and had a short talk with her. She was quite bloated in the face – probably the side effect of drugs – and had breathing problems (she was leaking air), and her voice was soft and very hoarse. Equally she was determined to look on the positive side. I remember her saying, "after all, the doctors can sometimes be wrong!" Finally, she grew tired and wanted to sleep, so I said my goodbyes and told her I would be back on the Saturday.

When I did visit three days later, I was informed that Doris had passed the previous night.

I cannot stress too highly how much I admire Doris and what she did for me – and many others. Not only did she teach me lots of techniques, a wide variety information and countless stories of personal experiences, she actually got me to think more deeply about all sorts of issues. Doris did that which spirit continually asks of all who become interested in learning about life – give out your learning to others, those not yet at your level, so they too may progress and in turn become teachers. If this were to be acted upon by more people, then perhaps that fear of death that pervades much of our society would be decreasing.

This book is dedicated to those in spirit who have done so much for my spiritual progress and help along my life's path – and that includes Doris.

CHAPTER 9

Toes in the Water

I will backtrack just a little to bring everything up to date. In May of 1998 I attended the AGM of the local Spiritualist Group, during which somebody suggested that that there should be a vice-president. In no time at all I was proposed, seconded and then duly elected! So began my education on the difficulties of committee life! It gave me an insight into the problems of change, and also made me think of what I could do for the Group, other than just helping with chairs and locking up etc. I helped initiate a membership, and introduced members only evenings, to try to broaden the focus away from just mediumship, but this was not very successful, as most seemed to be quite happy for clairvoyance all the time! But with the learning I was receiving from Doris, I felt impressed to try and pass some of it on. So in September 1999 I led a 'Spiritual Awareness' group that met once a fortnight. The numbers attending varied from time to time, but we managed to stabilise at around six people in the end, and it ran for eighteen evenings. It gave me an insight into leading a group, and I'm sure that I learnt as much as I hope the others did.

I also suggested that we should visit other Spiritualist Groups and Churches, and arranged to visit Irvine Church. The bus was booked, money collected from all who wanted to go, and the Irvine Spiritualist Church committee had even said that we would be greeted with tea and sandwiches before the service started. So at midday we assembled on a lovely sunny afternoon, and eagerly awaited the bus. As the minutes started to mount up past the appointed time, I tried to telephone the driver several times, but without success. Eventually I had to call Irvine and announce that we couldn't make it after all – they were not pleased after all the effort that they had put in!

This event just about summed up the doldrums that the Spiritualist Group was in; there was stagnation, little vision for development or progress, and disregard for the constitution. Several others on the committee felt in a similar vein and so we decided to close the Spiritualist Group, and then handed over the assets and money to the others, to form their own organisation that they could run as they saw fit. This was achieved in July 2000.

Meanwhile in October 1999, I and a few others of the Spiritualist Group went to Carlisle to see an apparently fairly well known trance medium. I will quote from my notes:

> *...Medium gave a good talk at the start about what was happening and what we should do. Then a Chinese personality took shape on her face, 'Chang' I think, and after him various others, mostly men, ... and an Alice – who said my voice was sexy! Some people could take the personality and transfiguration (perhaps more 'overshadowing') – but often it was "is that X?" first, as if they were not very sure.*

What was interesting was the great variety in the quality of the voices, BUT the actual mentality of each 'new' individual didn't change at all, indeed some of the phrasing was exactly the same. Into the bargain the 'trance medium' moved in her seat to make herself look smaller or taller! However, it wasn't entirely a wasted evening – I won a cake in the raffle!

In the summer of 2000, several others who proposed to form a circle approached me, and I accepted. However, there were different intentions as to why the group had been formed in the first place, and after about eight meetings it collapsed. However, always keen to expand my knowledge and eager to learn, I had decided to explore further afield, and in July 2000, I went to a "Mediumship & Awareness" course at the Arthur Findlay College, Stansted.

There were three groups of twelve; I was in the beginners group tutored by John Blackwood, the other group tutors were Val Williams and Simone Key, and other participating tutors were Leonie Kerslake Phipps and Sonia Driscoll. This was a very interesting course, with lots of new ideas presented to me, in addition to others that Doris had already introduced me to. There was much discussion, lectures, exercises, as well as demonstrations of mediumship. The main visual significance for me happened during the Divine Service that first evening. The mediumship was given first by Sonia Driscoll and then by Simone Key. I looked closely at Sonia, and although she moved about a great deal, a lot of the time she was against the background of the dark red curtains. I could see a slight whiteness near her head, and had a sense of an 'outer layer' at least one metre from her head.

Another high point was a few days later when John gave a lecture entitled "Reflections of the Soul". I found it very stimulating as it encompassed other religions and concepts. He mentioned that the start of modern Spiritualism is said to be the knockings in the Fox's house at Hydesville in 1848, and how this spread like wildfire across the USA and then over to the UK. He also said that he saw spirit as personality and the soul as a Godlike force, so that he did not believe in reincarnation, but incarnations of the Group Soul, which is made up of many, many spirits, like the many facets of a diamond.

Back in our groups later, he discussed Group Souls again, how these would change over time with 'parts' merging or going to other Groups. He thought that our guides exist, a multitude of them, all parts of our Group Soul. But he said there needs to be balance, so that opposites are needed. Talked about Hitler and Jesus, the difference was that Jesus was trying to give power to others, while Hitler was creating that ego and centering that power on himself. Then we had a discussion on morality and ethics that I found very thought-provoking.

Of particular interest was the way John used colour to enhance his work, taking not just a colour, but also a whole range of subtle nuances in each that he could relate to a wide variety of subjects. He asked his group, as an exercise, to assign a colour to the months of the year and to different age groups. I give my selections below, but have no notes to say why I chose these colours!

January: greys

February: dark brown

March: mid greenish brown

April: mid yellow

May: lime green

June: mid peach

July: mid blue

August: rich golden yellow

September: rusty red

October: gold

November: light yellowy brown

December: pale grey green

0 – 10: bright yellow

11 – 20: mid red

21 – 30: sky blue

31 – 40: light grey/blue

41 – 50: mid green + tinge of grey

51 – 60: navy blue

61 – 70: beige

Anyway, the course gave me much to think about and eager to try other courses in different places – if I could fit them into the school holidays!

The next 'event' occurred a little after this course, but for some reason I never made a note of it. Perhaps because it is almost impossible to describe to anyone, as it was 'an experience' that shook me to the core, and was so 'vast' and awful it is not possible to find words that can give a full sense of what I went through. The best I can do is to start by relating it to what might be its opposite! There are some people who say that they have experienced a moment of pure bliss, where they feel connected to everyone and everything, and are conscious of all being one in a moment of ecstatic love. That is difficult to imagine and can only be really understood when one has that same occurrence. Well, I had a moment of pure knowledge and understanding of the evil that the media cause throughout the world; it was a moment of pure terror, though it only lasted for about a second (thank God). But in that second I comprehended their immense power and ruthlessness, of what could be a help to humanity had been turned into a weapon of greed and materialism.

I doubt if I will ever be so terrified again, and the consequences have been taken onboard – I got rid of my television, now only buy the local newspaper, and listen to the radio for only short periods during the day. I will never trust them to tell me the whole truth, and always listen to their news with a critical oversight.

I next wrote a letter in August 2000 to establish a distant healing group, sending it to various individuals who I thought might be interested. A copy of it follows:

> This is said to be the age of communication, of e-mails, fax, mobile phones, computers, digital TV, the internet etc., etc. It also seems to be the age of blame, of finding someone to be at fault, to name and shame. There is a tide of negative comment, negative thought and negative energy constantly promoted by the media in general, where pressure of market forces, tight deadlines, instant opinions and jingoistic slogans make for a shallow and simplistic coverage of important issues that affect us all. There seems to be little that an individual can do to combat this state of affairs - but maybe we can try.
>
> Many have sat in groups or circles for such things as spiritual awareness, development, meditation etc., and will know of the enhanced effect on energy that such groups create. It is my intention to form a group with the specific aim of raising energy to be used in distant or absent healing. This form of healing is just as popular as 'hands on'; indeed many think it more effective with

less of the ego to get in the way. I expect that many of you already practice distant healing on your own.

It is hoped that by sitting in a group this energy may be enhanced and strengthened, and consequently the greater power can be used not just for individuals but in addition targeted towards groups of people. For example these groups could be local people involved with health and social welfare, old peoples' homes, hospitals, voluntary organisations, council committees and the emergency services, as well as animal sanctuaries, farming and the food industry. It is very easy in this age of constant world-wide news and information to be caught up in issues that are distant from us, and therefore to overlook the needs and problems that are present all around us. That is not to say that we would ignore other places, perhaps trying to help with the many natural and man-made disasters that frequently occur throughout the world.

In the future it may be possible to link in with other such circles to target institutions, societies, government, the environment etc. The purpose would not be to change these groups to our particular way of thinking, but to give as much love and healing energy to them as we can, so that they may with open hearts and minds arrive at the "best" decisions/policies that they can.

My tentative proposal at the moment is to meet once a month (dates, day and venue yet to be decided). If you are interested, please write to:-

Only a few replies came, but on 3rd October 2000 the first meeting was held with a total of four people. All agreed on the objectives, and soon we had a set day – the second Tuesday of each month. By the second meeting the numbers had increased to twelve. As it gradually settled down, the numbers averaged around ten, and as some left and others came in, the day and venues also varied, but it managed to keep going for over ten years. However, the inevitable change in people's lives, like moving to live elsewhere, having a family and so forth, meant that eventually that the numbers dwindled to three, and then just two. The last meeting of the Distant Healing Circle was held on 1st June 2011.

An organisation called 'Another Way' had attracted my attention, and I went to a couple of their meetings, but due to being so busy had mostly put it to one side. It was a charity that sought to educate and inform people regarding death and dying, as well as to promote green burials. They had produced an information pack that included Preparing a Living Will, Planning a Funeral, Green Burials and the Law in Scotland, Bereavement and Loss, together with a Resources and Contacts section. I renewed my attendance and at the 2001 AGM was elected onto the committee.

However, with the sudden departure of two important members who moved to another area, I found myself as editor for the newsletter, and elected as convener. Perhaps such an organisation would have a better chance these days of surviving with Facebook and Skype etc., but then it was a continual struggle. At the 2004 AGM we put Another Way 'on ice' for a year, to see if we could get a few others onto the committee, but not one could be found. So it was with sadness that at the 2005 AGM the vote was taken for the dissolution of the charity. The small amount of our funds were given to the Natural Death Centre in London, and the Information Pack was given to a new organisation in the Borders called 'Natural Way Burial'.

CHAPTER 10

Profit and Loss

2002 started with the death of Doris, which set the tone for what was to come later. I was busy with teaching, spiritual healing and the Distant Healing Circle. My mother had not been well for a few years, confined to a wheelchair, she still stayed in her own home but had a basic care package, which saw help arrive to get her up and fed in the morning, at lunch time and dinner, after which she was put to bed, and somebody would look in briefly during the evening.

In my holidays I would visit her, taking charge of the meals to give the carers a bit of a respite, and giving her a bit more choice. When the Easter holidays came I went over to stay. The weather proved to be quite good at that time, and the day before I was due to return I walked up to the village for a few small items. Deciding to have an ice cream, I went into a shop and I remember that the shop assistant had to stretch down to the bottom of the compartment to get one. Even on the way back I started to feel a bit unwell, and this feeling continued and got worse in the evening. Naturally assuming that it was the ice cream – perhaps an old one – I had little to eat and drank water, with the hope that all would be fine in the morning.

In the morning, after little sleep, I felt worse. My natural inclination was just to carry on and get over on the ferry, visiting my doctor if it was necessary when I got back to Scotland. But it kept nagging at me, and so I finally decided to see the local GP. He very quickly diagnosed appendicitis and suggested that I go to the hospital. I went home and told my mother, trying to calm her worries. Collecting a few things I went out to catch a bus, when I saw the neighbour and his pregnant wife getting into their car. I asked if he could take me to the hospital, only to be told that he was going there as his wife had an appointment! He dropped me off at A & E, and after a twenty minute wait I was seen by several staff. They all confirmed the diagnosis, but because I'd had some dry toast and a cup of tea for breakfast, they didn't want to operate right away.

Prepared for surgery, I was eventually operated upon. The first thing that I remember is coming round on the trolley that was being wheeled along a corridor, and one of the surgical team holding out a mobile phone to me saying, "It's your mother!" Groggily I told her that I was fine and promptly fell unconscious! My mother must have been pestering the hospital with phone calls!

Later I was told that the appendix had been gangrenous, so I was very lucky. Indeed, when I reflect on the sequence of events I can't help but think that spirit had a big part to play in all that happened – not just in keeping me alive, but more importantly, to ensure that I experienced what was to follow.

Initially I was put into a single room, but was soon moved to the main ward to a bed beside a window. I remember that there was a plumber opposite me who'd had his hernia fixed (apparently an occupational hazard), and in the bed next to me was a young boy who'd also had his appendix removed. Settling in, I experienced a bit of pain, but it was the plastic under the sheet on the bed that I hated. I would continually wake in the night totally soaked in sweat, and tried to spend as much time outside it as I could.

Then one morning a doctor came to look at me and asked me to remove my pyjama-jacket. Informing me that I had an infection, he got out his biro pen and drew a line on my body where the change of skin colour could be detected. It was a huge area! Immediately I was put on a drip and fed, roughly every eight hours, drugs to counteract it. The amazing thing was that I could actually feel a pronounced relief whenever I got this dose and looked forward to the next one!

However, there was another side effect that I couldn't really disclose to the medics. Whether it was the infection itself or a combination with the drugs I don't know, but the result was that I became extremely sensitive to people's emotions. The little boy was visited every day by his grandparents, and in the evenings by his mother and a much older brother or stepbrother, and once separately by his father. It was quite clear that the marriage of the parents was at an end, and that there were terrible tensions and conflicts among the rest of the family.

When they visited him I was subjected to these waves of negative emotions that at times I found almost intolerable. It was the most horrible experience, and I couldn't wait for the family to leave and to give me much needed peace. Indeed the situation was now reversed – I positively looked forward to night time for the mental peace and quiet that it gave me. Thankfully I made a good recovery and left after about six days.

I now see that whole event as an experience that spirit wished me to have – so that I would have a little understanding of what some mediums (they used to be called 'sensitives') go through. I had asked spirit to teach me as much as they could, that I wanted to know 'everything'. Well, they took me at my word! It has given me a greater respect for those who carry out great public service, sometimes at great personal cost.

My forced absence from work was a gain for my mother, who was in no hurry for me to fully recover and so leave! During this time Audrey, who had been ill for several years but refused to let it halt her work, somehow had got my mother's telephone number and gave me a ring. She was obviously in great pain and knew that her time was limited in the physical state, so wanted a final word with me to say goodbye. Audrey died less than three weeks later, and I was able to attend her burial, where she was interred in her hand painted cardboard coffin. Another of my teachers had gone back to spirit, indeed the one that started it all for me.

A month later I went to see Mike Peachey and received a healing session, during which I felt a hand on my right arm. Opening my eyes I could clearly see that it had not been Mike. Yet another little bit of evidence from my helpers in spirit.

In July 2002 I attended an 'In Depth Physical' course at Hafan-y-Coed, Abercraf, Wales, with the tutors Jean Duncan, Jean Skinner and Paulette Cove. I found the talks on physical mediumship interesting, especially where Jean Skinner explained how she had developed for transfiguration, having photographs for us to inspect and included a short video that she had herself commissioned when at Portsmouth. However, on the last night she gave a demonstration, sitting on a table with red light directed onto her face from two lights, one each side of her. An oriental guide spoke through her giving a brief bit of philosophy, after that mediumship was used to find the correct person, who was then asked to come and sit very close to her. I quote from my notes:

At times the face came very quickly and I could see clearly the differences in the mouth and chin area. All were taken and some of it very emotional. Lots of love. Being in the front row I had a clear view of all that went on and was very impressed by this display of transfiguration.

On the first night I had a dream that I remembered a bit about on waking, which is very much the exception, as I very rarely remember any dreams at all. The detail was hazy, but was mostly about healing – people helping each other. I was given a large basket of flowers and then found myself 'taking' a healing session, but it was as if I was about to go into trance – my voice was not quite my own.

Another aspect to physical mediumship is table turning, and my experience with this so far had not been very positive, remembering what had happened at the weekend in Lockerbie! But this was about to change with a morning session with Jean Duncan. Jean sat at one end of a rectangular table, inviting four others to sit two each at the longer sides, and then invited me to sit at the last side opposite her.

Jean started by giving the table a sharp rap. Explained that hands must be on the table - but lightly, so that if the table moves up or down there will be no resistance. Others were to stand behind our seats so that they could be taken away quickly if the table moved. Felt the ends of my fingers tingling, as did others, and the first sign was a quick movement. [It moved at Jean's end slightly to my right.] Then it went quiet again, and then the table started to move clockwise, got up and followed. It increased in speed until it moved at some speed, continually going clockwise as well as moving to other parts of the hall. Eventually it went so fast others couldn't keep up and Jean especially often had to let go - but it still went on for a bit. Luckily it often seemed to pivot around my end, so that I had the least running to do!! [On a few occasions I would be the only person in contact with the table.] *Then it went anticlockwise for a bit. We then changed and let others onto the table. Excellent evidence! Thank God that this phenomena has finally been confirmed for me. It couldn't have been better!*

Then Jean sat, with 'K' and 'B' holding the [far] edges of the table with both hands. They had difficulty and had to use some force to hold the table - then Jean asked them to let go and the table shot forward!! If Jean didn't touch it the table was still.

During this course we were all given a go of sitting in the cabinet, to feel the energies and see whether we were overshadowed or could speak in trance. One person – 'G', was extremely fluent in his trance speaking, bringing through a doctor, the famous Dr. Lister. Indeed, Jean Duncan said that 'G' had a marvellous gift and should develop it more, and that he was the finest trance medium that any of the tutors had seen. On talking to 'G' I said that this voice of Dr. Lister was familiar to me and that I would try to find out if I had a recording of it (suspecting that it may have been during one of Doris' workshops, but although I tried hard to locate it nothing came to light.) Unfortunately I don't think that 'G' was at all interested in developing any further. Jean Duncan remarked that I had some potential for direct voice, and asked me to turn my head, saying something about dark lines along the jaw.

In the evenings, although a non-smoker, I often joined the smokers in their caravan. This was set aside for them in case of rain, as no smoking was allowed in any of the buildings. There were always good discussions, many of which included experiences of physical mediumship and trance. I expressed my difficulty in sometimes understanding when people were actually in trance or just lightly overshadowed. Then on the second last day one of the tutors was missing in the afternoon, so both groups were put together to continue trance work. To my utter amazement I watched several people go into trance and spirit speak through them, and every time they talked a bright light went on and off in their larynx. It was just like they had a light bulb inside them! I looked around, but nobody else seemed to see any of this, so this incredible display was just for my benefit. Spirit were answering my doubts, saying in effect that 'Here Is True Trance'! This was on a par with the trumpet display with Stewart Alexander in October 1995.

On the fourth evening there was a séance. Seated at a table was Jean Duncan, with 'N' and 'G' seated on her right, 'X' and 'M' on her left, and myself opposite. The rest were seated around behind us, but only one behind Jean Duncan, as it was the door after that. In the centre of the table were a few toys and a trumpet, around which were placed four luminous rods, two long and two shorter ones, arranged in a triangle. After everybody was seated and comfortable the lights were put out and we were in pitch darkness.

First thing that happened was to look at the ceiling and see a green / purple mist (I didn't - but others said they could). Then the table received a loud rap - it actually felt as if somebody had kicked it from below. Raps continued at various stages - but all were at the other end of the table to me. A rod slowly moved and went towards Jean and ended up against her stomach, and stuck out at an angle of about 45°. Jean was told she was getting healing. Other rod moved, rested on 'N''s hand and played with her, then thrown back over Jean's shoulder, just missing 'L'. Throughout this a voice of 'David' from spirit (Cockney sort of accent) related the proceedings, saying that three little girls (two were twins) were doing the tricks and that all were orphans, including him. Rod was pushed towards 'G' and touched his cuff, and the two joined rods were both pushed together towards 'M''s hand. … Then gentleman came through tapping his finger, but wouldn't reveal his name, a little girl 'Ayesha', and later a Miss Corelli. 'G' had a really good chat with her - had read most of her books and had talked to her before in séance. Very saucy lady! … [She had the sexiest voice that I've ever heard in my life!] *She came to me saying she liked my voice. Did I still like being in education etc.? Said spirit was aware of a problem and will try to sort it out within four months. Then said she had my mother here - you look very much like her etc. Then, "also your father - but when he appears she goes away - did they not like each other?" I said I found that (and that my mother was there {unspoken}) perplexing.*

Then somebody wanted out! She was given water and we tried to carry on, but spirit withdrew, and the lights were put on and the atmosphere cleared. The person was then fine; saying she and others near her had been exceptionally hot and became distressed. The whole séance lasted about two and a quarter hours. Later I found out that the person who had talked to me was Marie Corelli, a well-known author of over thirty books and at the peak of her fame around 1900; she died in 1924.

I had lots to think about from that course, but had thoroughly enjoyed it and learnt a lot. On the morning that I departed, just before I left the Brecon Beacons, a red kite circling in the sky in front of me suddenly swooped down and flew over me. It was like an acknowledgement from spirit, and a sign that has been repeated since.

In September I went with Mike Peachey and a few others to the "Body & Soul Health Fair" in the Loreburn Hall in Dumfries, where we had a NFSH stand. However, the numbers were disappointing, partly due to poor advertising and plus the fact that the World Logging Championship was taking place in Lockerbie! During this day I gave a talk on Spiritual Healing in a very small room, just managing to squeeze in the twenty-five that were interested. It naturally got very hot, but most seemed to find it informative, and it was a new learning curve for myself.

My mother had increasingly been suffering medical problems, and had been admitted to hospital. On a few occasions I had taken the ferry over to Belfast for a day visit at the weekend, and it became clear that she was approaching the time of the end of her physical life. But my mother was always a battler, and would take her time about it!

Wondering whether I should go over at the approaching weekend in

November, I was eventually persuaded otherwise due to reports that she had made a bit of a recovery. In the event her death happened at that time, on the 11th November, so it is a date that will never be forgotten! I was sad and glad, but if the truth be known it was mostly the latter. She'd had a really difficult time; from being a very independent person she had become totally reliant on the help of others, and the last couple of years had been difficult and painful. So I was pleased that she had now left her material body to find a renewed and happy life in spirit.

Even with my outlook on the continuation of life, the next month or so after her passing was a strange one. I did feel a definite vacuum and for a while nothing seemed totally 'real', but this gradually faded.

In May 2003, on a sudden whim I booked a sitting with a young woman after reading about her in a local paper, in which she was described as a 'talented psychic'. She used tarot cards at first and gave a fairly sound description of my character, as well as predicting that I would travel a bit, especially between July and November, when I would be surrounded by lots of like minded people [This came true]. As regards health she said that there was a possibility of an operation in two or two and a half years connected with the leg area [Thankfully this has not been the case]. After more mostly true statements about work and home life, she took the crystal ball from me – I had been asked to hold it near the start of this session – and proceeded to talk about my mother and some of the ailments that she had, but reassured me that she was fine now. It was during this that I got a bit emotional, which was unusual for me, and I suspected that indeed my mother's energy was near me. At the end she gave me a cassette tape recording of the meeting to take home.

CHAPTER 11

Searching

The next four years saw me continue to look out for new venues and organisations, though the fixed holidays meant that these could only be accessed on certain dates, and so I was unable to go to some that I rather fancied or had seemed interesting. However, I remembered that when Doris had talked about various groups she had mentioned the Lynwood Fellowship; indeed she had lent me one of their newsletters. So when I saw their advertisement I decided to book for their seminar in July 2003.

Just before going to the seminar, I stayed with my brother-in-law and younger sister and their family. While there I had a dream:

Can't remember much, but walking down towards a beach and then my dad appeared - really clear and memorable. He was wearing a light grey suit and looked happy and cheerful. I think he gave a little wave, before he then disappeared. The vividness of the image was the main impact.

The Lynwood Fellowship seminar started a few days later at Losehill Hall, Castleton, Derbyshire. One of the first people I met was the chairman and founder, Don Galloway. He was very approachable and an attentive conversationalist; I remember a long discussion with him, another trustee Shonagh Moore, and a few others on the last night, that went on into the next day. He had a great command of the English language and was a pleasure to listen to. My short notes on his talk entitled "To Each Their Own" were: *Excellent speaker, has tremendous vocabulary and use of English, plus presence and projects his voice. Very interesting, involving a long sad observation on Spiritualist Churches etc., who don't seem interested in the 'how and why', just the messages. Held my attention totally throughout the talk.*

On the first evening I got talking to a tutor whose face I recognized. Her photograph had been published in the Tibet Society magazine, as she ran marathons to raise both awareness and money for the cause, wearing 'Free Tibet' sashes. Bridget Hickey was very open and had a great personality; we discussed all sorts of things and must have chatted away for nearly two hours! Bridget gave talks on Buddhism and Tibetan Singing Bowls, but what I hadn't realised was that she was a handwriting analyst and Master Graphoanalyst. A talk on "Awareness through your Handwriting" followed that was a very informative introduction to the science of Graphology. Intrigued, I managed to secure a private half hour session with her. At the start Bridget asked that I write out a couple of sentences on a piece of paper. I wrote: *By writing this sentence I hope to learn a great deal more about myself. If not I will be very disappointed, and go home.* Well I did indeed learn much about myself – and I didn't go home. I wrote two whole A4 pages of notes on that session, which was very accurate, so I won't include it! Bridget was so insightful that I found it astonishing; she knew aspects of my life that others have never identified. I will quote just two sentences from my notes that I thought very striking: *Highly intuitive - but not a great imagination. People often assume I know more than I actually do.* These statements are totally accurate; the first was a major reason for not pursuing a career as an artist, and the second is an uncomfortable fact that I have just accepted and live with!

I thoroughly enjoyed this seminar, everything seemed perfect, even the weather. Castleton was charming, the centre and meals lovely, and the other tutors gave excellent talks and stimulating workshops, plus the fact that other participants were friendly and welcoming. I knew that I would attend another Lynwood Fellowship course.

Making my way home I managed to fit in "An Audience with Colin Fry" at the Liverpool Empire Theatre, noting that he hoped to have seen 120,000 people by the end of the year from his tour! However, I was soon on my travels again, this time to the T&G Centre in Eastbourne, where the ISF (the International Spiritualist Federation) was having its Fraternal Week from the 2nd to 9th August 2003.

The first person that I met was Ann Luck, the General Secretary, who was very welcoming and led a wonderful Tai Chi group each morning before breakfast, on the hotel roof (the weather was again lovely). The next person I met was the President Margery Kite, also welcoming, and then Wally and Pat Wilkinson, who had been on the Hafan-y-Coed course in 2002, and who had told me all about the ISF and so were the reason why I had chosen to come. I thoroughly enjoyed the whole experience, especially meeting lots of like-minded people from different parts of the world. The hotel was superb, with up to date conference facilities, and the whole mood was uplifting and positive. Also I loved the character of Eastbourne itself. After reading the aims and objectives of the ISF I uncharacteristically decided that I would not only join, but became a life member!

Ann Robson was the tutor for the beginners group that I was in, and had an easy manner that relaxed all twelve of us, who came from countries such as France, Spain, Switzerland, Iceland, USA, Germany, Israel, Finland and the UK. Ann managed to form us into a most harmonious and supportive group, and I certainly made good progress.

One of the highlights was a trance demonstration where the medium Mark Brandist was particularly outstanding, being very lucid and relaxed. Near the end of the week I had a private sitting with him, where he brought evidence of my maternal grandmother, as well as my father and how he passed over: *"I'm having a feeling in my chest of a heart attack - massive heart attack - this person would have died before the ambulance arrived. I feel it is a father figure. You saw him in a dream - clearly"*, which was exactly right!

I had another private sitting – kindly given to me by a lovely American lady who had won some in a raffle – with the psychic artist Joan Walton. Joan drew the head of a man, saying that he had been a farmer in Australia. A whole group of people had gone over to Australia by boat before the war, when this person would have been a teenager; some came back but he stayed on. He was much taller than me, but not well educated, as he didn't like going to school. Joan got the names 'Will' and 'James' and the surname 'Crawford'. He had a great sense of humour. In the end he lost contact with the family. Most of this made no connection with me at all until the surname was mentioned. I knew that my mother had been in correspondence with a woman with that surname, indeed she had come over and visited us at one time.

When I got home I telephoned my brother and gave him the above information; he said that he would look into it. He called me back about a week later, saying that one of our relations on the Scottish side had memories as a young girl of a Jim Crawford staying for a short while one summer with her nana. He was tall and she thought that there might be a photograph somewhere. However, she moved house that month and we lost contact. So while I have no positive proof, I do feel that there is every likelihood that all this could be true.

In July of 2004, I was back in Hafan-y-Coed with "A Week With Tony Stockwell". On the second evening Tony gave a demonstration of trance, with two spirits talking through him, 'Zintar' (Tibetan) and 'Star'. Tony's face altered with each and I noticed as well that there was a bright aura around him. Spirit answered questions from the participants and I give my very brief note on this: *Spirit world is here around us all and 100 miles from here; they choose us not the other way round; this world will end for human habitation - but not in this lifetime; and he talked about the spirit world as "the land with the indigo sky"*.

There were lots of exercises in both dim and bright light, with trance, possible overshadowing, mediumship and so on, and one night we went to nearby Craig-y-Nos Castle to see Tony's evening of clairvoyance. This was good and well attended, and several of us sampled different spirits in the bar afterwards. The next day Tony had to leave, and we continued with one exercise called 'Looking into the Soul' that I found particularly interesting.

In pairs sitting opposite each other. Close eyes and centre on the music - get a feel of the vibration and get a feel of your own energy, your own vibration. Then eventually we looked into our partner's eyes and see what we got. With Joyce I got a feeling of deep pain in the past - but real inner strength because of it. She said she could take that. She got an image of Aristotle (or similar) for me - a teacher, a man of wisdom and philosophy.

We did it again, but this time just looked at the face generally and to see what we could get. Screw up eyes to get a better view or refocus behind the person could also help. I got a regal looking woman - somebody like the queen! Joyce got the same again for me but suggested this time it may have been Roman.

The last exercise was similar to the start, but this time invited our guide to enter us and show themselves to the person opposite. In the first 2 exercises I got calm water images, but inviting my guide to come gave images of sky, clouds - light, bright and an airy feeling. Joyce said she saw a northern African man, possibly Egyptian. When I looked at her, I half closed my eyes and at the start got a sense of a young man, but later saw a mutilated face with his left eye missing or blind, plus other parts of the face disfigured - either through war/fire, or maybe even from birth.

On the last full day there was another good exercise called "Body Snatchers". All formed one big circle and one was picked as a medium. All had to stand and as the medium gave out bits of information slowly, if it definitely didn't fit – then you sat down; otherwise you stood even if you were not sure. Eventually it would be whittled down to one person as the recipient.

All too soon it was the end of the course and I had to say goodbye to everyone. On the road back I came round a bend and there, hovering above the road, was a large bird of prey. Thinking it was likely to be a buzzard, I looked more closely and saw that it was a red kite! After passing under it I looked back in my mirror – but it was gone.

Two weeks later found me in the Arthur Findlay College, Stansted Hall, on a course entitled "Awareness of a Higher Life", run by the Avalon Project with Tony Stockwell. I had originally booked this course first, and later on seeing that he was also at Hafan-y-Coed earlier had decided to go to both, and was glad that I did.

Divided into groups according to our experience, I found myself in one of the two beginners groups, my tutor being Avril Price. Avril soon got us as a cohesive unit and we all sang our little 'ditty', tentatively at the start, but soon it was rendered lustily and loudly: "I am spirit – spirit am I". It certainly seemed to work!

On the first evening Avril gave a talk entitled "Working with your Doorkeeper", during which there was a visualisation to see if we could find a connection. Starting with going out into the universe, then back into a jungle and seeing our doorkeeper there, given a gift and ask for a name, before coming back to normal awareness and having a discussion about it. I got some light for the doorkeeper; the gift was a hexagonal box made from a light coloured wood, and inside was a die. I had rolled the die and got a one, then a two and so on up to six. During this I felt lots of energy around my head and very cool temperatures around my back and over my arms, especially the inside of the elbow joints; I did not get a name. Others thought that the die symbolised that I should take a gamble and go for it! However, I sensed that my gift was a reassurance, that despite my poor imagination I had actually got all the numbers, so although I might take longer than others to reach my destination, I would make it – step by step.

The next day after exercises in meditation and linking with a guide, we were asked to pick up four or five objects from around the grounds. Back as a group, one person was told to be on the platform and to choose somebody else; taking one of their objects, give what they get via psychometry / psychic level before linking with spirit. Then the 'picked' person had to go on the platform and repeat the process.

When it came to my turn I chose Sandra and held a piece of dark coloured bark. I talked generally at first, two different sides to her personality, potential etc., and then tried to link to spirit. Getting a vague light on my left that I took to be her grandmother, I then saw branches of a tree. So I suggested that this person may have had a lot of trees around her house [No]; maybe had quite a bit of wood in her house, like panelling [No]. As I struggled on with this, Avril interrupted and it turned out that her grandmother had owned a small wood of chestnut trees. I then saw a nice blue colour and suggested that her grandmother was bringing peace and calm to her, and that she often did this, as she liked to help her and guide her. Feeling that this last bit was a little lame, I thought that it was probably more 'me' rather than spirit influence. We then broke up for lunch. Meeting Sandra before the next group session, she showed me a text that she had got from a close friend and teacher at home, that said she felt the need to tell her that her grandmother was a helper and a guide for her. How good was that! There is nothing that spirit cannot do – when they think it appropriate!

Later that day I did surprisingly well in another exercise: sit facing the wall, link with spirit, and then give a reading for an unknown person who had been positioned behind me; no voice used, instead one tap on the shoulder for yes, two for no, and three for don't know.

The following day I complied with Christine's exercise of filling myself with white light, and in a large bubble float to the sky and find a door into the realm of guides. I saw a seated man, old, with a long wispy beard, but didn't really see the face. My first thought was that he was Tibetan, but on further reflection he could have been Chinese due to his dress of purple robes with gold embroidery. Three of the group saw a monk with me, hooded, a long brown robe with a rope belt at the waist.

In a later session I was asked to consider looking into shamanism as well as druids and druidic practices. Part of the time we went in twos and had to sense past lives; my partner saw me as a "Roman soldier steeped in blood". However, the next day we concentrated on mediumship, as we were being sorted out for our demonstration to another group tomorrow. I was asked to go third, but linking together with Rachael. Meeting with her during the tea break the following morning, Rachael told me that she had met my monk, who was called Jacob, and that he waddled slightly when he walked and had a low centre of balance.

We had our assessments from Avril, who was very encouraging to me, as were the others in the group, and early evening we did our demonstration. All did very well except for yours truly, but Rachael recovered it well. Avril must have been very proud.

Apart from the group work, there were lots of other experiences. There were several demonstrations of trance, the first with Donna Stewart – whose guide 'Toccana' gave good philosophy and encouragement – and Tony, whose face did change, especially later when linking with people to give an impression of their guides. Matthew Smith also gave a trance demonstration, with an eastern gentleman coming through at the beginning, giving some excellent philosophy about the power of thought and then answering questions. Then a different spirit came through, a little girl called 'Sunshine', who was very humorous and had lots of amusing mannerisms – a wonderful demonstration.

Tony gave a session on automatic writing; Eileen Davis a "Language of Symbolism Workshop"; Cassandra an interesting "Cycles of Life through Numerology"; Donna a talk on "Guides and their Purpose"; and a combined demonstration of clairvoyance and psychic art from Donna and Debbie: *Absolutely excellent demonstration - all the pictures were taken and the clairvoyance by Donna was superb. Very glad I had witnessed such an event.*

Regrettably the week just flew by and I left with lots to think about, but invigorated and satisfied, having met so many like-minded people.

The year ended on a melancholy note, with the death of my brother-in-law in Northern Ireland. He had been fighting cancer for some years, but eventually his body could not resist anymore and he was buried not long before Christmas. It was a sad funeral that I attended, and it must have been a difficult Festive period for the family.

During the second week in July 2005 I found myself on a plane flying to Västerås, Sweden, to go on a course at the 'International College of Spiritual Science and Healing' at Ramsbergsgarden. It had originally been billed as mediumship and psychic art (the latter my main interest), but I received a telephone call saying that due to family matters, the psychic art tutor could not come, so did I still wish to go? Without much hesitation I said yes.

About half way through the flight I suddenly remembered that I had forgotten to check on the currency! Enquiring from my Swedish fellow passenger, he told me that indeed they did have their own kroner – so the euros in my pocket were of little use. I doubt if I will ever make that same mistake again! Anyway, I was met by Jane, the organiser of the centre, and driven away from the big town into the forests, seeing several foxes but no moose. Jane kindly changed a small amount of euros for me, although it proved unnecessary, as there was nothing really to spend it on! The centre was near a small lake with houses dotted here and there, but it was mostly forest, making it incredibly quiet, and with the lovely weather and skies I was perfectly contented.

The light coming through the window woke me up at 4am, but I didn't get up until 7.30am. Walking to the fresh water lake I noticed pond skaters and fish, and going through the woods noticed a carpet of blueberry plants, together with a large number of bees that seemed to prefer a tall spindly plant with small yellow flowers. One could see why many would want to get away from the city and towns and love to come to places like this.

The other participants gradually arrived throughout the morning, a Norwegian, two others from the UK, two Swedes, the tutor Joan Hughes from England, (and the cook was from Ireland!). A small group, but all the better for that. The weather just got hotter and hotter, somebody during a tea break said it was nearing 40°C. Jane suffered a bit of heat stroke and later I developed digestive problems, though Joan helped with some Gaviscon tablets. However, that didn't stop me from going to the group sessions, where we started with psychic and then spirit linking. Joan mentioned that she saw my grandfather standing very close behind me, and that he helped me. Over the subsequent days we looked at the extent of an aura; trying to get a psychic or spirit linked reading of a stranger; inspired writing; table work; sensing colours in the aura, and much practice working in pairs and so forth.

Jane recovered enough to give us what she had learnt about psychic art, getting us to draw one of our helpers in spirit, and seeing what we could get for someone in the group, and then in pairs. Looking to get an image of one of our guides: I eventually got an image in my head of a young girl, late teens/early 20s, very dark eyes – all around the eyes (even more than Dusty Springfield) with blonde hair that stood up straight. She was laughing and had (I felt) a mischievous side to her character.

I've had many slightly different (but similar in feeling) images over the years, that I think are all the same spirit.

After this we did inspired writing, with Joan suggesting that my inspirer was a gentleman with a very long beard, but he went a very long way back in time, maybe pre Aristotle.

That evening though, became the highlight of the whole course, when we tried for EVP (Electronic Voice Phenomena) using a Dictaphone. *Met at 8 and went to barn - tried downstairs - but we got nothing and didn't feel anything. Went upstairs - but more or less the same, though at one point it sounded as if someone had put their hand on the player. However, we decided to go to the séance room. This was much better. First the batteries went dead. 'M' got a packet from his room. We found also the speed control had been altered. Then on the next run found the tape had slowed down and after that it went at normal speed ... On the 3rd try we got the bull's eye - a very loud "Michael" - as if said by a female Swedish voice! Brilliant!* For a brief moment or two I had thought it might have been my mother, but after listening to it carefully I dismissed that idea. *Pia was sitting opposite me and said she felt a cool breeze in front of her when I was talking. ... Lots of laughter as Joan's stomach started to gurgle - but only when the recorder was going! The last time 'C's, Pia's, Joan's and mine started! Fantastic result.* [Months later Joan posted the tape to me and I copied it onto a digital recorder and from there into my laptop. I produced some CDs and sent them to all for whom I had an address and one to the centre. Unfortunately some were unable to play them, but others were fine. Some years later the sound on the laptop ceased to function, so any CDs still out there are a rarity.]

The other interesting happening (for me!) was when we all sat to get something for Joan. I got a whole collection of disconnected images: a World War 1 gas mask, young girl with blonde curly hair, a black necklace of large black spheres, a 'funny' image of a young girl with blonde tight curly hair – but felt it was a doll although the eyes blinked and moved, etc. Much to my amazement Joan was able to take practically all of it!

During lunch on the last day Joan told me that I had a brother in spirit, my mother having had a miscarriage some years before I was born. That was interesting as 'C' had told me this earlier in the week when we were working in pairs. [This has been given to me by another medium years later.] Eventually, it was saying our goodbyes, and I got a lovely five minutes of reflexology from Pia that sorted out my back pain, and a lovely hug as well. Said goodbye to Joan and the other UK participants when we got off the plane at Luton airport, and arrived eventually at my destination to find my brother-in-law with the door open at 4.00am!

There was little time to get myself sorted as just over a week later I went to Wales and Hafan-y-Coed. This time for "A Taste of Trance" with Jock McArthur, who came from near Dunfermline in Scotland. The first evening we started with calisthenics, which raises the energy and extended the aura. Jock talked about auras, clairvoyance and the service on the last night, when the group will be taking it. Jock was not only a good teacher, but supplied us with many handouts, something that I really appreciate. I will not dwell on all the exercises etc., but confine myself to a few personal details and some experiences.

The next day we started using the cabinet, and when it was my turn:

Did feel my mouth was funny, that it needed to be smaller, and lots of energy around my head and shoulders. They seemed to think that an old lady was overshadowing me, with arthritic hands. The following day I was back in the cabinet: I went first - this time in green light. Tried to really relax and concentrate on deep breathing. Mouth again felt 'odd' and I felt I wanted to open my mouth, my lips certainly parted. Lots of energy around my head and shoulders. Very peaceful and calm. Some of them thought they saw a man with a long beard. Jock said he looked something like Stainton Moses or even a bit like Lenin. Jock said I was a bit like the carthorse - I'd get there but it would take some time, maybe 10 to 15 years!

After a disturbed sleep that night, in the morning we again had cabinet work under green light. *Second session we started in blue light. I was first. Didn't feel I went as deep as last time. Did see lots of decoration - like a Baroque hall with tall arched windows and doors - all very ornate. Then it changed to just strange decorations. Interestingly, some said I looked like Socrates or Aristotle! Jock said I should have my own group and sit for physical mediumship!*

That evening Jock gave us a demonstration, and I had the job of controlling the red light, so was sitting just feet from him slightly to his left. *Can't remember all that happened, but I felt the energy changes (most of them) and saw bits and pieces - but not all. Did see briefly a face of a young girl on his neck, but didn't see anything on the back of his head. Several guides / helpers came through + Winston Churchill in image only; 'A's grandfather; a wee girl John (Jock) had played with when he was in hospital at 5 years of age, etc. Best bit for me was when a Scottish accent started talking and it transpired it was John Campbell Sloan! - the medium who had convinced Arthur Findlay. At the end his main guide answered questions from anybody and before we knew it, it had*

*come to an end, and the whole thing had been on for 2
hours - it was supposed to last 1 to 1½ hours.*

On the last day, two of the women whose helpers had earlier come through
were talking, as they went for a tea break. One said to the other, "wouldn't
it be wonderful if our guides came through and talked with each other".
Resuming after tea, that is exactly what happened!

After the Service, which went well, we had a little ceremony on our
own with Jock, which proved to be quite emotional for some, and we
all thanked Jock for his teaching and his patience with us. Leaving in the
morning, which was dull and damp, I had my eye out for a red kite, but
this time none was to be seen.

There were only two other noteworthy occurrences that year, one
being a visit to the Cairndale hotel in Dumfries to see an evening of
clairvoyance with Stephen Holbrook. I found his style dramatic and he
was occasionally very loud. He had clairaudient abilities and that was his
main route of communication, but also clairsentience. There was some
very good evidence and lots of tears of release and joy. A friend who came
with me thought he was very genuine and was glad that she had come, and
I bought two books about him.

The other occurrence happened about three weeks before Christmas.
I telephoned my brother, and during the conversation he told me of a
dream he had years ago. He said that he had seen our father and grandfather
walking with each other, and that they had then turned and waved to him.

In January 2006, I stayed for a weekend with a couple who had been in
Doris' monthly sessions. We were joined by another lady from that group,
and decided to hold a circle. During a visualisation, my mind started to
wander and then I saw lots of cloth – tweed etc., being draped over each
other, all in different patterns and colours. For a second or two I couldn't
make it out, and then it came to me: I'm collecting too much 'material'
– the material side is too dominant and I should be doing more with my
spiritual side. I thanked spirit for making it obvious to me!

In the second week of April I attended the Lynwood Fellowship
seminar at Cober Hill, Cloughton, about six miles north of Scarborough,
Yorkshire. One of the tutors, Shonagh Moore, had brought her set of

crystal bowls (99% quartz crystal). She gave an interesting talk on the first afternoon, explaining the connection of sound with colour and light. The sounds from the different bowls were lovely, though a few could be 'penetrating' or even disturbing for some. Shonagh's workshops were equally intriguing: visualising images and colours from sounds, linking with a sound and singing Oms and noting reactions. There were very vivid memories that came to the fore, while one or two had to exit as they found the sound discomfiting. In another workshop Shonagh played five pieces of music, for about three or four minutes each, and then we related what we had felt or received in the way of images or colours.

On the first evening three of the tutors gave a demonstration of their mediumship, during which I saw unique (for me at least) images above their heads. *Donna Stewart, Shonagh Moore and John Conway - two messages each and then the three of them kept on the same link initiated by Donna. Very good most of it - some emotional messages and others hilarious! I was aware of an aura around them, Donna was first and I saw what looked like an interwoven 'crown', cone shaped, that stood out from the top of her head - in misty 'white' light - up to 6 to 8*

inches in height. Also etheric light around the head including the 'crown'. I saw exactly similar with Shonagh - though this was a little harder to see due to the background being lighter behind her. John also had this.

As the weather was so nice, I decided to go out for a few walks during some of the workshops, but tried to take in most of the talks from the tutors mentioned, as well as those from Bridget Hickey, Don Galloway and Peter Hague, all of which were good. Peter led the Tai Chi in the mornings before breakfast, which I always tried to join. However, time passes quickly and soon it was the end of the seminar.

At the beginning of May 2006, two friends and I attended another 'Evening of Clairvoyance' in Dumfries with Stephen Holbrook. It was well attended with over 500 people, and again was an excellent example of mediumship. Indeed, in September I visited for the third time 'An Evening of Clairvoyance' by Stephen Holbrook with four different friends. Another impressive night, and part of my note on it said it all: *All the people he went to needed messages - which is always a good sign.*

In mid June I again met up with old friends, and we had a circle, during which there was a guided meditation. *The meditation went quite well, I relaxed (mostly) and seemed to be attracted to the white flowers more than any others. Felt it was for purity - I needed to get to the heart of things - find the pure inner essence. The person who joined me was a hooded monk - so I didn't see the face - and he didn't speak - but the word 'Balance' came. Felt it referred to me trying to find that in my life - balance of the material to the spiritual, balance even in the material - not to go to excess in some areas.*

Later we attended a Spiritualist Church with the clairvoyance being given by a medium from the north east of England. He came to me near the end of the service. *He saw a gentleman with me who had a white beard - but much longer than mine, but well trimmed. He was not a family connection, more of an influence over me. He holds a scroll / papyrus rolled up under his arm and this was a scroll of knowledge and enlightenment. Some of it is a little heavy or hard going, but I will get there in the end. Then he got the word Michael ("I am Michael") - another Michael in spirit. Then he said, "Have you had your name shouted out?" (Yes !)*

Five days later found me attending the funeral of Mike Peachey. He was buried with Audrey, amid the drifts of drizzle. It was nice to meet and talk to the family, and say how much I owed to both their parents.

The next Lynwood Fellowship seminar ran from 9th to 14th July 2006, at Losehill Hall, Castleton. Again the weather was warm and dry, and I spent a morning drawing Peveril Castle and taking photographs. There was little in the way of significant personal experiences, but I enjoyed the talks by Don Galloway, and an interesting one on allergies and intolerances by Hugh Davis. Mary Cerrino, in conversation with Don, gave a fascinating life story of some of her family, starting with her great grandmother, who used to live in the Jews House, Steep Hill, Lincoln, and had séances with Rabbis etc. All the sittings were recorded and it was all done with letters and an upturned glass! During the tea break after this talk, Mary kindly came and showed me her book of the circle records.

Two weeks later I was down in Eastbourne for the ISF 29th World Congress Convention Week, at the T&G Conference Centre. It was nice to meet up again with some of the people I had got to know from three years ago. There was a choice of workshops for both mornings and afternoons, so for the morning one I opted for the 'Beginners Physical' with Robin Hodson as tutor.

First we went over the basics, what it is, safety and so forth. Then Robin gave us some notes and let us look at a few photographs. The second session was in the séance room, which was blacked out and had a red light. There was a cabinet with a circle of chairs. Volunteering to go first: *I felt very relaxed and soon aware of a 'presence' at my right-hand side - male energy. Then aware of energy around my head, especially at the back. Some saw a slight 'vision' of a man with a long white beard, then that changed later to one with dark hair; eyes 'blanked out' but no spirit eyes formed.* Then we changed places until nearly all the group had been in the cabinet. I saw lights with some, mist, and changes in features, and some even speaking.

The next morning we worked right the way through to lunch without a break. Robin started with a talk and showing us photographic examples of ectoplasm, how it can be in rods (for trumpet etc.) and figures, and even 'sheets' with faces on them. Then, sitting in the same positions we went back to cabinet work. Soon it was my turn again: *I felt less energy than yesterday, just slight energy at the back of my head, quite late on; at the start it was my jaw, I felt it wanted to grow! People said they saw me with a white face right at the start, then a long white beard (Father Christmas!!), some saw me with a large Roman nose, and somebody said I looked like a head on a coin. Next they saw a black hat on my head, as if I was a Greek Orthodox priest. Sandra said that I had what looked like shackles on my feet, others thought one was different from the other.*

One or two others had a go and then it was table work: *5 of us round a small table, and eventually it started to rock and spin a bit, and tip (very steeply). It may have done more, but I think '......' was a little scared of the procedure, and therefore there was no violent movement. We swapped, so that others could get on it.* After that we had a few more in the cabinet before the finish.

The next two mornings were taken up with the photograph, a business meeting and so forth, so it was not until the last day that the group got together again. After a talk, we were given envelopes, with a smaller envelope inside it that contained blank Polaroid film. We placed the smaller envelope on our person somewhere, and at the end gave it back to Robin. After a guided meditation we went back to cabinet work.

Sandra went in first, taken 'over' by somebody who spoke with difficulty: Joseph McCaffrey, who passed at midnight in a car accident on 13/14th Sept 1962. He was 46 years old and had 3 children and a wife, one of the children also died in the crash, (Steven or Stephen, aged 14), which was caused by faulty brakes ("loose" was how he described them). He came from High Wycombe in Buckinghamshire, was a carpenter making drawers and tables etc., liked to play golf, not very good but enjoyed the company. Very good!

Then Jim Robson - he sat without music (affected his hearing aids) and got overshadowing - two personalities.

Then …?…, who apparently changed features quite a bit, but I found it very difficult to see this - just very dark across the eyes, but others recognized a black lady with curly hair.

Then the other woman, who acts as an interpreter for the previous woman. Very good - personality that came through was very haughty and put her arms out wider than the actual chair she was sitting in - as if she sat on a throne. Very regal; she tried to speak but couldn't control the lips and speaking - so when she spoke the lips were closed so we couldn't hear. But it should come with practice. We then ended and I said the closing prayer. Excellent stuff! Tried to take a photograph but batteries depleted!!

We then went down for lunch. Sandra's room key had gone missing from her handbag. Everything was searched – including her room – but without success, and then it turned up this morning – in her handbag. When I went to put new batteries in my camera, it wasn't there! I searched everywhere, but no camera. Just before going to reception to report it missing, I went back upstairs (due to knowing about Sandra's experience) and checked there. It was on a table at the far side of the room, where I hadn't been!

Later that evening we all met up briefly with Robin Hodson. All the Polaroids had something on them, not much on mine, but lots on most of the others. A great success!

The afternoon workshops that I attended were for psychic art with the Swiss tutor Matthias Güldenstein. At the start he asked us to draw ourselves – just to show how hard it is, but then how difficult it must be for spirit to come through and draw themselves through a material person. Then some tips on drawing faces, before we worked in pairs, trying to link with spirit and get somebody that the partner would know. My Finnish partner got a grandmother image initially, but then it turned into a grandfather. I got an image of bright green sunglasses, and just added instinctively after that. My partner thought there was a family resemblance but couldn't place it. I had thought initially it was an aunt, but the picture felt as if it represented her image in the 1950s/1960s rather than when she passed over.

In the next session we started by doing exercises to loosen up: draw with a scribble; use your other hand; draw with your eyes closed. I tried the last two together, and then tried with two crayons held in my left hand – and was quite surprised by the result. Eventually we were asked to link in and get a drawing for anybody in the group. *I relaxed and asked for a link, but got no vision of any kind - so just started with my left hand and two crayons. An image formed of a young man - I thought 17/18, died suddenly. But after that I think my mind kicked in and I went a bit wrong. Looked around the room and felt it was one person - but another was directly behind him, so talked to them both. The first person took it - death was at seventeen and a half through a motorbike accident. Interestingly, the woman who was sitting beside me independently got the same link and drew for him, and she got the motorbike etc. Spirit must have influenced both of us at the same time.* Then there was the opportunity for some to draw, while others linked in and tried to give clairvoyance.

The next day we started with linking with a partner; then later several people did the drawing on the board in front of the group, while others gave a clairvoyant link. At the end I got up to have a go, with Eva Güldenstein helping with the clairvoyance. There was a bit of difficulty in placing the image, as there were two possible recipients, but felt it was for Carlo, who had been sitting beside me. A very interesting session, which unfortunately was our last due to other events.

This was a very enjoyable and educational week, and other noteworthy events were the talks/lectures. The first by Eleanor Landreau, who gave a very animated and passionate lecture entitled, 'Evolution of the Soul'. The other was equally fascinating – 'Reincarnation', given by Roy Stemman. So good was it that I bought the book!

Just one week later I was back at the Arthur Findlay College for Tony Stockwell's event, 'Reaching Higher', that ran from the 12th - 18th August. I had been lucky to get a place, being offered it by Joan (the tutor on my visit to Sweden) as one of her church group had dropped out. I was in Jean Blackabee's group and enjoyed her encouragement and optimism. We started with small exercises, then, in groups of two, sensing the aura and the colours that were there and giving an interpretation of these. Next it was groups of three: choosing a card, deciding whom in the group it was for and then giving an interpretation of the card for them and how it related to their spiritual path: *I felt spirit with me and got drawn to a woman on my right - can't remember her name. Gave the reading, with only a little hesitation; maybe it was true as she dissolved into tears afterwards and had to leave the room for a short while.*

The following morning we had a short meditation to link with spirit, and then Jean asked for volunteers – and I went first: *Didn't get an image in my mind, but a feeling of a person (ALL OF THIS VERY TENUOUS) elderly lady, slim, grey hair, glasses - but maybe not all the time, not sure of dentures - maybe half and half. (This was later confirmed as correct - top half dentures, bottom her own.) Felt I was with one lady - but it turned out to be the one sitting next to her. Wrinkles - smiles, was asked how she passed, but didn't really get any sensations except a slight feeling in my head, so said maybe a stroke (not known). Felt she didn't know much about spiritualism, but was pleased to come with her while she did these courses etc., and was there to find out for herself and also encourage her. Thought an aunt - but apparently not a family link (later she said it was her 'nan'). Later I felt lots of emotion and love. When asked for month for anniversaries etc., went through the list and got 2, March and July, as I had a slight feeling with these. Got the names of Joyce and Fred or Frederick, which were both taken. Got the feeling of something around her neck (necklace?) but this couldn't be taken. Also got an open white book - I suggested that maybe she read to her as a child - but no. However, on thinking about it later, the book looked like my sketchbook, so I asked her afterwards if she did drawings. She said her Nan used to sit with her and draw puzzles and pictures with her. So the book was a symbol.* This exercise continued after the tea break and again after lunch, then we went into pairs again.

Next day we were asked to volunteer and again I got up first: *Very difficult, but only had a bit of help as Jean sat down at the start.*

Said female energy and later got a vague feeling of a woman in a green suit sitting in a chair, dark hair, but got no sense of the face. I assumed the height as about an inch or two smaller than myself, and age about late 50s or early 60s. Struggled with sense of passing (Jean came to help me here) - found my left hand going to my heart, though wasn't aware of it at first - so heart condition, passing fairly quickly. Wasn't sure of where I was going but Jasmine said she could take most of it. Felt something to do with my hands and suggested knitting/crochet etc., (it turned out to be her mum and she used to do lace work), bubbly personality and also liked her moments of quiet - reading etc. Tidy, liked things to be in order. Coming through to give upliftment and humour and laughter. Glad of the progress that Jasmine is making. Felt I had made another little step forward. The others were very good and some very funny!

In the afternoon it went more slowly, with everybody seeming to be a bit tired. Noticeably, a few hilarious incidents happened, no doubt spirit trying to raise the energies. However, all had some success.

The following day we worked in pairs and in the afternoon we acted together with another group as guinea pigs for the more advanced students in Tony's group who gave one to one readings. However, an interesting thing happened just after dinner, when I decided to catch up with my notes. *Found I had to recharge my mobile phone (2nd time), plus my camera indicated low batteries. So took them out and checked them - they glowed 'good'; put them back in and viewed some of the photos - and the camera went dead. Took out the batteries which were glowing by themselves 'good', and they stayed like that for at least 5 minutes.*

We did inspirational writing initiated by selecting an Angel Card, before volunteering to demonstrate. Unusually, I didn't get up first! But by the afternoon I was back to normal: *I got up first this time! After a very slow start 'felt' tenuously a female energy, woman in her 50s, bright trouser suit, large pattern of flowers on it against black; passed to spirit due to a tumour or something similar in her brain (felt sensation inside my head). Felt this person to be very active, busy and happy, a large personality, very sociable;*

felt a car - red - was connected, a convertible, [Here I must add that my notes were often done in a rush, so they are just that – notes. My memory of the previous experience is still quite clear: I was in the Alps on top of one of the passes, I saw the car as a Ferrari, and instead of just saying that, I assumed it was my mind and said a red convertible, to which Gemma then said "yes, it was a Ferrari". I mentally gave myself a big kick!] *and that I was sure she was not Welsh, but felt I was being taken there or at least the border areas. [I had two possible links at this stage, then Gemma said she could take all of it.] Felt this person did writing - maybe a diary or something of that nature. Then I got lots of emotion and had to take some time before I could speak. Said I felt great love and I wished to express her thanks to Gemma and in return to give Gemma love and happiness in her life.*

Afterwards Gemma told me that she was a woman with a tumour and she was in and out of the hospice for some time; also that the woman was helped by Gemma to write her own personal story (memory book, that took over a year to complete) and letters to her husband, daughter and son. At the end of the group session Jean gave us all our tasks for the demonstration tomorrow. All of us are to take part – and I have to get on the platform for mediumship! After dinner Gemma proved to me that what I had given was correct, she let me see several A4 sheets that related to her experience with the woman, and then said that she didn't know why she had brought it, as it seemed to have no relevance to what she was going to do!

All too soon our demonstration came around. I went about third: *Felt really isolated - and really wasn't sure - female, motherly type vibration, passed in her late 60s, grey - pepper and salt hair, sitting in her chair, stick; felt she passed with a chest complaint, but it was just her time to go. A shawl round her shoulders, knitted. Felt she was a homemaker, and had all the abilities that go with that, baking, sewing etc. Lively personality, laughter, liked a dance in her youth, and felt this memory needed to go back the Second World War. (At this point it was taken.) Emotional, the month of March was significant, she wanted to give the person that laughter and upliftment to help her through all the 'stuff' she is going through at present in her life. All of it was accepted!*

At the assessment session, Jean said I had doubted a spirit link at the start – and now I knew I was linked to spirit – just go back and see what you get. She was disappointed that I had no circle to go to, but could see me running a circle in the future, and that I should practice meditation, link with spirit and use the Angel Cards. It was all very positive, but very much due to the excellent encouragement and teaching from Jean.

Before leaving this week, I must mention some other notable events: Tony Stockwell's talk "Great Great Granddads and Distant Friends", about getting a sharper connection with messages; the demonstration by Tony's group, which was really excellent; an interesting Angel workshop with Jacky Newcombe and the lecture by Leah Bond "Worlds within Worlds", what a lovely voice that delivers with passion and precision. Lastly, it was great to meet up with Joan and Pia once again, and to meet with other like minds.

CHAPTER 12

Seminars & Closed Circle

Visiting friends in November of that year, we had a circle, after which we all agreed to sit together more often. Deciding to try our best to make it on a weekly basis (bar holidays etc.), the first 'official' circle was held on 7th December with just four of us. We had many visualisations and meditations, seeking always to be guided by spirit. Some of the imagery was very symbolic, but at times it was difficult to come to any idea as to what it represented or alluded to: *The next image that I remember was that I held in my hands a giant mushroom, at least 30cms in diameter, but it was as if it was inside out, with the outside dome textured with lots of deep 'valleys', as if the inside 'fillets' were now on the cap of it. Nothing else happened - I just held the mushroom!*

However, it became clear fairly early on that Doris was in the background, and some of those spirits that used to be with her when she was in her material body were still with her now.

On the sixth circle, one of the sitters got lots of images connected with a cross, like hot cross buns and a house window divided into four sections. We initially thought that it might have referred to the four of us, joined in harmony. Then in the next circle another sitter saw an image of a beautiful solid silver roundel, with a deep turquoise stone in the centre and a cross, the whole thing connected to two solid silver chains that went over my shoulders. In the subsequent circle I got an image of a Celtic stone cross.

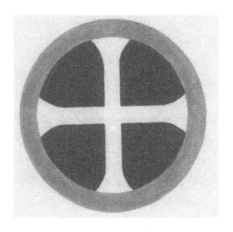

The centre had a blank smooth circle of stone, and the 'arms' extended more than would be usual. Eventually, we came to the conclusion that both the circle and the cross were important, and arrived at an image that became the emblem of the circle, a white cross on a blue background, both surrounded by a gold circle.

At the end of October 2007 we had spirit come through in the circle, though the voice was very soft and many of the words were lost. *"The colours that you have chosen, or have been chosen for this circle of light: the gold being the highest and the best, letting in the enlightened souls to come forward. The blue being the gentleness of the mind, and the body and the spirit and the strength ****. But above all the white cross, which ***... (Unfortunately the last bit was lost.) We wish you well in all that you do. We ask for the patience of those that are behind you and are trying to influence things to come."*

It was at this same circle, about a minute after what I've described above and while that spirit continued to talk to us, that I heard the fluttering of a bird, with its wings hitting something. This continued for at least a minute before it stopped. After the closing of the circle I looked in the corner behind me where the sound had come from, and there a small **empty** birdcage hung from the ceiling. Other phenomena included the altering of the intensity of the red lights; in fact on one occasion when I went to read out a short passage from a book, spirit immediately raised the lights as I found it difficult to see the type clearly. At another time the clock opposite me descended in three stages and quickly returned afterwards. Then there was the moving of a particular picture many times, not just up and down and from side to side, but once in a circular manner! Indeed, before even opening one circle I saw it move, and this movement was then confirmed by another sitter. It was good to get that verified.

Much of the early stages were sensing energies, meditating and using visualisations. I often had difficulties with these, so will give only one example, when although I was giving it out (inspired by spirit) I also got a 'result'! *Sitting on a bench underneath a flowering cherry tree, you enjoy the beautiful sunny summers day and hear the birds singing. In front of you is a path, either side of which are closely cropped grassy lawns; there is also a lake in which are islands, each linked to the other by wooden bridges. Walk on the path towards the bridge, and as you begin to cross look into the water and see the different coloured fish. Crossing the bridge, you approach a wooden building that looks a little like a temple. On the outside of it is a bell, ring the bell before you enter and note the tone of it. Sit down inside and enjoy the views, there is a beautiful mountain in the background, symmetrical in shape and snow on the summit; around you the trees and flowers give a variety of colour and scent, and there is plenty of wildlife. You see another person approaching the temple; this person also rings the bell and then enters, and takes a seat beside you. They may give you something or talk to you. I will leave you now to experience what may come ...*

I did my best to try as well - very fleeting. The bell was almost like a cowbell, tapering slightly at the end, and when struck it sounded very clear, just like a Tibetan singing bowl. I sat down and a Japanese lady appeared in wooden shoes. She was a geisha, dressed in a pale 'baby blue' kimono. She sat on my left and didn't speak, but got out a fan and handed it to me. I opened the fan, but the cloth was without decoration, a pale cream colour and this was on both sides. I felt my left hand go cold and sensed she touched it lightly and then took her hand away; it was like a touch of reassurance. Then she got up and left by a different exit.

During the first year and a half we had experiments with psychic art and psychometry, and spent some time on table work, before being asked by spirit to take part in 'saving lost souls' or 'rescue work' – which we did for about fifteen weeks. Naturally from time to time spirit would speak to us, to give encouragement, advice and so forth. Gradually, these increased to embrace philosophy and their concern at what was taking place in the material world. I give a short early example: ... *That is why we have brought the Sun Dance, to lift up all the vibrations. To bring great strength from the Great Spirit, for when you give respect to spirit you get it back. We respect all that we hunted, we gave thanks for everything. When we took out the heart of the buffalo and ate the liver of the buffalo, we held it in our hands, with the great blood running down our arms and held it up to the Great White Spirit and said our thanks. We did not kill for harmony, we killed for survival. But we showed respect for all things of the Pashamama. The Pashamama was our Mother. We respect our Mother with great hearts, with great trust and with great respect. This lacking in your plane today. We despair to see the devastation that man has been doing to other man, and to fellow creatures and to Mother Nature. But fear not, the balance will come about, when the divine plan bounces back. And when it does hit back only the strong will be left to continue. The strong being those in the mind and the heart, by doing what is right for themselves. But for men with the power of the spirit that your brothers know, there is nothing far greater.*

During this time I also tried to keep broadening my learning by continuing to attend seminars, though due to timing and circumstance this meant almost exclusively going to those run by the Lynwood Fellowship. The first one in April 2007 was at Cober Hill, where during an awareness group, Jean got up and said that she had been given a message for me: *It turned out to be both my maternal grandmother and grandfather were there. Grandfather was into Spiritualism but didn't take his interest any further. Grandmother held him back, as she didn't really approve - as most didn't in those days (especially in Ireland). Both were urging me on, to get over my fear that is holding me back, fear of failure, fear of looking silly - whatever. If I got over this and boldly go on with this pathway, everything will open up to me. There is a little health difficulty, not really heart, just a bit of blood pressure, especially when under stress. It is not serious, but if I go forward on my path all this will disappear. Grandmother was taking her bonnet off to me, to salute me and urge me on. Grandfather wants me to do what he would have liked to have done.*

Although I had discussed my interest in Spiritualism and other things with my mother, it was only about three or four years before her death that she had mentioned her father to me. Apparently he had an extensive library of books on this subject, but they had gone into storage and become 'lost'. How I would have liked to have read some of those books! Several mediums have mentioned him to me, particularly in connection with my spiritual healing work. An example of this happened in the closed circle about five months later when one of the sitters: ... *got two people for me, who are with me when I'm healing, and it was grandparents. Grandfather especially, but grandmother was around at other times too; grandparents were on my mother's side.*

Don Galloway gave his usual brilliant talks, but was not too well near the end of the course. Another tutor at the seminar was Will Pimlett, who gave two good introductory talks on shamanism, and I took part in a 'Medicine Walk' – a little like a walking meditation. We did other exercises to find our power animal, but being unsuccessful with this, I went one afternoon for a walk along the cliffs by the sea, and decided that the humble bumblebee was the candidate (even though I searched the sea for signs of humpback whales or even dolphins!). At a circle meeting two months later I was reminded of this when asked if I remembered the humming sound. When I didn't respond they added the sound of water, and I immediately thought of my walk along the cliffs. To confirm this I asked if it was near Scarborough, and got the positive response.

The next seminar in July 2007 was memorable for the statement from Dennis Russell (an interesting writer – I bought several of his booklets at the next seminar), who said that he had seen the end of a rainbow in Cross Street, Manchester. However, it was memorable in a different way; Don Galloway gave his usual excellent talk, but later that evening took a stroke and had to be taken by ambulance to hospital. He was later transferred to Hull. I never got to see Don again, and he eventually passed just over two years later.

Meanwhile in the circle we continued to get odd noises from time to time, some as raps, another time it was like someone slapping the wall twice, and a brief second of what sounded like a mobile phone tune. We had been told that some young Native American braves might be working with us, and soon after I got a condition that I associated with one of these who had decided to try and work with me. Throughout the next six months I continued to sense this condition not only in circle, but also in my own meditations.

The next seminar of the Lynwood Fellowship that I could get to was in July 2008, when Geoff Freed and Simeon Stefanidakis gave some terrific talks and workshops that were very thought provoking. Although Don was not present, Peter Hague took over his role. The beguiling voice of Leah Bond was present and Sue Odam completed the tutors. On the last evening we had a magnificent dinner that celebrated the twenty-fifth anniversary of the Fellowship.

The various noises in the circle continued, even after a few changes in personnel, though my Native American spirit friend seemed to depart by March 2009. However, I felt a new energy with me, much more gentle and subtle. In addition, I was beginning to sense changes in energies and temperatures better, and started to see things, like a blue mist and once what I can only describe as 'waves of energy' descending into the circle. As usual the progress that came to me was very slow – but at least I knew that I was gradually 'opening out'.

It was just before Easter in 2009 when my subsequent Lynwood Fellowship seminar occurred. Shonagh Moore again delighted me with the sound of her crystal bowls, but I was particularly taken with her workshop on the morning of the last full day. *There were only 4 of us – all men. Shonagh used the bowls first to relax us, and then used the drum (Hopi Indians) to detect and give healing to each of us. It was quite uncanny how she picked up the major problems – my sinuses, ears, tension at back of neck, a point in the upper back, my left arm being weaker, feet! When given the healing, the sound seemed to enter and fill ones body. Then she went through the bowls and grounded us and we closed. Very good and unexpected. Shonagh said that she had been given a vision of the future, where a patient was lying on a titanium bed, the patient was levitated and 'scanned' and given healing through colour and sound, without the need for invasive surgery.*

A new tutor to the Lynwood Fellowship was Andy Thomas, who gave a great series of talks. The first, "The Crop Circle Mystery", gave a brief history of crop circles and the latest developments over the last decade, illustrated through the use of computer. This was followed by an equally fascinating talk entitled "The Power of Collective Thought", though unfortunately I was unable to take any notes, due to the main lights being off for most of it! "Exploring 2012 Prophecies" was his third well presented lecture, which included a variety of astronomical data among other information. His final one, "Mysteries and Cover Ups", was a very thought provoking and powerful talk exploring lots of issues of which most of the public are unaware. In talking to him afterwards, I got an order in for his new book that was soon to be published – "The Truth Agenda". When eventually reading it, I discovered it contained some of the issues that concerned me, and brought others to my attention. At the time of writing this, I know it's on the third edition, and certainly think that it deserves a wider audience.

In the circle the noises continued and spirit gave advice to several of the sitters, including myself. We all smelt the fragrance of flowers in one session and others felt psychic breezes. Sparkles of light were seen and some overshadowing when we concentrated on one person at a time, trying to get deeper in relaxation and better attuned with spirit. Interestingly, in personal meditations at the end of April I again received the condition associated with the Native American. At the end of June spirit spoke through one of the sitters and spoke to me; I include part of my notes: *Your world holds many dark places, for it is you pupils that we need to send the message out to those that are in need of the Great Spirit's love, for it is the love that will break through many barriers. But if you my friend, sitting opposite me, will learn to love a little bit more within himself, those in the spirit will draw much closer to your heart, and as your heart will open so shall your mind. The masters are there waiting until at last the pupil has to be ready, thus patience is greatly needed. So fear not, those that are waiting with you my friend are waiting with great encouraging. As long as you play your part to have the peace of the mind that is required within you, then the greater the spirit will be with you. We know that you go on your travels, but those travels are only going to be spontaneous, then, we will make the breakthrough to give you time to think. For in the time that you think, you will receive more from spirit. You have had much on your shoulders lately, but this will come off in time. And time is the issue here as it is manmade, but there is no time in that of the spirit. So find time my friend, to yourself. In the next few months to come you will see those change or changes. We wish you well.* Then at the start of July one person returned to the circle, so we now comprised five in total.

The next seminar was again with the Lynwood Fellowship, from 5th to 10th July 2009, and this time we were lucky to have five tutors. The first that I saw was Alan Stuttle, who gave a talk on "Art and Mediumship" in the afternoon. In addition he gave a demonstration of his own spirit art using different methods, colour / black and white, right-handed / left-handed etc. Alan gave two workshops. In the first he gave us an example to get us started, and then off we went! I managed to get a picture of a military man in a green uniform, with various bits of landscape and a cottage, and a vegetable – all this was taken by the person who had been sitting next to me. After lunch I had a private sitting with Alan, so I got my own picture, with quite a few symbols in it that were very relevant.

I will give my notes for the last workshop. *Same as previous workshop (and just as full), though this time he started with an egg shape for the head and then half divisions. I found myself with a face that started as a female, changed to male, back to female etc.!! In the end I settled for female, but couldn't get the hair; had a 'glimpse' of blonde tresses, but in the end decided that she was meant to be bald. Then put orange round her shoulders and felt she was a Buddhist nun, who seemed very serene and young. We were told to write some words and I got the following - which is not exact, but the gist of the meaning: "Bring the Light into yourself, and then you can help to light up the world". Also got the wooden food bowl - but it was symbolic of 'Simplicity'.* [When another person was talking about her drawing she mentioned 'cancer'. I immediately felt that was appropriate to my drawing. I had the feeling that this person knew she had cancer and decided to follow her inner feelings, which were towards Buddhism, and she was happy and at peace before she finally passed to spirit.] *At the end Alan asked me to stand up and give out what I could [nobody could take it] but it was Peter Hague who suggested that maybe this was not 'for anybody' but for all of us, the message was the key. Got Alan to kindly sign the book I had bought, and he encouraged me to continue with this work.* Alan also gave a service, in which in just over an hour he executed five separate portraits, all of which were taken. The way Alan works very much appeals to me, especially as I have been interested in symbolism for some time.

Another tutor was Levi Attias, a barrister from Gibraltar and a person

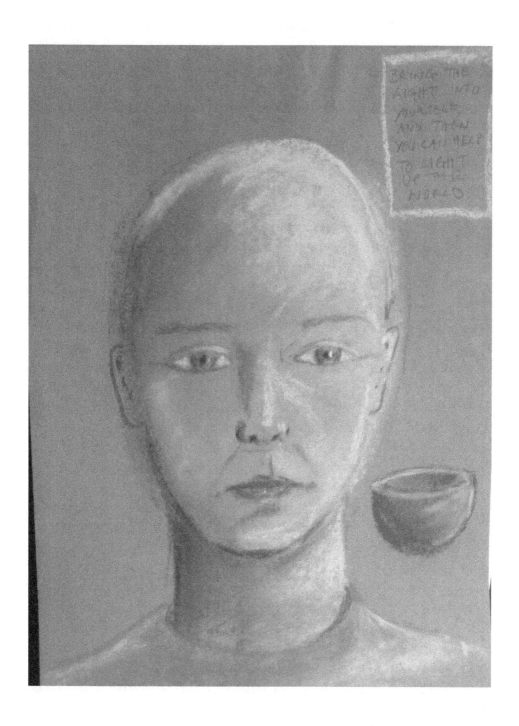

of many talents, including graphologist, writer of lyrics and a good talker. He began with "Mind the Healer, Mind the Destroyer", that was about the power of the mind – for good or ill – with many examples. A comment that I found thought-provoking was that he has acted in criminal cases quite a bit in the past, and a common factor that he found was the emptiness in these peoples lives, they had nothing to fulfill them. Levi gave a workshop on graphology and two more talks, the first of which was "The Sounds of Silence". It was all about taking the time to connect with our inner self and spirit, with wonderful stories and quotes from philosophers and poets, and ending with the advice: walk, don't run, otherwise you may miss the point of your life! Levi's last lecture was called "ESP, animals, plants, birds and people". It went from trees to lizards to his personal experiment with plums! The audience was also given the chance to give their own stories of extraordinary animal behaviour.

On the first evening there was a demonstration of mediumship by several of the tutors. Donna Stewart was the first to start and came to me, though I could not relate to most of what she said. However, at the end of the evening demonstration I got talking to the woman sitting next to me, who said that she could take **all** of what Donna had given to me – but hadn't spoken out! Donna also gave a lecture, "It Should Never Happen To A Medium". This was a story of some of her early life when she became aware of spirit energies and had prophetic dreams, but was scared of it all. She related some amusing, horrible and wonderful experiences on her journey to be a medium.

Another tutor was Melanie Polly (now Blyth), who gave a lecture called "Alive and Kicking", which was an engrossing account of her early life. No words that I could use would do it justice, but the final sentence from my notes was: *Fascinating tale, could have listened for another couple of hours to the tales she came out with.* Melanie gave a workshop on various breathing exercises and techniques, and another lecture called "Beyond the Delivery of Platitudes". Very down to earth and incisive; I will give a bit from my notes. *She wanted to focus on trance and started by saying that it once was quite prevalent, but now few are willing to sit and develop it. Many want to be showy; they want the appearance to be right, but not necessarily kind in their work. Mediumship does not equate to spirituality,*

*though spiritual practices may very well develop mediumship.
All mediums are trance mediums, everyone is clairsentient, and
every form of mediumship can be done in a deeper trance state,
the deeper the trance, the deeper the connection with spirit. In
trance, never mind trying to 'get out of the road', of clearing the
mind etc., just link in with that deeper essence inside, do your
meditation and try to get closer to 'God'. Very good lecture.*

Lastly, but by no means least, there was Gerard Smith, who gave a
workshop and two lectures. The first of his lectures was entitled "They
Walked Among Us". This was about the mediums and pioneers of the past.
He included excerpts from books and a brief recording of Ernest Oaten
speaking in 1937. Gerard said it was important that mediumship should
'touch' you deeply, as it needs to change you. We have to learn from the
opposites that we meet in life; we need both the positive and the negative.
Material things will come and go; we must garner to ourselves that which
is eternal – truth and love. His second lecture was equally as good, "There
is no such thing as best in the world of Individuals". Interesting as always,
he made us think about the deeper things connected with spirit, mixing it
up with quotes, stories and music. Gerard always speaks well, with feeling
and sincerity.

Back in the circle, the first one after the seminar, I was asked to relax and
the others would direct energy to see what may develop. After a while one
sitter said that he saw a Quaker's hat on my head, and all picked up a soap
smell. Then in the discussion afterwards, one of the circle said that he had
seen a man with a towel over his arm and a bowl of water, with soap in it.
The man's name was George Hamson, Hampson or Hanson. Not long
after this 'George' came through:

'George': "Good evening".
*'Me': "Good evening. Do you wish to speak to anyone in
    particular?"*
*'George': "You have to bear with me. This is my first time.
I have tried to come through before. I have been in high
realms since 1746. I am a Quaker, from the day I was
born, as my mother and my father. We were taught and*

brought up in a simple manner, for it was the simple things in life that brought us through. I wish to say to the young lady, she looks very like my sister, she reminds me of her. My sister was younger than me when she passed away, unfortunately with a dreadful fever. We tried all we could to help her. I passed away with the same thing in 1746. That was what you were smelling before."

'Me': "Right."

'George': "It was the warmth of the water and the perfume that was in it, my mother trying to cleanse my brow and cleanse my body to get rid of the fever, but alas, it was not to be. But my passing was peaceful, I was glad to be rid of the body, it was so feverish and hot, and the pain that came with it. And I was feeling, once I had left my body, I was happy when I arrived in the spirit world, because then I met my sister. My sister was Florrie by the way."

'Me': "Florrie?"

'George': "Yes, she was Florence, named after my mother, because she got Florrie."

'Me': "And your name?"

'George': "My mother was Florence Jane and my father was George senior, and I am George junior. I also had a brother called Bertram, but Bertram was older. But he was not with the same likings as we are, because he was on a different wavelength. Although he was into Quakerism, he didn't altogether follow it. He followed what he thought was right for himself, and quite rightly so, for everybody and everyone is entitled to their own opinion." George went on to give some advice to two in the circle.

At the next circle I was told that a man had placed a lightweight chain with a cross on it in my hand, a gift to me as it was one that he used to wear himself, and in my other hand was a quill pen. Shortly after this another of the circle (who had been absent last week) said that there was a Quaker bit to this. The man was in his black clothing, pointed shoes and a big hat, and a date of 1727.

During the next month or so, we once had spirit children, and spirit came through to request a slight seating change as well as some music before the start. Several different spirits came through, but most would not give a name, though one did, 'Raimos', who was an Egyptian snake charmer that died from the bite of a cobra. Many gave advice for us, and I was told that 'George' was there to help me.

At the beginning of October I sat at home in a long meditation, aided by a particular piece of music. I hoped to get a bit closer to 'George', and unexpectedly got my condition that signalled the Native American brave was still there with me as well.

One fascinating spirit called Hafed came to us half a dozen times before the end of the year. At the beginning he said that he came from Persia and had worn the crown, was a priest and that he brings the star. During his next few appearances, it was evident that he had a connection with Y, asking her if she remembered the Temple of Isis, "where our great friend of the Egyptian Hermes (was)." In October he was much more forthcoming. He talked how he had sat still with a clear mind and had heard the voices of spirit clearly.

Hafed: "That day I knew I had the inner strength to continue with that which was on my shoulders, for I had a big responsibility in trying to lead my people in the best way that I knew how. Though my father was a great example, I tried to follow his footsteps, but unfortunately I was thrown in the deep end, so I had to find faith and courage within, in order to do what I had to do. From a very young age I discovered the horrors of war. ... Eventually I lost my wife and my son at a very young age. They came upon us one night unexpectedly ... we heard nothing, saw nothing - they were silent. And they came and they murdered and they took away that which was dear to me. That, my friends, took me a long time to overcome. I had to overcome and then learn to forgive and to forget and to move on. It was one of the hardest tests of my life." Then he conversed with Y again, mentioning the holy waters of the Nile and the temple, before saying, *"Then I may leave you with the light, the light of the Eastern Star, which shines upon each and every one of you. May I leave you with that."*

The next week he again spoke, saying that he knew Jesus.

H: *"He went to Greece, he went to Portugal, he went into Egypt, he went everywhere, as I did myself. For we were seeking to learn from others at that time, and Jesu also did this. And then came the time he realised that what was within him would come out. So he went his own way, and in his own way he learnt from his mistakes. And he became more aware of that which was in him, the ability, the ability to see, the ability to hear, the ability to heal, the ability to love, a very vital ingredient, to love his fellow man, to share it. He spoke of this to his people there and to his friends. … But through patience and perseverance Jesu spread the word of truth and showed them the truth. …one of the disciples called Judas had turned against him, but he forgave him and friends again could not understand why he did as he did. He told once again, if you do not forgive then that which is within will never leave, for if you forgive then that which is there with you will leave, and that love will flow through once again. For if you do not forgive, then you are holding that to which is there all the time, unless you forgive, you let it go. And they began to realise that this was the way, by forgiving."*

In circle, one of the spirits that came through – giving her name as 'Red Wing' – claimed to be the mother of the helper connected to another circle member. Right at the end of her talk she said: *"Watch for smell. When you smell, spirit is near. Watch for scent. Remember."* Then in the next meeting, after several spirits had come through, we sat in silence for the last ten minutes. *During this period (and earlier) I experienced a beautiful smell of flowers, but could not distinguish which type of flower, roses and freesias came to mind but that didn't seem quite right.* After the close of the circle

I made a point of smelling the small bunch of flowers on the table, but it was not the same scent.

Unexpectedly, I received an invitation to join the Board of the Lynwood Fellowship, and feeling greatly honoured, accepted.

In the circle meeting prior to Remembrance Day in November 2009, the spirit called 'Matthew' came to speak about his experiences. *"I do not have many memories to tell you my friends, because this was part and parcel of my problem. I could not face what I had to remember, that with the terrible wars that I went through in my time. I'm talking what in particular should be the First Word War, when many lives of innocent men, women and children had lost their lives unnecessarily, for what? Even although we were fighting against the enemy, there were times when the enemy themselves had wondered if they should have fought on or what. Even on the Christmas Day I well remember when both sides did cease fire. And oh what a joyous moment it was when peace fell at last, and everybody put down their arms and the men began to sing. Singing songs of the carols, 'Good King Wenceslas' and 'God Rest Ye Merry Gentlemen' and so forth. And it was surprising that even the enemy, the Germans, could speak a lot of English. And for that moment in time men were playing football and so forth. But then the moment that the Xmas period had ceased, the fighting began again. It was incredible, one minute was (?) and peaceful, then the next minute it was uproar again. ... The horrors of the cold and the water and the mud, and the digging and the tunnels, the darkness, the clamminess and the cold etc., but luckily I survived this.*

"... when life was also hard. There was no food, our life was starving, children were unclothed, many families were struggling to survive. Even now, here on the earth you talk about your recession and so forth, on that which is coming on, and I look at it myself and wonder, could those here on earth survive that which I had to go through? Especially in the 20s, when there was nothing, when food, water and all else was scarce,

man really had to struggle to survive, he really had to grab anything he could in order to feed his family. There was no work for the men to do and so forth. And then when you get to the 30s, especially 38 and 39, and then again when we were facing the troubles … but we only survived because of the experiences that we already had gone through. …

"I learnt to realise I had to switch off, I had to forget. It was the only way that I moved on. Since then, since I've been in the spirit world for quite a long time now, I found my peace, and the only way I found my peace was by forgetting all. If only you could fill your hearts with the peace and the happiness from the spirit, the rest seems to follow on itself. If one plays the part, as I discovered when I met up with my colleagues and family and so forth, I learnt that they too had learnt their peace and their happiness because they moved on themselves, they put behind what they had gone through. But they tried to pass on that which we see fit to those here on earth to get them to that stage, that little bit of understanding, to make them realise that you are better off than what we had to go through. Even children of today, why do people not leave them alone? Let them be in their own thoughts, let them be children, let them be happy, let them teach for themselves, let them find their way, and as they find their way they learn a lot more. …

"I never had much in my life. I left home when I was very young, I did not know what I was going for, but I knew I had to go through it. But at the end of the day for the grace of God I survived it. How I survived it I often wondered, yet then in my faith, I knew that someone was watching over me at the time. I well remember the time that there was a group of soldiers who had absolutely nowhere to turn, and they were under constant fire, and how they survived it they never knew. But those twelve men, they saw the angels, the angels of Mons, they actually saw that vision. And the angels as I say, floated past their First-Aid shed. They could not believe their eyes and they lived to tell the tale, they saw that. They had said that the angels had gathered there and guided them. How I often wondered about that tale, I wondered what it would have been like for me to see that vision myself."

'Matthew' went on to have a personal conversation with one of the circle before returning to his theme. *"So please, lift up your heart, do let it be strong and go forward. Find the peace better; switch off as when you need to, that is the best way to deal with it, is to switch it off. Do not let things get to you. That is how I did it; it was the only way I could do it, because I did not want to talk to anyone for a long time. I did not want to talk about the wars and what I had to go through. In fact, very few of my comrades, very few men had talked about their experiences, for their faces alone and their bodies were there to tell. So it is little wonder that people did ask them how they got through it, or what happened or what they had seen or what they had heard. In fact there were many, and many my friend, who had actually lost their minds, for the pressure and the intense 'horribility' of the memory and so forth. Their bodies and their minds just could not cope, so therefore they had broken down and many had died young because of it. Many even cannot breathe because of the gases; many of their bones were damaged. But I do not wish to go on my friend, but these (?) (?) and things that we had to endure, especially in the First World War going onto the Second. However, I have found my peace as I have said, and that I wish to pass on to each and every one of you. For all you people have got work to do and it's the work of the spirit, and please do not forget that."* Although 'Matthew' would occasionally speak at other times, it was usual for him to do so around about Remembrance Day. Also that evening two of the circle saw the presence of Helen Duncan, the famous physical medium, and she was said to be there on several other occasions, and eventually did speak to us.

Very slowly, I was starting to build up a connection to my spirit helper 'George' and beginning to sense what he looked like. In the next circle my notes started thus: *Managed to get down earlier and felt this was beneficial, as by the time I opened the circle I felt George's presence with energy around my head and the bottom of my beard - which made me think that his beard went around his chin and not just at the sides as I had imagined last week.*

A spirit helper for another in the circle came through, talking about attitudes in the past and the changes to come on the earth in the future. I give some extracts from his talk: *"However, my friends, I want to say this, that there are many challenges ahead and those challenges will be met, and will be met in truth, in honesty, in respect, in trust. For the natural law of the spirit is perfect and so shall it be here on earth. So those who we trust and know to be of service, the spirit will not let you down, but only yourself. But if you are strong and you not let your great enemy get to you - that which is your ego and yourself. If you rise above all that, then the rest will follow in a smooth manner, like the river that flows gently. But if you go against this river then its currents and its tides will make things harder. So I urge each one of you to keep it as simple as possible within your own thoughts. …*

"There is nothing better when one sits in the quietness, to hear the sound of a cricket, or a butterfly or a bee, or whatever, or better still, the sound of one's own breathing and heartbeat. This takes time. But do not worry, if you put your mind to it then that alone can achieve a lot of results.

… "It is good to see a spirit like you evolving, getting stronger each time. It gives me and my friends great joy to see this. And once again I say unto each and every one of you, how wonderful it is to be sitting in powwow like this. We know there are many, but this is one here … it is still important and special to us in spirit. …

"My father once gave me a bitter lesson. I thought I was clever. I saw gin trap. I used to tease gin trap. My father told me once to leave gin trap, and I did not. What happened? I caught my finger in gin trap, so quick. My father never said a thing, but I never went near gin trap again. So you see, my father let me, for he knew that I had to learn my own lessons even if it was the hard way. He let me go, for he too knew … it could have taken my arm off. But luckily it took tip of finger. So that is the way it should be. You should let your children, let them be free. And when they come to you for your help, that is the time you give your answers to them, the honest way."

A different spirit spoke at the next circle: ... *"And blest are the pure in the heart, to those who sit willingly and listen, and listen intently in silence. For not only is it golden, but it is your strength. ... How sad that we see those who shut the door on many, whose deaf ears and whose eyes are closed and hearts are closed, and minds. If only they would open them, it's so much better, with help and the strength can be given. Many people say, "why me?" or "why us?" This is not so, for everyone is in the same boat, for to go through whatever in life. ... It is there for you to overcome, and it is in your overcoming that you gain the strength, and your wisdom, and your answers to your prayers, as you walk through it. ...*

"What joy and happiness it makes to us that we can reach to those that see the light themselves. For we know that the torch of light will be passed on, as it is given. At the moment we do struggle to strive to share that torch, for there are so many dark corners of your world. But we try to pierce through, to hand that torch to man, so that the light once again can be shown. ...

"Your thoughts are very much alive, in everything that you do and everything that you think. For what you think you become, as it is in the spirit world, for we go or where we wish to go, we think and we are instantly there. For we come from the land of anywhere. It is easy in that way for us. We know that. But it is not easy for when we try to reach out to the hearts and then minds. The only way that can be achieved is by that inner calm, that stillness, as you are in now."

In the last circle of 2009 spirit gave individual advice to members and then said: *"We shall meet again on the 14th of the next month, which we feel will be suitable for all of you ... So therefore we ask - now we come to the nitty-gritty my friend - when we said to you that you had much to play, that indeed you have. May we ask that you my friend, along with the young man when the time comes, can you consider to help to build a three-sided cabinet please? [The answer was in the affirmative.] And that will be done so that when the time comes we can place this young man in this cabinet, and it will hold the energy contained therein.*

… Also my friends, we ask that you will bring some toys for us in the spirit world, the little children also. … It will be a slow progress but a good one and a steady one. … This will be the time of testing. This will be the time of patience. That which has happened up to now, this is what we would call a preparation period. Not only that which has been taking place now, but for each one of you, you have come along in your own sense of development."

This confirmed our thoughts on the direction that the circle was heading towards, though we knew that it would take some time to come to fruition. At this stage in the circle we were experiencing many different spirits coming to talk to us, often giving advice on a personal basis, but equally giving talks on many subjects. Perhaps the most concern expressed by spirit was about the wanton destruction to the earth by humanity, due to greed and materialism. However, we were ever exhorted to do whatever we could and to try to 'plant seeds' in the minds of those who would listen.

At the start of 2010, one spirit gave a talk on love, and I give a few extracts from my notes. "*…There is the greatest gift of all, in that which you know and that which lies in each and everyone of you, and that is the gift of love. God's greatest gift to man, for it is in their choice as to whether they share that love or not, for love conquers all. It can shift mountains; it can bring the brightest of the bright along with the stars and the sun. For love is that which makes the spirit world go round and also here on the earth plane. … But you need not search for your love, for that is something which is already there, from the day that you came into this earth plane. It is your most treasured gift of all, and it is thy choice whether you share that. It is unconditional because it is so special; it is your utmost jewel, the jewel that lies deep within you. …*

"*We hear the cries of help on prayer, the true essence of the communication, and in that outworks that love. And it is that love that helps you to keep you going. So you see, it is a valuable tool to all. … it is the key to everything; it is the key to all forms of life. Every creature and every human being and every flower* and every tree ... even the flowers are filled, even water my friends, is filled with love. It can't be seen by the naked eye. It can certainly be felt. How many times have there been occasions when you know that something has touched you, and touched you so deeply? That comes with love. ...

"Those who will not use it, those who do not use it properly, those who do not wish to use it at all, those who do not love it at all, those who do not wish to know it at all, they are the ones that tread a hard pathway of life. ...

"And when you use it the more you will grow, and the more you will feel it, and the more you will see and understand as you go through your daily life. ... When you think of it here on earth ... all different characters, all of different images, all of different makes, all of different cultures, and yet we all belong to the one, and that is being belonging to God, the spirit. So we have come from there, they are your brothers and sisters, but again, each one has their choice, has their freewill. ...

"And if you fall, you pick yourself up again, that is the reason for falling. And never lose sight of God's love, the true spirit's love, hold onto it, for it will never and never let you down. It is thy greatest tool and thy greatest gift. I leave those words unto each and every one of you, and I say goodnight and God bless you."

At the next meeting 'Ho-Lin', a spirit who had been with Doris, came through and gave a long talk (comprising eleven pages of notes). He began with the evolution of man's spiritual thinking, mentioning the Egyptians, Greeks, Vikings and so forth, and then went on to talk of other things. I will give a few extracts.

"There is such a thing, as we call it from the spirit world, is the astral world or the astral plane. The great grey area or forestry as it were, where the souls upon souls who are lost there for whatever reason.

"So now we come to your motherland and your modern day here on earth. What a mess it is! Simply because it is slightly overpopulated. Oh yes, and not only that my friends, it is also full of materialism; your world has become a materialistic world. It is fast and furious with it, yet with all the modern technology that comes with it. This is what's happened. It is the great involvement in Mammon. …

"You are first and foremost a spirit. It is only thy physical body that is your overcoat. Now if I put it to you this way, if you were all walking here on earth now and you had no overcoats, you would get the biggest shock of your lives. Because you would see that every one of you would still be different, because every one of you carried a light that would be your own. Some would not be so bright, some would be bright and some would be very bright, and so forth. … So when your soul comes into its own as it's growing, the brighter and stronger it will get, and the higher you will reach when you arrive here in the spirit world. …

"So what is the point of having a lot of money if it's not going to be of great use, or any use? Ah, but yes, I know what you are thinking, you're thinking, yes, well it would be nice to have a little or a lot, so you do not have to worry … But my friends, it's not always the case. It is who you are and what you do with your life that matters, and how you overcome that which you already have, and what you have. And if one counts ones blessings and is grateful at all times, then no more or less will be asked of you. Because remember, your friends and your loved ones, if you are true to yourself and carry the torch, they will not fail you. The only person or persons that fail, I've said this time and time again, and that is man himself. And he must realise, that is why the world is in such a state as it is now, because their souls are over here, everywhere. But he is not listening, his ears are deaf and he is spiritually dumb. …

"How I yearn for the great guides of the past, to hear their voices once again. How I yearn to hear their philosophy once again. How I yearn to hear their great teachings. But where does this come from? It comes from the higher souls in the spirit world, there is no other. … Day in, day out, they studied, they asked, they fought and they went through some terrible times, because even then there were people who would say what they would do as coming from the dark and so forth, and shouting about the devil and all the rest of it. But they were the ones who were the devil my friend. For there is good and bad in each of you ... It is thy choice ... to obey the devil within you or the good in you. It is as simple as that. ...

"It takes time, because our work is slow, it has to be, we cannot do it any other way. For there is much preparation and effort that goes behind it each time, no matter what we do. Even if it is communicating, because communicating is the essence of that which we do, and we do it as you know in many ways and many forms. But has one sought to think of the effort that it has taken for that to happen? That is why we preach to you at all times about patience, for there is nothing greater than that, to have patience, to practice and to wait. ...

"It has been said many times that each thought you have is real. It is a living thing. It is a bit like electricity going through you and reaching to us. So you safely say that nothing, but nothing goes amiss. But having said this my friends, as you should understand and know by now, we cannot and will not interfere with thy lives. It is thy freewill, thy choice, because it is law. For if it would not be, then how would your life be worth living? How would you learn, how would you gain knowledge, how would you become strong if it was not? ...

"If you are willing to share and show that torch to others and do the work for spirit, then, each one of you will not get a greater reward other than to see joy, happiness, love, compassion, understanding, bringing the ultimate happiness to those that are in need of that great help through the teachings of spirit, or whether it be healing. So remember that my friends, and I say to you continue your great work once again, for there are groups like this who continue the great work. It is like going back to the very beginning where it all began, in simplicity and in truth and honesty and dedication. Goodnight my friends."

It was interesting to note that once again I perceived a flowery scent about half way through this talk, and it persisted right to the end of the circle. Also that I was aware that 'George' had been with me right from the start.

At the next meeting, which was at the end of January 2010, 'Ho-Lin' spoke to us again, but I will first start at the very beginning of those notes. *I managed to get down early and set up the music and red lights. Even at that stage I noticed the middle picture of three moving slightly, so I changed seats to look at the left hand one and saw it move too. When everybody was in and settled, I felt 'George' with me, and said the opening prayer. After about four minutes spirit came through.*

Ho-Lin: "He who is still keeps calm and is wise. This I take note among you all my friends. And yes, I chuckled my friend when you used the magical word of patience. What a marvellous word patience is, for it colours everything, to let go, to understand, to bring about awareness of oneself and the stillness of the mind, and being in touch with those who are near to you. I teach unruly souls, souls who are ready to seek that help. And the first thing I do with them is to let them be, to be like a child, for a child is an innocent one, and their thoughts are their thoughts alone. They have their dreams, they have their visions … and that is the way it should be. For if one tries to interfere or impress upon it too much, then not only does it make it more difficult for the master, but also more importantly, the pupil as well. So it is important in that stillness, to let the child be, to discover for themselves what they are capable of. And the master can only give one or two hints, in the hope that the child receives, and when the child receives then further instructions will be put upon them, in their learning. …

"It gives me no greater pleasure to share my wisdom and my knowledge, that which I had many, many years ago when I was here. I was privileged to have served a wonderful lady, who now resides in the spirit world, as she is now content and happy in the knowledge that this particular school is continuing its good work, and that her seeds are being sown, and have flourished in each

and every one of you. She is the fine example of what a fine instrument one should be, just like the great many mediums of the past. To serve mankind, to serve spirit, and there is no greater reward when one serves humbly, and keeping ones feet on the ground at all times.

"So it is wise to have your feet on the ground, firmly on the ground, for it is the way of the spirit. For you will begin to understand the t'ai a little more. That is my word for mother earth, and the chi - the spirit world. [When Ho-Lin said what follows, the medium had his arms forward and hands apart, palms facing each other, as if holding a ball between them, turning it one way and then the other.] I know about this, my people today practice the art of the t'ai chi...breathing in...breathing out. ... You can almost feel it, through practice and dedication; one becomes a perfect balance in mind and of the spirit. The body then comes into its own with that balance, and the greater the strength and the knowledge that will come through understanding the works of mother earth and the spirit world. The two go hand in hand, and this is very important, as you all sit here now. ...

"So therefore, now, we come to the all important thing, for someone to take the responsibility, the responsibility of overseeing that which is going on. And you already know, for that has been given to you. I say unto you that you listen also to the one who takes responsibility, for that help will be given also to that person, in times of need or as and when required.

"I speak to my friend on the left. Hello my friend."
Me: "Hello."
Ho-Lin: "Thank you for your patience and your time my friend. We do see that you are trying, and it will only be a matter of time before your dear friend is able to speak to you, or through you shall we say. But it is only thyself that is holding back in a little way. You just need to bring down the barriers a little in your mind." ...
Ho-Lin: "And take the weight off your shoulders! For some

of thy responsibility is not yours, as I am talking of the material."

Me: "Yes."

Ho-Lin: "You speak about overload, you know nothing about overload, not when it comes to the spirit. You have to be responsible for your own, but not of others. So take it off! Do you understand my friend?"

Me: "Yes."

Ho-Lin: "It is like the rucksack sitting on your back, and the weight you carry with it. Take it off. But do not let those of the earth plane give you any more than you can take yourself, my friend, for you can only do so much. For that is something that one has to take into consideration, for you are important to those of the spirit. And it is important that you are finely tuned and balanced within yourself for that which is to come also. The day will come when there will be far less of the material for you to do, but more of the spirit in the work. Then this will bring a big smile to ones face."

Me: "It will."

…

Ho-Lin: "Thank you for listening, I like one who listens. For those in the spirit world listen intently and this many people not see. For if there is not one watching you here, then you can be sure one is watching you over there, and vice versa. It is the way it works. … I love you all as much as I love my friends in the spirit world and my fellow masters. But masters only become masters by earning that which they have came through themselves, through hardships, through dedication and difficulty. And it is in that, that the soul comes into its own and the brilliance of the light that comes with it. … This is what we see and seek from those of the higher realm in the spirit world. For it is vast, a real place of beauty. This is why it is so hard unless one has seen it for oneself. That even those who have seen it, they find it difficult to describe because it

120

is indescribable, because it is non-physical. This you will understand even more when your time comes to pass. But for now you have to be content while you're here on earth. I will leave those words with you my friends."

It was significant that school matters were brought up. Due to circumstances, events, timetabling, etc., the last few years had been extremely stressful in my teaching. With the increasing interest – and importance – in my 'spiritual' work, my thoughts about leaving my job had accelerated and I had made the decision that I would indeed go for early retirement, and it would be 'soon', in about eleven months.

After 'Ho-Lin' had finished another spirit spoke, and that brought us up to 'closing time'. When the medium came back to normal awareness, he complained about having such a dry throat, and we remarked that he had talked longer tonight than usual. He also said that it felt as if there was a ball of energy between his hands and we explained about the t'ai chi. He then commented that it may be something to do with a voicebox, but it was just a thought. A statement that I found very interesting. The circle was then closed.

CHAPTER 13

A Few Surprises

The very next circle (4/02/10) was a totally different affair, and I will give an abridged account of it because it is a lesson that all prospective circles and their members need to know and take into account. All must strive to be at one and in harmony, otherwise spirit have difficulty working with us.

Having arrived early I was taken down to see the newly erected cabinet, which certainly fitted the instructions that had been given by spirit, though I advised that it should be moved as little as possible as it may come to pieces with a bit of wear and tear. Chairs were set up in a semi-circle facing the chair in the cabinet, so that all of us were in view to each other. The energy was there and quite quickly I noticed the presence of 'George'. When the others came in Y was clearly shocked to see the cabinet with the chair inside it and the curtain at the side. She said that she had been told not to do it and was clearly upset. After some discussion Z took the curtain off and put it away, then he pulled the chair out of the cabinet and left it in front of it. All seemed happy with that and we relaxed to the music. When it was time I turned the music off and opened the circle, asking spirit for advice, help and their love. The incident seemed to have altered and flattened the energies, and I wondered if spirit would actually come through. It took over twelve minutes before the first word was spoken.

Ho-Lin: "*Sometimes...* [It took nearly two minutes before spirit continued. The medium's legs seemed to be trembling, and although his posture was not erect and despite the totally subdued nature of the voice, I had a feeling that it might be Ho-Lin. During the following talk I noticed a few times a light mist at the right side of his head, and a few speckles of light near the back of his neck.]...*the masters are to be patient...*"

Y: "*Yes, thank you.*"

Ho-Lin: "*...for they know when the pupils are ready. A true master has the ability to see through the pupil themselves and their capabilities within. It is only the pupil themselves can discover that which truly lies within each and every one of them. The master can never force anything upon the pupil, for he knows only too well that he cannot make the pupil do whatever. And one of the greatest obstacles he has to overcome is not only responsibility, but the responsibility of themselves. No matter what training or knowledge one has, it lies within the pupil themselves, and that something can be called ... fear. We all have to overcome this at sometime in our lives, for fear is an awful thing, which can and do cause more problems than anything else.*

"*I remember a classical pupil, who was strong within himself, who had compassion and desire to become whatever he wanted to become, but he had to overcome his own fear, and he knew of this. No matter how the master taught him nor how correct or true it was, and even though the pupil knew of this for himself, the master could still not make him do whatever he wanted him to do. And that was a certain kick he had to do, in the form of a martial art defence. The pupil knew that it was a difficult one and he knew himself that he could do it, but he just could not bring his mind to do it at the time. So when the master had told him that he wanted him to do this, the pupil immediately said no. And each time he was asked to do it, the answer that came was the same answer, was a no. That was his fear. It was the fear of knowing that* what could happen if he had not got this right, because the pupil knew it had to be right. No mistakes could be afforded, even though he made mistakes and he learned well from them, but this was different. Even though he saw his fellow pupils do the same and they got through it, but he just could not bring himself to do it.

"But eventually, one day came, he steeled himself up. The master knew this was not so, he told him not to do it. But the pupil thought by summing up the energies that were steeling himself, preparing himself, he could not see any other way. His mind was hard and focused on this particular kick that he had to do, and the master had warned him not to do it. However, the master said it was his wish, but nevertheless he went ahead and did it. The master stepped to one side and said to the pupil, "you may go when you are ready". So the pupil stood and got himself worked up, really focusing on this kick that he had to do. He went ahead and alas, he almost broke his back, he was badly injured.

"The master rushed up to him and calmly told him that he was not ready because his mind and his body was not in the right frame of mind. He did not do what he was taught to do, he did not see what he was taught to do, and that was the result and he told him this. The pupil turned round and said to the master, "But master, are you not annoyed with me, are you angry? You are ever so calm master." The master replied, "My son, if I were angry I would not be a good master. There would be no point in me being angry even though I knew this would happen. I could not tell you, you had to find this out for yourself and this is the result. What is important now young man is that we get you fit and well again". And it was quite a number of years, at least three years before the pupil was able to do whatever again.

"It was a real battle, now law had it and he survived this, law had it that he was able to walk, law had it that he had this chance. But he learnt from this harsh lesson, and the lesson was to take the full responsibility unto oneself properly, and not to allow any fear to come into the frame of mind. For he knew that fear distorts the mind, confuses ones thinking, and not realising and allowing the true peace of mind and the calm thoughts for the proper instruction to be given. He realised that if he had stood and listened to what the master had been trying to tell him before, that he would have got through that kick and no harm would have come to him, because his mind, his body was right, and the timing would have been right.

"However, he did not do this kick in time to come, but he went on to be a great teacher. He passed on the knowledge that he had from his master, and he began to realise that he was then able to see the gifts that other pupils had and how they can use them. So he began to teach them in the way the master had taught him, so all was not lost. No fear ever came to his mind again. This he passed on to others, and others realised in sorrow what can happen.

"So what we say to you, each and every one of you here tonight, is always remember that those who are true to yourselves will never fail you. As we said before, the only person that fails is themselves, nothing less, nothing more. True spirit will always be there to guard and guide. There is no way they would allow anything, except if the pupil themselves do whatever regardless, then so be it. Then spirit is powerless to stop whatever, because they know it is thy choice, thy choice alone. They cannot interfere."

Z came back to normal awareness and drank some water. After stretching and a very brief banter, he sat back and relaxed. Several minutes passed and this time his right hand slowly became clenched as if holding something. He sat erect and his hand also rose and spirit spoke forcefully. [*This was the same spirit that came through on the*

10/09/09, who had brought his band of brothers for us. Z identified him as White Cloud.]

WC: "I bring back tomahawk."

Y: "Welcome."

WC: "We are ready. I bring back tomahawk, for Great Spirit is always there. I have my band of brothers around this. [Indicating the circle with his hand.] To protect you. Fear not, for we are ready." [During this time the lights went down very low, and I was conscious that my legs were quite cold.]

Z came back a little slower this time, but after a brief drink of water relaxed in his chair again. After about five minutes Z asked what did we see behind him. Typically I said "wood", but a more perceptive V said "balls of energy".

Z: "The reason I ask, is that all the time I've been sitting here, if I put my hand back, it's like putting my hand into a cold fridge. I've never felt that before, it's as though the power is directed into it, it's contained, and it's coming out from it as well. I can feel it all the way up from the bottom of my back, all the way up my spine."

Y: "are you comfortable with it?"

Z: "I am comfortable, yes. I'm impressed to say that, you know, not to expect anything miraculous, because it will be far from it, far from it. For example materialisation, you would never get that, you would not expect to see that or look for that. … But this is based on the foundations that we have been building, in the offering to spirit in the hope that they can do further work within ourselves. …

"That if we leave certain things sometimes in their hands, or if you surrender as it were to them, then they are more than capable of, say for example, of putting you to sleep just like that. But this what we see here is only an example and that whatever spirit may wish to do, then it is through the experience and experimentation to see which field that we could further ourselves on in that which we offer and see here now, the little bell, the trumpet. Now even with that I wouldn't build any hopes up there, even though it's there. But that does not mean to say that nothing wouldn't take place, far from it, it could. But it's up to spirit. But we can only offer ourselves for them to do whatever, they cannot do it without. So there should not be, what shall we say, any hesitation between ourselves or whatever, because that would only hinder not only ourselves but for spirit as well. ...

"Yes, you can take myself, you can take Y, you can take whoever else, you can take the training and the teaching that we've had and that which we've seen and witnessed ourselves, and we can learn from that and we're grateful for that, because it is something that which once you've seen and heard it, and so forth, you can never forget. But it's also there to share, and this is what it's about. So we have to put ourselves in spirit's shoes as well, in what they would want or what they would like to try, because of the way things are today. And this is what we have to bear in mind. This is why we have to stick and be strong as we are, because there are other groups of the same calibre, of the same like of mind. This is the only way that we can pass on that knowledge, we can pass on their teachings, it is the only way we can get forward, so the only way that spirit will push [is] forward as well. They cannot do it any other way. [Z went on to talk about the things that Doris had given him, even offering him her cabinet, but he didn't take it, as it was so heavy. Doris had just smiled and said that he could always make one.] ...

"And hopefully I'm thinking of putting my trust in spirit, because, yes, I know all too well what can happen in the good sense, as well as the other. But we have to start somewhere, or we have to put our trust somewhere. So if the group is not all together happy with this situation - fine, it doesn't bother me, it won't bother me at all, I will *not be offended. But, I would appreciate if people would speak their mind, or be honest. That's important as well, because without that, then, as a team, as a group, it's worth nothing."*

There then followed a long and often confused discussion on the subject, often with many talking at once. I tried to keep out of it for the most part, only commenting when asked directly.

Z: "What about you Mike?"
Me: "I'm quite happy. I've always been happy with spirit - no problem. And we were asked to build it. It seems silly to build it and not use it."

A little later I again responded.

Me: "I'll go along with anything that everybody agrees with, but I'm quite happy to go along with spirit and what they ask and what they say."

As the talking continued, I told them that I would make a copy of the last circle meeting and this one, then they could read over it and think about it. My last contributions came close to the end of this discussion.

Me: "I don't think we're going to go that fast; think how long it's taken to get to this stage. They are going very slowly with us, because they need to, and they said that."
U: "Why do you think they need to?"
Me: "Because we've all got to be there together. It's not going to work if we don't all go together. It's not going to work."
Z: "Do you feel it's right Mike?"
Me: "To me, yes. Absolutely. But that's my opinion."
Z: "But you see I've got to take U's opinion into consideration, there's also Y's, but more so U's. Because you see, everybody has to be in harmony, got to be in tune."

Me: *"They know that as well."*

That was my last utterance, though the conversation went on for several more minutes and then stopped for a healing section, before the circle was closed.

Naturally enough, there was a lot to think about, what had happened and the opinions of the rest of the circle members, so it was my main focus of contemplation over the next six days. So eventually the next circle came on 11/02/10.

I got down early after giving everyone notes from the last two circles. The red lights were already on, and I put on the music, arranged the chairs with Z's only just inside the front of the cabinet, and checked the pictures - no movement. When the others came down and settled, we sat for about six or seven minutes until it was 8pm. I opened the circle and then said that there would be a talk first, to give everybody a chance to air their views, and that next week Z would be fully inside the cabinet.
Me: "What I want to say is, that last week was an example of where a disruption can cause a lowering of the energies, and we saw that spirit struggled to get through with Z. Indeed, I was surprised that they actually came though. So it is an important lesson, that we need to be together, we need to be in harmony. I want to say that all of us here, each single one of us is meant to be here.

"For U and V, this circle began in November 2008, for them; for the rest of us, we decided to sit in November 2006, two years earlier. However, I do not believe the circle started then. It started before that. One afternoon, one weekend, I decided I would get in my car and I would go down the west coast of ...... Why I don't know, but I did. And after driving past ...., I was driving along and I saw a man and a dog. So I nearly drove on by, but I thought, "I recognise that person", and I stopped, and there was Z. So we were reunited again, as I didn't have

Z's address and I didn't know where he lived. And that is how we all got in touch together. But it started before that. When we went to Doris' and we sat with others and with spirit, with Ho-Lin there and others we know are around this circle, they were there. And it started before that. When Z and Y were together in ...... itself. So it goes back a long, long way.

"Spirit work in a different time to us, they see possibilities, they see opportunities, and they arrange things so that they can work. And they work ten times, a hundred times more than we ever work here, and they never ever claim any credit. They see the potential in us, that we don't even see ourselves. But it is up to us to realise that potential. So you may be called a weedling or an acorn, but you've been told what the potential actually is. There is a tremendous future."

U: "Well whilst you were saying that, I just had a reassuring stroke on my left hand."

Me: "Because I remember when I was at Doris', and Y, Z and others were there, and they were getting things, and Doris would come to me, "and what have you got?" and I would say, "nothing", or very occasionally I got a colour. And I never understood why I was there really. But they, Doris and her helpers, saw something in me, and I have stuck to it, and I have been given fantastic evidence. I've been given experience of clairvoyance - with proof! I've been given experience of clairsentience - with proof! Otherwise I would not have believed it. I've been given experience of trance, real trance - with proof! That's how much they actually think about us and work for us, and I'm very humbled by that, that they have gone to that trouble - because it must have been a considerable trouble - to bring that to me.

"So if that potential is there...they obviously see some potential in me, in you, in Y, in you, and even in Z. There is more to come, we never ever stop. And if they are prepared to do that for me, I will sit in this circle for as long as I can. I will do my best for spirit, not only here but in Lynwood and other places, because that is the focus of my life. I now have less than a year to go in teaching, that area in my life is going to come to an end, and I will concentrate almost exclusively now, getting a closer link to spirit and doing my utmost for them. And I think we should aspire as a circle to be the best we can. I would like us to be the best circle in the world. I'm not quite sure if we have the potential to be that. However, that should be our aim, we should go forward, and we must be in harmony, we must be together, and we must feel we have no doubts. We have to put our trust in spirit, that they know what they are doing...and go with them.

"As for the direction we are going, it is quite obvious that with the cabinet, we are going towards, as we thought, maybe something physical. Exactly what we don't know. I have hopes of maybe independent voice or whatever, but we'll have to wait and see, that's up to spirit and us. They have hopes, they can see where this can go, but it is up to us to realise that. And lastly...well not lastly, two things. One: that was confirmed with a little sign with the Sudoku in Psychic News, I won a book that...Z was talking about one of the mediums, the two best mediums that he was talking about, and one of them was Alec Harris, and the book is about Alec Harris, so there you go.

"And in the previous, not last week but the week before, spirit came through and said it was time for somebody to take responsibility for the circle, and that has been given. Now as far as I know, the only person spirit has asked to take charge of this circle has been myself. The last time I shirked that responsibility I got a telling off! So I am taking responsibility unless anybody here can tell me otherwise. Ok, that's all I have to say. Anybody else want to say anything?"

U: *"I thought that was very well said."*
V: *"I do and all."*
U: *"I feel quite emotional."*
Y said something also, but it was too soft on the recording to make out.
Me: *"Good. Ok, right. You want to say anything Z?"*
Z had his mouth closed and brought his index finger across it!
Me: *"Ok."*
Z: *"I would like to open my mouth, but they said no."*
Me: *"Ok, right we shall settle down and give out our energy, and hope that spirit will come through and give us some advice."*

Some two minutes later spirit spoke through Z.
Ho-Lin: *"Good evening friends."*
Me: *"Good evening."*
H-L: *"Wise words from our brother. But I am afraid that you are all like pigs in a barn dance! All out of tune, not in harmony, for several reasons. However, we in the spirit world do understand that it is not all easy, but after all you are as human beings. It is only thy nature that one may think or feel as they are. But now the dust is blown over, and that which matters, for as other brother say, we can but only now go forward. You cannot go backwards, for if you do you only go back to square one, but you only do that in the reasoning that you have to back to square one. For if you were instructed to do so, then there would be a reason.*

"But fear not my friends, as I speak of you as brother and sister, you are one and one of a kind, you are special to each of yourselves and to those of the spirit world. We do not ask a lot in that which we try to do, we only ask that you understand our ways and through that will be harmony and love. For the two go hand in hand, for those two vital ingredients cannot go hand in hand if

it causes a lot of upset. But you must remember that love and harmony is always there from your spirit friends, it is only thy selves that holds it back.

"Your brother spoke of responsibility. Take responsibility to all yourselves, it is to be shared among you all. You are in a position now to look after each one of you, even at this stage, for it is called teamwork. It is the same with thy friends in the spirit world; it cannot be done in any other way. Always speak the truth, always be honest with thyself. Again, we do not ask for a lot, nor are we expecting great miracles. For we know only too well the state of thy world as it is today, and how difficult it can be for those in the spirit world to try to do what they wish to do.

"When you think of your past history ... the great masters and the great pioneers and mediums of the past. You my brothers and sisters, you should know the difficult times that they had to come through, the tests that they had to come through and so forth, for they lived and breathed in that which they did. They are nothing but the fine examples of what a true medium or channel should be, in order to bring true survival, love and harmony among fellow man. It was their purpose to serve and this is what it is all about. Even here and now, you are serving now, each and every one of you. ...

"Spirit is closer to you than you'll ever think, for they know every thought and everything that you do, whether it be spiritually or materially. We can do a lot more spiritually, for it is thy way, it is our way. But it is not our way to interfere the ways of your thinking and the ways you lead your life, for that alone is thy responsibility. ... You are only answerable to yourself. That is why it is safe to say that no one judges you except yourself. This you will all find out and realise when you pass over. ...

"But at this moment in time, this is your special time. ... This is the top class as it were of your learning, putting aside your daily thoughts and the work that you do. This is where you will break the chains free, to become once again like a free bird. By being happy and content to be among friends and that which you do now, so that you soak up the knowledge like a sponge, to gain more strength and understanding in the ways of the spirit, and the ways of your spirit friends that are trying to impress and teach you.

"Yes, there is much to come. For as I've said before and I will say it again, that our work is slow but very sure. And I can promise you this now, for it is a while since your circle started, and would it not be so that you would have left or folded up by now, for we would have sorted it out by then, has one not thought of that? So this should tell you that we are and will be sticking with you, for there is much yet to come. …

"So be more in harmony with one another. It is the balance of the circle that is important, not so much the knowledge and the understanding. Yes, that is important, but there is nothing to stop one learning and gaining that knowledge, for it can be passed through those who already know of it. That's why it is said that it is not yours alone to keep, but to be shared. So if you share it, then it will not be too long before the others will gain and climb the ladder as it were. …

"Like I said before my friends, you have the blessing of spirit upon this circle, may you walk in beauty with it, may you be happy. May you go with it like the tides of water, not going against the tide. May your hearts and minds be forever open, to listen intently to those who are trying to teach you, or to pass on words of wisdom. May your eyes ever behold that wonderful light of the spirit, for it is there in front of you. Never let go of it, keep hold of it but let it grow. We know it is not easy at the best of times, but remember that it is through thy experiences and thy difficulties that the soul comes unto its own, and the dealings that come with it.

"So move onwards and forwards, for there is much work to be done, for we are and will be calling upon you, because that work, that teaching has to be spread, has to be shared. For your world is bad enough as it is, with all the dark corners, with all the unlit places and the things that go with it. This alone is one of the reasons that you are here, so that you can work with spirit and to spread it and share it to wherever it is needed in thy world today.

"I will leave you those words with you my friends and say goodnight and God bless to each and every one of you."

There was a break of about seven minutes before another spirit came through, one called 'David', who had been confined to a wheelchair most of his short life (he died when he was eighteen years old). He explained his family life, urged us to continue our work before giving personal advice to several members of the circle. To me he said: *"Now if it helps, I would like to say unto you my friend, in time you will get stronger, for your friend George has plans for you, and he could also speak through you as well my friend. But keep going as you are, for you will get there. And as I say that, I say that unto each and every one of you, keep going."* After the close of the circle there was a brief discussion, during which V said that he had seen a light at my left side at the start, when I had been talking.

From this time the circle seemed to get back 'to normal'. Spirit made references to the approaching date of 31st March (when in 1848 the knockings were heard by the Fox family in Hydesville, USA, and are seen as the birth of modern Spiritualism) and to the pioneers of the past. Ho-Linn gave us a quote of Silver Birch, the spirit who worked through Maurice Barbanell: "If you have not made an enemy, then your work has not been done".

Hafed gave us another talk, beginning with: "My friends, I bring to you the Star of the East…" and then: "I recognise thee as disciples of the East…" Then he surprised us with a visualisation, which was to focus on the Star and then take that focus down to our feet and take a good look. As is usual for me I didn't get anything, but knew that I should be seeing my bare feet in sandals and sand. He went on to give a long talk, some parts of which were as follows.

H: "I speak the truth, for God will out and the truth will out. So therefore when you see that which is on your feet now, you will know and understand that you are part, because you are truly like the brother and sister that you had met up (with) before. … Each one of you here tonight will have a very important part to play in thy material world, to pass on the seeds of knowledge, the seeds of truth. …

"The Circle of the Eastern Star is the vital jewel to it all. This is why it has been formed in the first place. For not only for progression within thyself, but to take seeds home with you or wherever you go, and to use them and share them.

"We saw spirit through the flames of our fires at that time. We heard the voices of spirit coming through the very walls of our temple. We heard the high notes of the angels that sang at the time and also we heard those whose mouths were ready for spirit to speak through them.

"See your feet once again and feel the golden sand … that even the ships of the desert are your friends too. Ha, ha, ha! For I know that you don't like them! You think they are big horrible animals that spit, but they are your friends. It took you a little while to master the art of sitting on the ship of the desert. You [U] were not so bad, but you [Me] were terrible!

"I will leave you with the crook, the crook of peace, in compassion and understanding … along with the Eastern Star and its power that comes with it. And may God bless all your wonderful spirit friends who are truly with you. And perhaps I will say it this time as well, that your friend George may well still get the chance to speak through you, if you would only allow him to do so. But in *time, it takes time, but in time ... he will. It may only be a short few words, but at least it will be something, and that something is important."* He came through several times after that, giving long talks on Jesus and his life, but nothing that is not already mentioned in the Bible. I did some research on Hafed and found a book that I recommend to any who would like to know more: "Hafed, Prince of Persia: his Experiences in Earth-Life and Spirit-Life" by David Duguid, Hay Nisbet. The original was published around 1875, though I ordered a paperback version via the Internet from Amazon.

White Cloud took a more prominent part; even his son came through once to give us a blessing in his Native American tongue. White Cloud sometimes gave advice, and while doing that for me said the following:

"Many people say we need more people. More people, maybe, more people maybe not. But it is not the amount of people that really matters, it is what is within the people that matters, and that is what we look for, and that is what we see within each and everyone of you here tonight. It is what you have got to offer."

At another circle he gave a nice morality tale. A young boy approached his father and said that he was intrigued by the wolf. The father answered by telling him that the wolf was a 'sacred one', same as the buffalo and the eagle. That the Great Spirit made all forms of life, so one must respect them all and only kill for the means of survival and no other. The little boy listened intently and said that he could not understand why he was mesmerized by the wolf. His father replied, saying that the wolf lives in you, is part of you, you can feel its strength and its spirit. But to remember that there can be two wolves. There is a good wolf in you and there is a bad wolf in you. One does good, one respects all, one is trusting, one is loving, one is understanding, one has compassion and the other is not. One is bad, one is untrusting, one is unloving, one full of anger or bitterness, or whatever. His son asked him what he meant by that, to which his father replied that he should think about it, and that two wolves lived in him. When the boy wondered which one wins, his father declared – the one I feed my son, and the son nodded his head in understanding.

Just before Easter there was the first Lynwood Fellowship seminar of the year. I was not in good health and found it hard to concentrate on much of the lectures/talks and workshops. Indeed, several times I took time away to walk in the fresh air and try to clear my head. To be honest I needed a good rest and complete relaxation, which I tried to do when I returned home.

The circle continued with spirit giving philosophy, encouragement and advice. In May 'Bluebell' came through to give much advice to each of us, as well as generally warning us to watch our thoughts, and this was a topic that several spirits had highlighted, often giving proof that they knew what we had been thinking. Her advice to myself included to not eat hot curries (something I was beginning to work out for myself), to eat a bit more fruit and drink more water.

Due to a school parents' evening I missed the next circle, and at the subsequent one at the end of May I was surprised to discover that the circle seemed to have now reduced to just four of us. 'Matthew' came through; using experiences from the war to give us an idea how necessary it was to be a unit, each supporting the other no matter what occurred. He suggested that our absent member was not quite suitable for what was to eventually come. However, he insisted that one of us had to write to her, a duty that I undertook. Before he left, Matthew told me to keep in touch with George, and that a French man is coming in, who was going to bring a little bit of excitement!

Before I knew it, it was time for the second Lynwood Fellowship seminar, 12-16th July 2010. The problem this time was not illness – I was in full health – but rather the difficult task of choosing which person to go to see, as there were five tutors! I attended informative and interesting workshops and/or talks by Joe Wilcock, Sheila Green and Angela McInnes, but found that I had only seen Irene Hartley when she did a demonstration of mediumship with Angela on the first evening. Therefore I made a point of attending her workshop on the last full day. It started with the fire alarm going off, but it was a false alarm, and we eventually settled down to try some inspirational writing.

After picking a card out of a bag, I asked 'George' for help, and contemplated the word 'Health' that was on the card. After a bit of time, we each in turn read out what we had written. I wrote the following:

HEALTH

For most of us who are healthy, this word does not really register in our daily lives. A few very fortunate ones will go through their whole lives in good health. The rest of us will experience varying degrees of ill health at various times throughout our lives, and some will have it for most or maybe even all of theirs. Ill health is a restriction; it debilitates a person in some way. This is added to the restriction that all who incarnate into the material from spirit experience.

Some of ill health is there to slow us down, to get us out of our usual pattern of life, to give us space and time to think, to make us more aware of others and a host of other reasons. So although we may dislike the condition, it may be just the thing for our soul. It will hopefully expand our consciousness, deepen our awareness.

Some illness may not be necessary for us alone - it gives opportunity for others to help, to care, to open their eyes to another rather than self. So we learn from each other, and gradually see our fellow travellers in the material as the brothers and sisters that they really are.

These may seem as obstacles and hindrances to us, but they are just stepping stones to 'heaven' and our merging with spirit.

Rather than for an individual, I felt that it was for the group as a whole. Interestingly, Irene asked me if I had a monk that worked with me.

A month later found me attending the 31st Congress Week of the International Spiritualist Federation in St Andrews, Fife. Apart from one afternoon of torrential downpours, the weather was exceptionally warm and sunny, and I had a marvellous week of learning and meeting distant friends. Interestingly, at the start I had to choose quite quickly whether to opt for physical mediumship workshops (that I had originally intended) or spirit/psychic art. On the spur of the moment I opted for the latter.

The next day I started with my other choice of Shamanic Journeying with Steve Vogel, which involved seeking a power animal to work with. This was not a very successful session for me. The following day we had to journey to a pool of water to see the salmon and ask our questions. Eventually I got to the pool to see the salmon that had its back to me. When I asked my question (Is this a good path for me now?), the salmon swam away! I interpreted that sign as meaning not at this time anyway! After discussing this with Steve, he agreed with my explanation.

Midweek there was an evening demonstration of mediumship by four people. One, Simone Rüegsegger, came to me saying she had my father with her. She related that he had passed with a condition that had been with him for a long time. Then Simone stated that he read lots of books and newspapers (I could understand this, though it was a slight misinterpretation), didn't like being disturbed and was not a very demonstrative individual. However, he was pleased how much I have learnt; that I need to write, including a book, as I had a lot of knowledge to impart. [Only took me four years to get started on that!]

Coral Ryder took the spirit art workshops. At the second one Coral started with pariedolia (seeing faces in anything). We scribbled all over a sheet of A4 size paper and then tried to find faces. I found two, both together, but only the eyes were showing as the top part and the bottom were covered with close fitting 'hats' and 'masks' that suggested surgeons. I distinctly felt that this was important and not mere accident, but nobody could take it when I showed the image to the class. Then I put it away carefully in my folder.

The last workshop was the exciting conclusion! We all had to focus on a young Swedish woman and see what we could get for her. However, most linked in with the woman next to her. With a change in seating we tried once again. I found it very difficult; I got just the eyes and one minute they would be male and the next female! Then it dawned on me that the rest of the face was hidden by a surgical mask, and I remembered the sheet I had done earlier in the week that I had been sure was linked to somebody! Coral intervened to help me, and it transpired that it was not a normal spirit link with family or friends, but rather a couple (of some renown) who were part of the young woman's healing team in spirit. Fascinating!

I could add more from that week, but will confine myself to just mention some of the evening demonstrations. A psychic/spirit art one with Colin Hall, Matthias Güldenstein, Coral Ryder and Joan Watson; it was interesting to see the different styles. In addition there was an exhibition of trance and later an evening demonstration of the Scottish mediums Sandra McFadden, John Alexander and Bill Coller.

Little did I know that the surprises were far from finished! At the next circle on the 26th August 2010, I said the opening prayer and then thanked spirit for their help at the ISF Congress. Within a few minutes an unknown spirit came through and gave long talk on shamanism, with a hee hee at my attempt in St Andrews! This continued with aspects of Native American culture and giving us power animals. After he withdrew, there was a gap of about five minutes – I will continue from my notes:

> *I waited but nothing was said, so I opened.*
> *Me: "Greeting friend."*
> *There was a noise from Z's throat but no words, so I suspected that it might be somebody coming through for the first time.*
> *Me: "Take your time."*
> *Then 'he' started to make signals with his hands, touching his head several times.*
> *Me: "Think?"*
> *More hand signals, with him touching his body and pointing at me.*
> *Me: "Connection with me?"*
> *More signals.*
> *Me: "You to me?"*
> *Then after some more signals the penny began to drop.*
> *Me: "Ah! Drawing...you were with me...you helped me ...*

thank you very much indeed…I am most grateful."
Then there were more noises as if struggling to speak and pointing to his mouth.
Me: "You can't speak…right…your tongue was cut off… right…right…you spoke through your hands…and your art…thank you…and writing…just drawing…thank you…I am most grateful…you control my arm…thank you …yet… even when I'm going like this (as if I'm scribbling or going all over the place)…very good…right…you can't speak, I understand…maybe one day you could write through me." Then the person relaxed and with difficulty started to speak through Z.
?: "I can speak. I have been…in spirit long, long time."
Me: "Right."
?: "Your friend George …?… me to him."
Me: "Right."
?: "I would like to paint through you."
Me: "Oh right. Certainly."
?: "I love to draw, to paint. It gave me comfort. Gave me comfort. I was a slave, but no more! Many years ago during bad times, in Greek times, where great Pharaohs were not so good."
Me: "Yes, I understand."
?: "My memories are not very good I'm afraid. My family was broken up. I was accused of wrongdoing, but I did not do it, so they cut my tongue regardless. It was the Romans who did that to me. But I found good comfort in drawing what I used to see and used to use pigment of… eh …colour of white, red mud and things like that. Even of the leaves, colouring, used to make different colours, ambers, sienna, umber, even blues. So I got great comfort from that. Just for, even for food, to make money just for food. I write too. It has been me unfortunately who has been trying to influence you where your drawing has been concerned. You sort of understand that?"
Me: "Yeah, yes I do. Thank you very much."

?: "But...but forgive me, I can't speak. It took me long while to get used to it. You understand?"

Me: "I understand."

?: "Because my memories not of good one, my life was not of good one. Nothing of good quality as it were, it was harsh and hard, as many of my fellow countrymen were. But we are now in the land of happiness, of richness and beauty. Where we enjoy and just succumb to the great wonders of the peace of the Great Spirit and the beauty of the land that's around us, in our own creation of love and understanding where we can still draw and paint, etc."

Me: "Good."

?: "So there are many great artists still doing wonderful works even now in the world of the spirit. Well my friend, I need not say what you experienced was the classic example, that two great surgeons, as you've seen."

Me: "Yes, yes."

?: "So you see, they carry on the great works of the Great Spirit. Do you understand now how your little piece of the jigsaw is coming?"

Me: "Yes, yes."

?: "So this is why I have, what shall we say, surprised you!"

Me: "You certainly have!"

?: "So, it's one way of getting through. Do you understand?"

Me: "Yes, I understand."

?: "Pardon my hands from going all over the place, because my hands were like that all the time. I could never keep still, I was always...had to be doing something. Because it kept my mind off a lot of things, kept my mind off the horrors of what was going on, kept busy." ...

He went on to talk about some of the other spirits who have visited the circle, and then continued: *"I am very proud to be part of your great plans as it were. That's why I come forward tonight in this manner, so forgive you for my interruption as it were. I just thought I would surprise you."*

Me: You certainly have! It is great to hear from you."

?: "And my name, I will proudly tell you my name because you have been asking for it. My name is Ramos."

Me: "Ah. Ramos."

Ramos: "Ramos, that is the way you do say it…Ramos."

Me: "Ramos." [Pronounced and slightly extended 'R': Rrramos.]

Ramos: "Ramos, I like to hear the little bit of 'rrr', Ramos."

Me: "Well I am very pleased. Thank you very much for your help."

Ramos: "But I am quite confident that my name will be mentioned again to you in some way my friend."

Me: "Right, thank you."

Ramos: "May I perhaps, if I'm given the strength, because I'm not in good state at the moment to tell you exactly about my life, my lifestyle. My memory is not very good at the moment, but not a happy one, but it's taken a long time to come to terms with what had actually happened, what was happening all those years ago. But this is BC mind."

Me: "This is?"

Ramos: "BC."

Me: "BC!"

Ramos: "Yes, oh yes. … But it was far, far from what would imagine, lifestyle as it were, was not what you would say…aristocratic, or like that. Far from it, there was very hidden, sinister ..?.., with people that were of great ignorance and barbaric mind. That wouldn't think twice about taking your eyes out, or your ears off or whatever. So, unpleasant place, not nice at all. …

"But I offer this in sincerity and in truth. That even although my tongue was cut and I could not speak, my lips and my strength and my faith, and everything comes together made me survive it. My pathway became much harder and then I was able to build a house with my hands, putting mud together, building it up. I found my peace, my understanding in that hut. People would come *to me for their painting, portraits, whatever, some come for plans, some come for this some for that. So a little bit of everything, a little of whatever.*

"I was able to use my hands, but my ears became very sharp, that I was able to hear and listen, a sound of a cricket in the sand or the sound of a snake or whatever. So even without the words of my tongue, I could smell a camel a mile away! Goat! Everything around me became a lot sharper. Who knows, maybe, I'm not saying it was meant to be or whatever, but I'm only saying what actually happened. But I got used to it, I got better, I got better, but it took me a little while. But at the time I call on Allah's help, Allah was close to my heart at the time. But anyway I'm not going to say too much more. My mouth shut, because that you know fine, as if and when I do come, or hopefully I will come through to you my friend, that [There followed several sentences that I was unable to decipher.]. Anyway, I must go now and say goodnight and God bless."
Me: "Well thank you."

Ramos then left, and it was not long before the circle was closed. Needless to say I was on cloud nine by this time!

Notwithstanding that, the surprises for this year were not over yet! Just two weeks later a spirit that I documented as D(s) came through. He had been a shepherd called David a long, long time ago, and had talked to us several times. However, I need to start at the beginning, before the circle opened. *I arrived a bit early and chatted to Z. He said he had been on the internet and come up with a list of things that happened in a physical circle, and that we had experienced most of them at some point: raps and taps (✓), pulling from the solar plexus (✓), severe itching to nose and face (✓), scented smells (✓), water (✗), earthy smells - maybe sign of ectoplasm (✗), psychic breeze over face or from floor to knee height (✓), spirit light (✓), whistles (✗), light touches on hair and body (✓), lip smacking noises (✗), voice box (✗). As regards the last one I expressed the hope that it would come. Then we had a mug of tea and then went down to arrange the room. I relaxed to the music under the dimmed red lights, and when all were assembled and settled I opened the circle at 8 pm.*

Me: "Great Spirit, once again we meet to join with one another and with our friends in spirit, in an hour of love and understanding, to listen to the voices who give us food for thought. May we continue in this way giving our energy, giving our love, so that we may join together to build what is needed to be built, here and in our lives. Amen."

Within a minute and a half spirit spoke through Z.

D(s): "Greetings my friends."

Me: "Greetings."

D(s): "Short but sweet my brother. And how are you may I ask?"

Me: "Very well thank you."

D(s): "Indeed I hope you are my friend, for once again thy inquisitive mind has been sending out thoughts to those in the world of spirit. Patience I ask my brother, for the answer shall come, or answers shall come as and when required. Hee, hee, hee, I chuckle at the thought and when I heard you say you wished to hear the voice box, that we will give in time my friend."

Me: ""Thank you."

D(s): "For it is a great preparation for such a thing to take place. ..." He went on to outline a little bit of what had been his material life before commenting on the spiritual beings from the angelic realms.

"Oh yes, they are the most beautiful souls you will ever see and hear of. They are very rarely seen and heard my friends. I myself perhaps have seen only once or twice in my time here in spirit, which has been a long, long, long, long time. But I know there are such beings. I am not going to speculate and say they are, well... their wings are there to be seen and to cover you in

their protection and love combined. Oh no my friends, I am saying to you that most definitely there is that love and that protection from such high beings. That their power is unbreakable and the power that comes with it is something else, for it is the purity of thought that comes from these beings."

David went on to talk about spiritual law, answer a question, and then spoke to us individually.

[There was a very long pause here while he stroked what would be a moustache and a beard, and sniffed at his fingers a couple of times.]

D(s): "You have good man with you, the bearded one, George. He very good man, very trustworthy. He will help you a great deal. Please allow him to influence your mind for you can and will surprise yourself, from time to time. That is where you can help each other grow. Have you got that?"

Me: "Ok, yes."

He returned to discuss his time on earth and the cruel nature of some of the people before he departed and the circle finished. This time it was more like I was on cloud nineteen rather than nine! So we were going to experience an independent voice box!

At the end of September, after the circle was closed, V reported seeing a flash of light in the corner to my right near the start. He also saw a few orbs of light and a large 'ring' of light on the wall to his left. He also commented on feeling the energy being pulled from him and that at times he couldn't keep his eyes open. Then Z suggested that we should sit for V next week, and Y agreed that we should all take a turn. However, I told them no – that it would come but only when spirit told us, as this had come up before. During this part of the discussion the red lights went up and down dramatically. I mentioned that I had seen a green/blue coloured light/mist over Z's lips, and that I had seen it on previous occasions. Y mentioned that she had a very close link tonight and could have said the words before Z spoke them.

In the next circle a spirit named 'Red Cloud' came through to give us a bit of teaching, and also to give me another reminder.

RC: *"That to perhaps spend a little more time also with pen and paper, if you may."*
Me: *"Thank you, yes."*
RC: *"In your own time perhaps. But may I ask that you continue to do such work for us in spirit world."*

During the discussion after the close of the circle, V said he had seen loads of small lights and I told him that I had seen a bright one by his right shoulder in the early part of the circle. V then asked if it had been Red Cloud who had first come through, as he had got a feeling for that before spirit actually spoke. Also he had seen a light by the edge of Z's right eye, and again noticed the big circle on the wall that he mentioned last week. I reported that I had just finished a book by Red Cloud – through the mediumship of Estelle Roberts. I thought we had a Grey Eagle speaking previously, but Y confirmed that we never had Red Cloud. As this discussion went on the red lights started to go up and down, and then Z reminded Y that they had been talking earlier today and Red Cloud had been mentioned. The rest seemed convinced that this was indicative that it was indeed *the* Red Cloud. Then Y and Z got back to their conversation of today, and Y reported that last week she had Sitting Bull with her; this was confirmed when Z had shown her a picture of him. Y also said that Sitting Bull had some connection with children.

I was absent for the following circle meeting, but returned to the next one from holiday, so without the music that was normally played at the start. The red lights dipped slightly and there was a little 'nod' from the picture as I sat down to relax before the others came in. At eight o'clock I said the opening prayer, reminding everyone that there would be no circle next week, and about a minute later spirit came through.

RC: *"Hail thee, my brother."*
Me: *"Good evening."*
RC: *"I hear thy words, for I come from the land of anywhere.*

   I have spoken before, but those who choose to speak through the vessel have and can be welcome to do so.

Fear not, for who I am is not important, but the words I have to say maybe of some use if I may be permitted to speak through this vessel. Yes, there have been others who have spoken for they have had their opportunity, for that opportunity has been right my friend. For if it were not then it would not be so. You've heard in thy Bible that it says, 'hear ye spirits, test ye spirits', is this not so?"
Me: "It is."
RC: "So there you are, for we are testing all the time the vessel and himself, and that which is there in front of him. For we understand the importance of an inquisitive mind, but it is thy part and parcel of your nature, but do not worry for all will be revealed in time. But let us just say that the more you are doing this the easier and higher it is getting, so they are reaching those who matter in the realms of the spirit world. Do you get my meaning my friend?"
Me: "Yes I do."
RC: ""This is what it is all about. For I am a simple man...

He went on to say he was a Lakota, and became a chief. He talked about the Native American culture and attitudes to Mother Earth and the Great Spirit. As he was nearing the end of his talk he said:

RC: "What is thy question you wish to ask, if you have any? For I am aware that you my brother have a particular question to ask."
Me: "When did you first become aware of Jesus?"
RC: "I knew of Jesus my friend a long, long time ago, for I go back as far as even then."
RC: "Does that answer the question?"
Me: "It does indeed."
RC: "And do not take this wrong way, but you have to understand that there are many lifetimes and that one can and will travel along that long and weary path."

Me: "I understand."
RC: "Have you got that?"
Me: "Yes, I have."
RC: "So I even knew of Egyptians also, I even know of the Indians also. Do you know for example, that it is only twelve and a half...maybe...yes...twelve and a half/ thirteen thousand years ago since first Indians came to view? Did you know that my friend?"
Me: "No, I didn't know that."
RC: "You had no idea?"
Me: "No."
RC: "Well now you know."
Me: "I do!"
RC: "So you see, but time is not in the existence of the spirit my friend, what is...is the ageless body and the timeless mind. It is the mind my friend, the mind that carries the secrets and memories. ... And look forward to thy retirement, for you will have busy hands."
Me: "Good."
RC: "Busy, busy hands."
Me: "Very good."
RC: "Be careful what one wishes! ...

Several weeks later when our circle fell on the 11th November, it did not surprise us that Matthew spoke, to talk about the horrors of war in the past and of today. For the next few circles Red Cloud also came through to encourage us to think a bit more, and to offer individual advice. He warned me to watch my weight, not to worry unduly about my hernia, as well as offering a little guidance on my thinking regarding the Lynwood Fellowship.

A new spirit talked to us. He did not give his name, but was obviously active around the early part of the twentieth century, as he said he knew Sir Arthur Conan Doyle and the Rev Vale Owen. On his second visit (when Y was absent) he advised us that Z was needing a rest to recharge his batteries, indeed he said that the next meeting would be the last of this year and would be one of discussion between ourselves. During his talk he said that they were going deeper and it was more testing for the medium, and also made a remark: "*Hence the lady that was sitting here tonight, who full well knows what can happen in consequences, for such event or events that we take place...*" When the medium returned to normal awareness I asked him who had been sitting in Y's seat. He responded by saying that he thought it might have been Doris at the start, but got Helen Duncan after that.

As there was still some time to go I suggested a visualisation: walk down a street in a large town, see a library and go in, feeling which area to go to. One book will take your attention, take it out and sit in a chair nearby, look at the title, then open the book and note what you see.

Z said that everything had been so clear. He was in Sauchiehall Street in Glasgow, instead of the library he went into W.H.Smiths, saw all the books, when he turned around found himself in a chair like the one he was sitting on now. He saw three books: 'Trance', 'Physical Phenomena' and 'Transfiguration'. Next he found himself sitting in front of Sir Arthur Conan Doyle and other people. They greeted him and said that they were interested in what was going on. Conan Doyle remarked that the circle was giving out such a good light that it had attracted these men. Then one came up to him and shook his hand and announced that he was Stainton Moses, and another that he was Alfred Russel Wallace. Z recognised some of them as he had studied them years ago, but that they were clear as day and were wearing Victorian type clothing. Our group was one of seventeen others in the world who were similar, in places like Denmark, Sweden, Norway, New Zealand, Africa, and in Britain.

V had found himself in York where everybody was wearing old style clothing. He went down to a selection of books and chose one with a rainbow on it. The title was 'Mind, Body and Soul'. When he opened it a blank page fell out. He picked it up and asked what it was for, and got the answer, "The chapter is not writ; what the mind wants to do the body and soul will follow". He went blank after that and then felt as if he was falling down, and that was when he lost the book.

I had walked up stone steps to a huge library, going along to the main area. There were corridors with books everywhere, so decided to go into a wee corner somewhere. I went to the right and eventually saw one book sticking out; it had a light grey cover but nothing else on the outside. I sat down and then opened the book only to discover that there was nothing inside except lots of blank pages. It had not been written yet!

We had our discussion at the next meeting, and settled on the 10th February 2011 as the date of the next circle.

CHAPTER 14

Big Changes

Undoubtedly the biggest change of all was that I retired after thirty-four years of teaching at the same school. On my last day some of the sixth year students, ones that I had taught, presented me with handmade ties that they had created secretly, and one of them had painted a symbolic still life picture. It was very touching that they had all taken so much time and effort to do this, especially as they had lots of other work to do. Indeed, as I write this now I can see that still life hanging on my sitting room wall. In January of 2011, I invited them out for a curry at the Merrick Hotel [now called Momtaz], an Indian restaurant that I have frequented for many years – and still do. I had made it plain that it was my treat, but at the end, after I had paid the bill and put on my coat, I found a load of notes in one pocket that covered half the cost! Teaching can certainly be a trial at times, but I have come to understand that it is also a great privilege to have met so many wonderful human beings, and they have taught me much into the bargain.

The final act was a dinner at the Urr Valley Hotel, organised by the school. I had a thoroughly enjoyable meal with colleagues and friends, some of whom had travelled quite some distance. They had to endure my speech, which was basically a thank you to the many who had enriched my life during my career. Into the bargain, I received some lovely presents, including from the school a crystal glass bowl that had been engraved by my old boss and friend, Ron White.

In January I got a sudden urge to visit Z, and we had a long chat when Y also arrived. Previously, just the two of them had sat and an extraordinary event had happened. A mist formed between them that was also seen by Z, but then he "went out like a light". Y then saw an overshadowing/ transfiguration of a large man of about 40 to 50 years of age, with black hair that had a 'kink' in it, and was clean-shaven. Y said that it was so detailed that she reckoned that even I might have seen it if I'd been there. She thought he was some sort of professor. We had a look in some books for photographs and also on the Internet, but didn't find anything to fit. We then discussed the circle, and Z said that he thought that Y should take over the leadership. I agreed, because if things were going to move a bit quicker now it would be better if the person with the most knowledge was in charge (and it would give Z more reassurance).

V was having a continual medical condition and was advised to wait until he improved before attending any meeting. It happened that Z was having problems with sciatica, and into the bargain he developed influenza, so the planned first circle didn't take place until the 17th February 2011, but it was worth the wait!

Just three of us sat under a dim red light and it was not long before Ho-Lin came through. He spoke to Y for a bit and then said: "*And that may I say first of all that things are beginning to move, as you have witnessed. That was the reason of the exercise, so you were not instructed for nothing.*" Then he gave us four instructions: 1 – to play the music gently for some time before we enter for the circle; 2 – take out the clock for total silence; 3 – have the lights as they are now; 4 – to observe very closely. In addition he told me that although I had retired, I would be working more than ever! Also it was important to be in tune with spirit. It was very important that all the sitters were of the same thoughts, but not mind necessarily, but the same thought is given out as spirit does. We were to remember that as you think you create – it was as simple as that.

After Ho-Lin left, White Cloud quickly came to give assurance of protection for the circle and emphasised the importance of working as a team. Z came back to normal awareness momentarily, drank some water and stated that someone had been sitting in V's seat, before settling himself again. About ten minutes later a voice attempted to speak with difficulty. There was a delay and Z cleared his throat several times.

Y: "Can we help you?"

HD: "Well thank ye, but I'm getting there. I have been watching. I just wish to say that there is much preparation still to come."

Y: "Yeah."

HD: "And that there is a great source of power coming from the realms, or the other side. I wish to take upon gentleman's thoughts that one stage that there is possibility of building a voice box. It is or has been considered, but would be best advised to go along with the tide as it were. But I just wish to let you know that it's mainly just observing at the moment. For I wish not to surprise you too greatly, for it is I, Nellie, who wish to be remembered to you, for you know my granddaughter."

Y: "Oh, yes."

HD: "And that which the promise was made many years ago.
   For now you know and you ken who I am."

Y: "Yeah,"

HD: "That I can see and understand that which is going on.

   For when I was here in my time, on the very day I thought I was bacon, but didnae ken and realise the sticky stuff that came oot of my stomach, the sticky stuff that the spirits could use. I was just naïve and oblivious to it all, I didnae know what was happening and nor can my man Henry tell me what it was too. But then again you learn as ye go alang. But I'm not here to say for one moment that that is what is going to happen, for it is a very rare occurrence. So rare indeed, that blessed in disguise it is and may God be thanked. But there is such a thing, the thing today.

   "For in my time I went through a terrible, terrible time, and even mind the day when I lay down and spirit did the operation on me. There is so much, and so much to understand, sometimes best no to understand. But for what I see here and now am quite pleased and proud that there is such a work going on at the moment. That even in the transfiguration is something in itself, but it is a marvellous thing to see and to have, for you have witnessed it before. But these things above all else are to be *treasured, and in this small foundation is just right for it. For I am pleased to pass on the information, so I wish to bid ye a good and happy successful working with spirit.*

"I still have my fond dogs, even though I brought my man and my family. But what happened to me all those years ago, I not think of myself as a hero or a martyr, but just an ordinary Scots woman trying to do the best in the service for God, and God alone it was indeed. I wish not no harm on anybody or anything, for it was long ago and I have since moved on. I still have my dogs as I say, and my man and my family and Albert, for he was a good and steadfast of a person that served the spirit world, in all honesty. But alas, in a lot of stages of my career was not to be, for whatever reason or reasons to be, but hopefully one can only learn from. That is all I have to say. So goodnight and God bless you both. For I may return sometime."

Y: "You are welcome."

HD: "But forgive me if I have poked my nose."

Y: "No, you are quite welcome."

HD: "For it was that I was sitting there before."

Y: "Ah, thank you."

HD: "And the gentleman in front of me reminds me of myself. That I say to him to be content and be happy within yourself sir, and better that way the spirit. And I wish to say goodnight and God bless ye sir."

Me: "Goodnight."

HD: "Ah, happy retirement, but a happy retirement indeed, but you will be working more than you will realise, so be prepared Jimmy as I would say!"

Me: "Thank you very much."

HD: "Or perhaps Andrew, but you do not go by Andrew, you have always stood by Michael."

Me: "That's right."

HD: "Yes, we know you see, for I am no smart alec either. I know, so there you have it, and goodnight and God bless you all."

Me + Y: "Goodnight."

HD: "May I extend my best wishes to you my friend, for we
*   indeed go back a long way."*
Y: "Yeah."
HD: "But that long way is nothing, for the time in the spirit
*   world is not there my friend. But the connection will always*
be and shall be for evermore. Goodnight."
Y: "Goodnight." Then after a long pause.
HD: "Will you send a wee thought to Gena please?"
Y: "Yes."
HD: "Thank you. I just thought I would leave you with that."

Soon after that the circle came to a close. In the discussion afterwards Y related how she had seen a light surrounding Z, not his head, just around his shoulders and down, very faint. She also could hear the drums with White Cloud, and stated that there had been one squaw between Z and myself. Z then said, "Mary many days", and wondered where that had come from, speculating that it might have been a wife.

When I got home I looked at the printout on Chief White Cloud that I had found on the Internet: His mother, Mary Many Days Robidoux was a daughter of Joseph Robidoux, founder of St Joseph, MO and an Iowa Indian woman.

At the subsequent meeting Hemron spoke, and during his talk he included a little more on the subject of 'rescue circles'.

Hem: "And may I remind you, for perhaps one has
misunderstood, that when we said about the rescue,
that yes indeed all circles no matter what they may be,
I repeat, all circles no matter what they may be are of
the rescue. For they will attract those concerning to join
in the joyous moment of the connection to work, to do
whatever, including those that perhaps have lost their
way. But only in the specific purpose of this ..?.. ..?.. in
itself, for it has to be, then you would most certainly be
well instructed. So there is the difference, so please do
not be alarmed or think for one moment that this can
be probably used for the rescue purpose. For one thing for

certain my friend, there is not enough numbers to do the job as it were. But there is sufficient numbers now if no one is absent, that what you do now there is sufficient, and we ask for further patience on our behalf."

I saw speckles of light during his talk, and Hemron went on to give some advice and a warning on a situation that had impacted on my life. At the end of the meeting there was a long discussion that covered many subjects. When the conversation turned to automatic writing, Y gave a suggestion that I should sit still and let a word come to me, then write on it. As it so happened, something of that nature did come about later in the year.

Seven days later, before starting, Z asked me if I would get in touch with Jock McArthur and maybe invite him to come to see the circle and give us some advice, and I said I would. In the meantime we continued with just the three of us.

A spirit, who had been murdered the previous year, came through to express his thanks to Y for her thoughts and to say that he was all right. Red Cloud returned to lament humanity's attitude to Mother Earth, and emphasized that everything on earth is accountable, "even down to the humblest of the bees". He kindly confirmed the name of Henry Sidgwick (first President of the Society for Psychical Research) as being one of those in the background; for I had been doing my homework with the very few hints that had been given over the last five or six months, and his name was on my list of four or five possible candidates.

On 17th March, the circle was notable not so much for what happened in it, but rather after it! I had a narrow escape from serious injury or even possible death, when driving home on a dual carriageway. Passing a lorry on the brow of a hill at 70mph, I suddenly encountered a wheelie bin! Instinctively I swerved a little, and lost all control for a few seconds. During this time the car jumped and bounced from one wheel to another and I thought that it would overturn. Luckily I regained control, at the same time as knocking the wheelie bin off the road with the front left of the car. Quickly I moved left off the road and came to a halt, and just sat until my heart rate lessened. I got out and inspected the impact zone, to discover a light trailing underneath, still attached by its wiring. I yanked it free, and cautiously made my way home. Going over the incident in my head, I knew that I had come very close to losing my life; it would only have needed a little more turn on the steering wheel. St Patrick, or whoever, was guarding me that night!

At the next circle we agreed on a date in August to go up to see Jock McArthur. When sitting, Bluebell came to speak to us. Now, to be quite honest, when first encountering her I had found her a bit tiresome. She comes through as a little girl (at the age when she died) to bring laughter and upliftment, while at that time all I wanted was to get on with things and find some of the answers to my long list of questions! However, I had since discovered that she has a great depth of knowledge as well as compassion, and I now hold her in great respect. Since she spoke at length on several interesting subjects, I will give an abridged account of some of them.

> B: "So do not worry, we're trying to adjust to conditions of the room and its surroundings. It has taken me a little while to get used to my instrument, for I have been with [him] for quite some earth time now. It has taken this time even for me to get adjusted to coming in to speak, and to have that closer influence of ones mind. It is just the same as those that are working with you now to create the right sorts of vibrations that are needed. Such as thinking or the thoughts of perhaps voice-boxes or whatever, that they wish to desire, to try to do or to think. That everything is in the power of thought. That the essential part of life comes from the spirit world to here and so forth. Hence that is why you sit together as a team, to work together, to generate that wonderful power as it were. For we need the harmonious and the upliftment of the vibrations and so forth. That is why I am always happy you see, because I bring laughter, happiness. It is my way of letting my instrument know that I am there. We are a jester as it were, or shall we say a harlequin as it were.
>
> "I also want to say, you were well looked after my friend. That incident as it were, has served its purpose in

a round about way. For one it would certainly make you come more alert as it were, here."

Me: "True!!"

B: *"So therefore, hee, hee, hee, you would not have had your eyes closed, they would have been wide awake, wide open, because of the state of shock. But I have to say to you that you were being looked after. So do not worry, that all will be well at the end of the day, but put it down to experience, that one has to be 'on the ball' as it were. And this includes what is happening now, and that we ask that you be more observant. Hence you will get your answers to your questions you perhaps wish to ask and all the rest of it. So if you ask the right question you will receive the right answer as it were.*

"You may think of me as a dear little child, but I wish to assure you that I am a child that is full of wit and wisdom, and I wish to pass that on and to let you know. For I am not saying for one moment that I am perfect, but I wish to tell you that the experience is there if and when required.

"You will notice that the instrument is wearing black here, he is being influenced to do so, because if you look closely you will see. And if you think and you remember, one of your dear friends who…what's her name again, em, [Jean] Skinner, she wore black. So you see she wore black because you could see spirit better. You could see spirit better all round, if you look closely around the medium's body and leading up onto the face here as well.

"Ah! But I know what this man is thinking! He's probably thinking, well I've seen Jock, didn't he do well, yes, so. The conditions have got to be right in certain areas of where the experiments or sittings are taking place, it all depends. For example here, water and the air, and there is the temperature, there is the atoms and the elements, there is the solid objects that we have to by-pass as well. We have to get round the best we can.

So perhaps in the future the room would be tidied up a little bit more as it were, but for now we have to be content and be satisfied with what is being achieved at the moment. For after all you have only sat for four years and five months. Therefore you have to take into consideration the time and the scale on your earthly side of life as opposed to our side.

"*You must remember that our business is strictly business, is the strict business of the spiritual business. For example, I have never ever interfered with my medium's life at all. I have been there at times of need, oh yes, he knows that, but I have never interfered in any other way because my business with him is strictly at the spiritual level. Now this should perhaps answer a lot of questions as I speak of this now to both of you, that is applied to the self same as yourselves. Meaning that all questions you may ask or whatever, that is why perhaps when you ask a lot of questions that you don't get answers. Every thought and everything you do is already recorded. How when the right one is there then you will receive the right answer as it were. Does this make sense?*"

Me: "*Mmmm, yes it does.*"

B: "*But on a spiritual level as opposed to your material level, which is your daily life. We can influence, we can certainly help and guide to some extent. But our job and our jobs is not only to look after the instruments, but on the spiritual level, that is our estate, yes it is. Because I chuckle and I shake my head in sadness when I see here some of the instruments who even say, well my guide says this and says that. Oh, no, far from it my friend. For they do not understand that if that were true, then, how could one learn? You would not find out for yourselves, you would not learn or understand. They have got to understand that it is only on a spiritual level, that it is strictly business.*

"*I have to say too, there are other circles going on.*

Some you will hear, others you will not hear, and they're going across the globe or world as it were. Some are even out in the open and even in Mother Nature, even when the sun is warm, so it is there. So they're all working together to generate that wonderful power through God's love as it were, or spirit's love, to influence where the great power is needed at this sad times of need of your earth plane. So it's not just this one, it is all the others included. It's just like having one big happy family as it were, working for the good of mankind or the earth, or whether it be for the good of spirit itself.

"So we all do play an important part of helping wherever we can. That's what I enjoy about it here, but I am still the child that I am. But I've shown my instrument as I was and that I could be in that moment. He saw that twice, but he could not understand why I showed myself like that to him. I was telling him how much I had progressed, I was showing him how much I had grown. I would have been as a young beautiful woman in my teens or in my youth as it were, as opposed to when I passed away when I was seven years old. I was happy when I arrived here, because once again I saw my brother and my sister, my mother and my father.

"I remember when I was in the orphanage, we helped each other in times of need. I've told you about the time when I took the apple which was thrown from a wonderful gentleman, and I was staring out of the window at the time. But that was my luxury, my only time that I saw some luxury. For there was nothing but gruel at the time, it's just like a watery bread, water and whatnot. So we weren't fed very well at all here. Rickets was rife, polio was rife, TB was rife, malnutrition was rife, consumption and so forth. I remember seeing many souls who just withered away, just like little broken dolls. Whose bodies were taken away, lifted at the time to unmarked graves. Mine was, my brother and sister, I know they too were the same. But

the toll of the health had taken the time when they went to the workhouse."

During the talk by Bluebell I saw some lights, one very bright electric blue that shone for over a second just between the eyebrows, and the next one at the left eyebrow.

At the end of the first week in April, V rejoined the circle and was welcomed by both spirits who communicated, George and Red Cloud.

G: "I speak on behalf of those that are in the spirit world. I speak for the brothers and the sisters who are eager to speak their own words of wisdom. For I was a simple man also, that I greatly believed that there was an hereafter and that there was no such thing as the word death. And that my mind was always open and understood that all man, no matter who they were, is equal and that we are all equal. Just perhaps one may be more advanced, or less or whatever, it does not matter. What matters is what understanding and knowledge that they may have to impart with themselves and to others. My life was simple and my routine was simple. I enjoyed when people gathered together for it gives a sense of well-being and unity among my fellow men and my fellow sisters. It was good to hear others speak also.

"This is why I am speaking in this manner now, for what you are experiencing here is giving others who stand behind here now to speak their views and to give their thoughts and their words of wisdom. For it is building a picture, a picture of that which is to come. You were given the road, it was spoken, it is a long one but is the road to greatness. For that which is to come out of here to be given out to others and to be shared, and to be shared among yourselves and for those who may come in contact with you also. This was the work that we did also, we spread the word. And seeds are being sown here and now.

"When I was here I always had a great and utmost

respect for Mother Earth. We were very closely associated with land because we were self-sufficient. At that time our potatoes were a reddish colour, and it was passed on from generation to generation. Through these generations are spoken the words of wisdom. What is happening now is using this vessel to allow others to come and speak, and building the picture for that which is to come.

"You're probably thinking, well who the devil is this? Well if I point the finger to the friend on your left that would be the clue, because I cannot get through to him. So I'm using the opportunity, although I've stood behind him, but I am using this opportunity to speak.

"I certainly wasn't perfect, but I hear about God, I spoke about God, because I believed in God. I spoke about the afterlife because I believed in the afterlife. But my meetings with my brothers and sisters was a routine thing because we felt it was right, because in things we did we all felt unified. And everything you do here and now is only for the good and is right. But it can't be done without your cooperation of giving out where necessary, and to observe and to listen, for it is the only way you can all go forward as a team.

"We used to write hour upon hour, the feather quill is imprinted on my brain and the writings that I did, including my fellow brothers and sisters. For it was a great source of wisdom, not only wisdom but communication, talking with God or spirit, or to our higher self or whatever. It was right and we also got answers from the wrong.

"We are evolving all the time, slowly progressing all the time, everybody and everything. I am so looking forward to see the great picture and to see it with you. I hope I have given you something to think about. And remember, each one of you is special, each one of you has a part to play, so work as a team. Thank you."

During this long talk (over 40 minutes) there were lots of sparkles of light around the head, especially in the early part of it. Later V reported that he also had seen sparkles, with the person being quite young, a thicker neck, curly hair, but no hat. While Y was impressed to say that she was getting that George had sandals on his feet, aged in his early twenties, a hot country and desert like, and he was herding goats, and that this was going a very long way back in time. Red Cloud was very brief, just to welcome back V to the circle and give a little advice.

During this time I was doing some work preparing for the first Lynwood Fellowship seminar, as I was a co-organiser with Shonagh Moore. In truth, Shonagh did most of the work, but as this was my first time, perhaps that was to be expected. The tutors included Andy Thomas, who again gave informative talks. The first, "Crop Circles of our Times", was a brief illustrated history that led to the main circles, from all parts of the world, over the last couple of years. "The Truth Agenda" was the second while his third entitled "The Real 2012 Prophecies" was a very professional presentation, starting with the Maya calendar and ending up with the science of cosmic waves. The one on the last day, "Creating Global Transformation", brought it all together, suggesting that we **can** change what is happening.

Tim and Janette Abbott gave a demonstration of mediumship on the first evening, while Tim gave an experimental demonstration of trance on the Wednesday evening. Both gave talks and workshops on the process of spirit communication, as well as the levels of consciousness and altered states.

The other tutor was Rosemary Stephenson, who used both angelic and Om tuning forks, crystal bowls, drums, cards, mantras and her voice (and ours) in her workshops. Rosemary also gave a good talk, "Animal Healing ... Experiences of Telsa the Healing Dog", in which she showed pictures of her dog while telling us of the healing exploits. At the end there was a bit of video showing Rosemary meeting with tigers in Thailand. So an interesting and varied seminar!

When I got home I started to transcribe two booklets that had been written by Don Galloway. These were typed into my laptop, a procedure that took a considerable amount of time due to my inability to type properly. Two fingers, one on each hand, were the sole instruments used, but the work got completed eventually and were then put on the Lynwood Fellowship website.

Meanwhile the circle proceeded, and on the 12th May 2011, Hemron gave a very long talk on the importance of spiritual growth, a special flower in the mountains of Tibet, patience, making time for quiet thoughts, and several more topics. Despite the length of time, Z didn't return to normal awareness or even take a drink of water. In a few minutes another spirit spoke, and within seconds I knew who it was, as I'd heard that voice nearly six years before when I was in Hafan-y-Coed, Wales, with Jock McArthur!

JCS: *"I've been listening to ye. You no ken who I am? Ach, you ken who I am? Well, can ye understand me?"*
Me: *"I understand you."*
JCS: *"Oh can ye! Oh come on, there's never a chance a penny before I heard youse."*
Me: *"Aah! I know who you are!"*
JCS: *"Aye, maybe the penny's dropped."*
Me: *"Born in Dalbeattie."*
JCS: *"Aye, that's it! So you remember me noo do ye?"*
Me: *"I do."*
JCS: *"I just sorta dropped by ye see. I ken ye're going to see Jock, just tak as it comes. Fair busy?"*
Me: *"Reasonably busy, I think I'll get busier."*
JCS: *"Ye should tak your retirement then. But the trouble with youse man is that ye dinnae ken what you're doing yerself. Och, ye've got yer fingers in too many pies. Ye want to tak yer fingers oot and just tak yer time. Patience is a virtue man."*
Me: *"True."*
JCS: *"Aye, but ye dinnae listen. Then listen intently, ye ken what I'm saying?"*
Me: *"Aye, I ken."*
JCS: *"Aye. That's a brill beard ye got, all trimmed, I just had a wee tash. Ma missus wouldn't have liked me with a beard. But ma missus was a grand lassie, she was a braw wee lassie, she did all things for me.*
  "I never charged a penny for my services, oh no, but

at the same time, working for spirit, it's enough. And I admire those who do the best for spirit and be of service to their ain fellow man. The world 's greedy as it is the noo, man pulling himself to bits, och, what's wrang wi it? Aye, it needs a guid kick up the a***. Spirit kens, and there's nae a thing that gangs amiss, it's all accounted for and that's most important. Aye, it's aw taken into account.

"I'm just a humble wee man. I did ma best for spirit, because I love spirit. Och aye, I could be a cantankerous wee s** and the grumpiest of all men, but that was me. But at the same time I was an empty vessel for those who came who spoke through me, to gie the greatest of all evidence to the families that needed it the maist. And it's those that need it the maist get the greatest benefit.

"But when I think of the hard days and aw the weans and the bairns, that they're bare fitted, they had nothing, nothing. Then there were the poor wee souls, poor wee souls that needed the pump up of spirit and the loved ones the maist. That they dinnae ken what had happened to them but what was wrang, where they were and where spirit world was or what it is, aye man, ye know both. However, I'm trying ma best even noo to pass on what I ken. But I wasnae perfect, so forgive me, but I wanted to let ye know that there are those, including myself, are listening intently and only too willing to put our thumbs up. So, just be patient wi yerself man and you'll be richt."
Me: "Good."
JCS: "So I'll say guid nicht to ye."
Me: "Goodnight."
JCS: "Aye, and to you madam."
Y: "Goodnight."
JCS: "And to you wee man."
V: "Goodnight."
JCS: "And I say wee man because he's just a wee boy. Guid to see your wee floppy feathers starting to come through son. You've a lang way to go, you're near pluckét. But

dinnae worry, dinnae fash, och no, just tak your time.
The slooer the surer ye be, the greater ye'll be, so dinnae
fash, just tak your time and do the best ye can.
"I'm awa noo. Oh by the way, Mr Findlay's no
impressed, och no, the big man himself, but he kens, he
kens."

Z came slowly back to normal awareness and then drank gulps of water.
We commented on the timing, dead on 9 o'clock, and the circle was
closed. In the discussion afterwards I commented that it was interesting
that the second spirit that came through had also come through Jock
McArthur when I had been on his course in Wales. V reported that there
had been a lot of movement when he had come through, and that there
had been somebody near me as well. I decided to put Z in the picture
and told him that John Campbell Sloan had come through him. V then
said how he could hardly keep his eyes open when Hemron had been
talking, and I stated that I had seen lots of speckles of light around the
face and hair, and some even 15 to 20cm away from the head. As well as
that, I had seen a couple of large 'bars' of electric blue light on the bridge
of the nose, and also dimmer lengths of light by the side of the face. Z
then talked for a time about different aspects of physical mediumship
and some mediums of the past. He also mentioned when he first saw
what he took to be cigarette smoke at the time, but was spirit 'mist'. Y
then related that this week she had two instances of this when she was
outside.

The beginning of June saw what was to be the very last meeting of
the monthly Distant Healing Circle, with just Vera Middleton and myself.
Then the next day there occurred what I felt as a slightly 'uncomfortable'
circle. Before the start I had gone down to put the music on and help Z
arrange the chairs. Z adjusted the red lights to a lower level. I went through
my usual sequence in preparation for the start with my eyes closed, and
sensed the presence of George. When I opened my eyes I saw that the
lights were brighter, and as I turned the music off Z asked me to adjust the
lights to a lower level. However, I told him that spirit were dealing with
it, and at that point the lights flashed lighter for a second. Throughout the
whole circle – though less so near the end – the red lights were almost

constantly varying in intensity.

Very quickly a spirit came through who was a joker, said his passing had been quick, had liked cricket and Brylcreem, had been a 'journalist cum accountant', like dancing and had worn spats, and gave his name as Dick Somersby. During this I saw one very bright flash of light from a point on the inside of the right elbow joint. He had excellent control of Z's body that moved in quite an animated fashion, giving all the actions with hands, arms and legs to complement his chat. I'll give a bit of the latter at the end of his talk.

> DS: *"Time will tell, yes. Here I go again, I'm at it again. Do*
>
> *I look smart? Like my dicky bow, with the wee dots on? Does my hair look alright? Well, ladies and gentlemen I'm being called now and I'm going to have to go. Please do indeed keep up with your wonderful work, for without that we cannot come to entertain you as it were. I'm sorry about my bad joke but I didn't mean it, I love Irishmen. But I know there's loads of Paddies over here - there's loads of Paddies everywhere. Having said that, I do like the Irish you know. But he's a bit of a cad, oops, oh dear, it's me that's the cad, oh I'm so sorry."*
>
> Y: *"Yes, I can go with that."*
>
> DS: *"Do you like my trilby? Oh, my hair. Anyway, I've got to go now my friends. I'm so sorry, I've extended my welcome. May God bless you all."*
>
> Y: *"God bless you."*
>
> DS: *"Thank you."*
>
> Y: *"Be happy."*

Z relaxed and spirit seemed to be withdrawing, but about 70 seconds later there was laughter from Z and I thought 'Dick' was back again. [***I should add here, that it was my practice when writing up my notes that I used the spirit's name/initials or other designation from the start, even if the name came later. For this book I have changed this briefly below, the reason will become apparent later.***]

[DS]: *"Oh dearie me, it's me again. You thought for a minute that I was gone, didn't you?"*
Y: *"Yes we did."*
[DS]: *"Oh dearie me."*
Y: *"A bit of a joker."*
[DS]: *"I'm afraid so. I feel a little bit ruffled there. Oh dear, oh dear, oh dear. Actually, it's his twin brother that's here."*
Y: *"Oh."*
[DS?]: *"Yes."*
Y: *"There isn't two alike is there?"*
[DS?]: *"No, no, not alike, not too bad. I'm Ronnie by the way."*
Y: *"Oh."*
RS: *"Yes I'm Ronnie, I'm Ronnie, that was my brother that's come before here you know."*
Y: *"Are you sure?"*
RS: *"Yes, because, yeah, he wouldn't mention me because you see, well I'm afraid, we didn't see eye to eye if you know what I mean. He thought I wasn't good enough, sort of thing. But we've made up our differences. I just want to put my two pence worth in you know.*

He went on to say he was a twin brother, and that there were other brothers as well in the family. He had passed with appendicitis, was born in the 1920s, liked Jimmy Hendrix and other guitarists, and tried to remember one called Hank but couldn't get the surname. I suggested it was connected to the Shadows. He replied: *"No, no, no, I was long gone before the Shadows, a long time pal. I've been to the spirit side of life for a lot, lot longer than that. Shadows my foot. What do you think I am, eh?"*
Me: *"I'm not sure yet!"*
He talked for about a minute or so further, calling me 'Paddy' and then mentioning Roy Walker and the programme 'Catchphrase'!

After a gap of about seven minutes the circle seemed back to 'normal' when White Cloud spoke about the American presidents, the world needing harmony, and the advice to feel Mother Earth through the soles of your feet. In the discussion later Y said that it had been amusing tonight, and Z related that he had just got "it was a little reward". Y remarked that there had been lots of changes in Z's face and there had been lots of green behind the first person, while V said that he had seen a green and red hat on his head. Y mentioned how she had seen the faces of the American Presidents just before White Cloud had mentioned them. The others thought the first person was Irish but I was not sure. I also had reservations about 'Dick', took a dislike to his character, and didn't know why he had come through, but I declined to voice these thoughts just yet.

Next circle was more 'normal'! Hemron came through to briefly talk about it.

> Hem: "And it takes a little bit of effort and a little bit of time. And as we stand beside the vessel and as we go deeper, to finally when we get to stage of perfection, that the vessel, he will have left to one side and we will take the full and utmost control. But we are pleased with the way things are going. ...
>
> "You'd be amazed and most surprised when you finally come here. One of the things I learned about myself was just how much sharper I became, how youthful I was. But even more amazed to find that my memory, my mind was even greater to that when I was here on earth.
>
> "So we know that you cannot fully be expected to fully grasp and understand just what we are about, and any description of the spirit world and our life in the spirit world. It has been said from time to time again that until you pass over, only then, but then will you only realise and fully understand."

He continued with personal advice to each of us. To me was the old admonishment "to keep as many fingers out of the pies as you can'. But how can I dismiss my natural inquisitiveness and my wish to know 'everything'! However, during this talk I saw speckles of light, and then a small dot, dull white in colour and about the size of a 5pence piece, streak quickly from my left at head height straight to the ground beside Z. V was able to confirm this and the colour later.

After Hemron, David the shepherd came for a brief moment and we closed the circle. As Z came back to normal awareness he started to sing "by the rivers of Babylon". After a bit he then said that he had just found out about the song, as he had been asking. It was related to the one who had come through last time, the one who was musical and gave laughter (Dick Somersby), and that he was a new member of the group. Y then commented that he was a little like the 'Harlequin' she had known about 23 years ago. She then related disturbing stories about what happened, before she had got rid of him at Blackpool. I was not pleased at this news, but if Hemron, White Cloud and so on accepted him, were my negative feelings really to be taken into account? I certainly didn't want to introduce any disharmony or negativity, so went with the flow.

The circle in mid June had only one spirit come through, but this 'Lady Nunnington' spoke for at least fifty-three minutes. It did seem to me that spirit were gradually testing Z for longer periods. The arrival of LN was signalled by a change in the lights, and this continued at intervals throughout the rest of the meeting. When she first came through I saw a flash of turquoise light at the right side of Z's head, where I had a sense of something being there, and although I couldn't actually see anything 'ringlets' came into my mind.

LN: "Oh, isn't this a lovely place! When I was here my place was full of grandeur. It was full of my, what shall we say, posh friends and doctors and solicitors and one thing and another. But now I realise that I am just an equal as you and I are now my friends.

"Oh those damn corsets, oh dearie me, how I wonder … there were many times I fainted you know. But it wasn't because of the sight of a young man, it's because I couldn't breathe because of this damn corset I had on! My servants used to pull to get it on, some used to get

172

their foot up and pull, oh terrible, terrible, terrible!"
[During all this Z's body and arms were very animated,
describing actions such as waving a fan in front of the
face, indicating parts of the body, putting on boots and
showing the width of dresses etc.]

LN gave us lots of information on a variety of subjects: two offspring, a boy, Louis, and an older girl called Amelia; wigs; whale oil lamps; tea; an episode with her brother and a toad; Jenkins the gardener, and the butler. *"Right, I tell you about the time with the butler. Oh yes! Well I had a little of you know what with the butler. But nonetheless, what shall we say, well there was no TV then! I'm sure you get the picture. But oh, the butler was a charm, he was an absolute boon, yes he was."*

Going on to tell us that her son passed away when aged 15 and the daughter at 23. She herself passed in 1799 when aged 37 years and six and a half months, and her husband outlived her and died in 1810. Her portrait was painted by 'Drysdale' (a friend who was not well known) and cost five guineas; knew about the French Revolution; read Sir Walter Scott, Robert Burns, Wordsworth; came into contact with a lot of Quakers. She then talked a little about Bluebell (who had brought her children over to the spirit world) saying she was wise and had evolved. She then talked to Y giving the names of people she might remember and then withdrew.

V confirmed the sparkles of light and agreed with Y when she said that she felt a lot of energy being taken from her. Z mentioned that he had heard at times very gentle music, like wind chimes or panpipes, soft and beautiful. Z also felt that his mediumship was getting stronger and his awareness was sharper.

With lots of information given by 'Lady Nunnington' I started to do a little bit of research to see if I could find proof of a material life in the past. Using the Internet, I didn't get very far at all! Then I remembered that on my way to Cober Hill for the Lynwood Fellowship seminars, I passed several signs advertising 'Nunnington Hall'. So made a mental note to take a little time either on the way there, or the return, to check it out and see if it had any link to our circle guest.

At the next meeting, about thirteen minutes from the start, an Arabic shepherd spoke for the rest of the time. Even though it was time up Z did not come back the to normal awareness. Within a minute our joker was back unexpectedly.

DS: *"Ha, ha, hee, hee, oh dear, I'm back again friends. I've been waiting for my chance. I went to the doctors the other day, oh aye, yes. I said to the doctor my arm hurts when I do that, the doctor said well don't do it again. So there you go. Never mind. Oh ah, dearie me, dearie me, he was a lovely chap before wasn't he? No? He was alright wasn't he?"*
Y and Me: "Mmmmmmm."

There followed his usual stuff, though mentioning my upcoming trip, and Y's 'Harlequin'.

DS: *"I could never play a tin whistle or anything like that. I thought I could play, but people weren't kind enough to tell me that I couldn't play, but ah, I'd rather be told the truth you see. But they didn't tell me so I carried on regardless, and the more I did that the more they started to laugh. So that was it. People never really took me serious."*
Y: "Not surprised."
DS: *"You're not surprised! Oh now, you don't know me yet."*
Y: "And I don't want to."
DS: *"O, come on now my friend, it's not as though I'm going to bite you is it? I'll be kind, I'll be gentle, but with a twist."*
Y: "That's the problem."

There followed a bit more chat and a 'joke' before he got onto his clothing.

DS: *"Nice dicky bow, I'm smart. I love Jimmy Hendrix. I met him you know, he still doesn't know how he done it like. … I'm working behind the scenes along with the big chiefs as it were. … Concerning your question sir, the lady that was here last time, mind you, she was a madam as well like. I spoke to her you see, I gave her a bit of help to come in here. She had, what would you say, her wires crossed as it were, hence the reason you were poking your nose in. Yes, we know about that, the ever inquisitive mind. The reason you couldn't find her was because it was the wrong location. However, I'm instructed to tell you that in due course, when she is ready, she will correct, if she decides to come back again. She will rectify the situation for you, if that helps you sir."*

There followed a bit of chat to Y and V, before mentioning leprechauns, meeting Frank Carson and Arthur Askey.

DS: "Certainly got my eyes opened when I came over, I was amazed, I was amazed. I even spoke to my old pop, pop I hadn't seen for years! He passed away when I was a baby. I tell you one thing, I do miss my fat cigars, I used to love big fat cigars, big long Havana ones. You smoked at one time didn't you? You were told if you did not stop you'd be dead,"
Me: "That's right. The best thing that happened to me!"
DS: "You know the reason, it's because of exactly what you're doing now. Don't you think?"
Me: "I would think so."
DS: "So it's just as well you did take heed."
Me: "Aye, it is isn't it? Otherwise I might be talking to you!"
DS: "I used to love the cigars, it made me feel important, that I had money. But I was poor; I didn't get a fantastic wage. Well, I 'll say goodnight and God bless you all."

As Z slowly started to come back I looked at my watch, it showed that it was almost thirty minutes over time. Y was not happy about that. When Z was told about it, he said that it would not be tolerated again; otherwise he (DS) will not be allowed to use him again. The circle was then closed, and in the discussion afterwards all of us expressed our concern about what had happened and the way DS had come in. I mentioned that in the previous circle when DS had first talked to us, it had been the **other** brother that had talked about Jimmy Hendrix, so I wondered if the 'two twins' might not be the same person. On reflection later at home, I thought that DS was an actor (natural or as a hobby) and that 'Lady Nunnington' was him as well. Into the bargain, in the first session he had talked about being in the bathroom getting ready to go out dancing, and his pop standing outside waiting to get in – now he tells us that his dad passed away when he had been a baby! Can you trust someone who deceives you? I reckoned that this change in 'normal' proceedings was one we could do without. Naturally, those in spirit have to learn just we do in the material, but this was beginning to put huge doubts in my mind.

Glad to say that DS was absent during the next two circles. Hafed came and Bluebell, who advised me to listen to George, do more writing [I had started to do small pieces], listen when in my bath and to watch my tum-tum! The following one brought David, who gave his surname and date of passing, and a new spirit 'Damascus' whose job was to take notes on what was happening.

Then I was away for the next Lynwood Fellowship seminar, and it was a relief to leave all my worries behind. The weather was lovely, even giving me a little sunburn on my face and hands just driving to it. Levi Attias gave more of his varied and thoughtful lectures, all with great titles: "Wherever we go – there we are", with the clever double meaning 'HAPPINESSISNOWHERE'; "To knee or not to knee", that included a personal story of disastrous surgery; "Sympathy, empathy, God's symphony", witty, with humorous stories – but all with a point. Then on the final evening he amazed us with his feats of 'magic'.

Brian Lynch and Sue Odam gave a good demonstration of mediumship on the first evening. Brian brought in all sorts of aspects, including reincarnation, in his excellent lecture "Evolution of the soul", while his second one was "How angels work among us". Sue gave a very informative historical talk on "The aura and the mind", while the second

"Our journey of spiritual awareness" involved the changes in sensitivity that we all experience. In addition, I enjoyed several of her workshops.

Shonagh Moore stepped in to replace the original tutor, who was unable to come. Shonagh presented many scientific aspects during her lecture on sound, and worked with the crystal bowls while the rest of us were having a blissful meditation. Her workshops proved how intense some sounds could be. Of the first I made a note, "but the noise of one particular bowl was so powerful, it reverberated and rumbled like a jet airplane engine". In the second several participants perceived the figure of Jesus and one saw the Virgin Mary, while another saw a column of white light in the centre and heard three sayings spoken in Latin, roughly translated as "the love of the angels, the love of the Christ", but the third was forgotten. It had been another illuminating seminar and so refreshing to talk to so many with 'like minds'.

At the next circle on 21st July I discovered that the seating had been changed the previous week, when I had been away. Three chairs were placed in a row in front of Z's chair. It had been suggested that Z wear a black hat on his head to make it easier to see 'things', so he was going to wear a black 'beanie' hat tonight. After starting the circle, I noticed that the lights changed quite a bit throughout. An unknown spirit was the first to speak, but only briefly, though he did mention that the cabinet would be used again, but altered, and that there was no set date for this. Soon after this George came and said that he wished to speak to me.

G: "What am I going to do with you?"
Me: "I'm a bit distracted at the moment."
G: "Not to worry my friend, I have ways and means of
    dealing with certain things. I shall let you know what
I require of you, but you will get to pen and paper first.
And watch for thy thoughts alter, for I will inspire you.
Not with long fancy words but straight to the point, simple
matter of facts. For I spoke here on earth with a clear and
unrestricted voice and straight to the point, there was no
in-between. That I will inspire with you my friend. For we
have travelled a way together, it's been a long tedious

*journey. But you are getting there slowly and much surer.
You will feel my great hat on your head at some stage
and you'll know that it is I. But alas, thee have whiskers
as well as I have."*

Me: "Yes I do."

*G: "Oh yes! I have a lovely beard too you know. I was proud
of it. The thicker it was said the man was to have more
wisdom. And of course, as he grew old with age, like his
health unfortunately, that ones beard has gone whiter.
So that too was a sign of true wisdom and stability of
the mind. And that I will try and inspire with you my
friend.*

*"And I will be there on the day that you meet your
fellow friend Jock. So keep up thy good work dear chap.
And watch for the silver buckles on the feet, that you will
see. And my tight pants, oh, I used to sweat in them, that
we did."*

George then left us and shortly Hafed came through to talk to Y and give
all of us encouragement, and then he left. While waiting for Z to slowly
come back to normal awareness, I looked at 'the picture' and saw it move
quite obviously and deliberately for several seconds. Both Z and V picked
up an earthy smell, but neither Y nor I detected this. V then said that when
the first spirit had spoken, there had been somebody different there just
before, and Y agreed with this. She also confirmed that somebody was
with her when asked by Z, but declined to find out who it was. Z was
silent for a time, and then commented that what he had seen was way
back in biblical times, by the river Jordan or the Nile, but knew it was 906
or 926 AD. He had seen very briefly a woman, like a princess, with a gold
band around her head with a 'pointy' thing at the front; there were other
people around and he had thought of Egypt. Z also said that 'the shepherd'
stems back to then, as he had been in the background, and that either one
of them could be close to Y, which was when she gets her coughing fits. V
related that he had seen the differences in build between each spirit; also
he had got the date as 926 AD. Before we broke up, we arranged what
we were to bring with us to the meeting with Jock McArthur, as there

would not be another circle before then, as Z was going on a well deserved holiday abroad to recharge his batteries.

Meanwhile I continued with my typing, and from the end of June had started to do some 'notes' for what I thought of as 'spiritual cards'. These later expanded to include my own photographs and eventually became to be classified as 'Meditation Cards'.

The 6th August 2011 came round soon enough. I left home at 7 am and met the others while crossing the Forth Bridge. We were welcomed by Jock and introduced to two others, J who was local and acted as Jock's assistant operating the lights and infrared camera etc., and M who was a medium from further north. After the brief introductions, getting a mug of tea and going to the toilet, we all sat down for an informal talk from Jock about his circle.

They sit for anything – trance, transfiguration, voice, materialisations and so forth. He insists on putting luminous bands on the trumpet at both ends, and had a large board, at least 18 inches by 24 inches (45 x 60 cm), that was black on one side but had luminous paint on the other. Jock declared that he did not accept anything as an apport, except that which appears in his 'dome' of Perspex, the entrance of which has several right angles so that people are unable to drop or push anything in. It was decided that the four of us would sit in turn and just see what occurs. This would be taped on a four hour VHS tape. That, he said, should take us up to about lunchtime.

We then all went into Jock's 'garden shed', which was quite small but adequate for us, though I would have thought that eight people was just about maximum capacity. In one corner there was a chair onto which lights were directed, and behind it was black cloth. Under infrared this 'black' cloth will come out as white if synthetic dye has been used. So Jock went to some trouble to acquire cloth that was dyed from black vegetable dye. Similar black cloth was made into a simple garment to put over sitters, with a hole cut for the head and sleeves for the arms. The camera gives a view from above (located in the ceiling) showing the person down to waist level, but with quite a wide area around the figure. The rest of the room was laid out as shown in the diagram bellow.

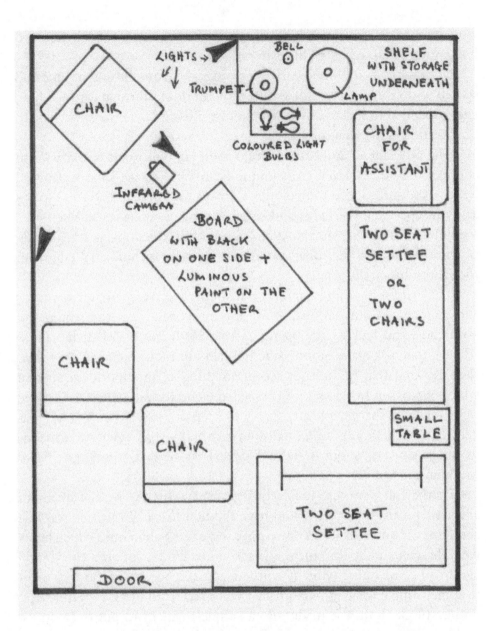

When all were inside, Jock taped up the door to keep the light from coming in. There was very little preamble – just went straight into it. V was first in the 'hot seat' followed by Y. With Y I got a vague idea that something was on her head and Z said it was a hat. Several others thought there was an elderly woman there who could possibly have been

V's 'nan' or grandmother, as a stroke condition was mentioned. Later Y said she had felt old and was wearing a long dress, and that her hands were 'funny'. In the blackness I noticed that there were large patches of purple and saw several sparkles of light around Y. Then it changed, a young boy with a cap and an air of sadness that Z thought would be a spirit connected to Y. M saw lots of yellow. At the end Y reported that there were tears running down her face, and Z said that was spirits way of releasing energy.

Next it was my turn. Looking later on the video lights could be seen. Jock thought he saw "shades of Conan Doyle". J declared that she could feel a real sense of space and a cooling in the temperature. M thought she saw a quill in my hand. Jock said it was like the Victorian era and somebody else saw a top hat and fob watch and chain. Then it changed to a thinner faced person, smaller than before, with a scar on the face.

The light bulb was changed, first to green and then to a blue one. Jock thought it was a heavier energy. A new face, a vicar's collar was seen. I felt at this time as if I was smiling and wanted to laugh. Y thought it went back to biblical times and M confirmed that with bare feet and sandals. J thought that there was a statue of this person somewhere and Y seemed definite that there were 'pictures of him'. Z heard music in the background, like hymns, while J got a sense of linking of arms. Jock felt it was physical power there.

Then Z sat under red light. Again lights were moving around and M saw a woman with long dark hair. Jock said there was something vibrating around M's chair, and then explained that the chair had come from a local Freemason woman's group 'Eastern Star', that they had got seven, each a different colour, and that M's one was one that sometimes levitated. On the video Z can be seen rocking from side to side. Jock said it was somebody with a Tony Curtis style haircut, sort of Teddy boy etc. Then the lights changed a bit and very slowly and gradually Z raised his right hand, and I felt it was 'wrong', deformed or useless. Jock thought the spirit trying to come through was wheezing. Eventually 'David' spoke, "this is my medium. Thank you for the opportunity. I'm among good friends. Happy for you all, it's a pleasure..." David also gave praise to Jock, especially for his work over the last twenty years. Then it changed again and after a little singing to energise the atmosphere, 'Bluebell' came though briefly but didn't talk much or stay long.

We broke for lunch then. I have no notes for what happened in the session after lunch. However, I do remember standing on the 'board' and being told to look at my feet and asked what did I see. Nothing was the answer, though I presumed that I had been expected to see silver buckles! Jock also gave a little demonstration, but it was nothing like I had seen before in Wales, and that told me that Jock, who never had great health even from childhood, was in a poor condition. After thanking him for giving his time so generously, we collected all our stuff and were given the VHS tape, and headed home.

At the next circle on 11the August, I put the music on and then went upstairs to watch the video with the others, seeing some of Y's spot, then mine and some of Z's. V offered to copy the video so that we each could have a copy, and he thought that he might even be able to get it onto a disc. [*However, I never received a copy despite leaving my address, and hence how I have no notes at all on the second session of our sitting with Jock.*]

Y asked me to open and said she would close the circle. In opening I asked spirit for their advice. We sat quietly but Z was not sitting as usual and had his hands together with fingers intertwined, looking as if he was thinking deeply. After about two minutes, it appeared at first as if spirit spoke. However, it didn't take too long before I realised that this was coming just from Z himself. He spoke for at least forty minutes, outlining the dangers of physical mediumship, citing examples, and saying that he had researched on the Internet and found similar experiences of others feeling sickly like he does. Finally he had decided that it was not for him, and was happy to stick to mental mediumship. At the end of this long explanation he then asked V what he thought.

V stated that he was not happy with the physical, that he had been going through a difficult time with his health, and now just wanted to do mental mediumship. Y agreed, but said that she had not been listened to, and was thinking of dropping out altogether. She had been told not to do physical and had told us this when she found the cabinet up. Things had to be done properly or not at all. She definitely wouldn't sit for physical. By the time it got to me it was a foregone conclusion! I was numb, just stunned, I couldn't believe what had taken place. All I wanted to do was to get out and think things over on my own, so I initially said I'd sit with them for mental mediumship. They then realised that it was past the usual closing time. Z decided to do the closing prayer.

> Z: *"Divine Spirit, I wish to point out from here on that we will no longer, and I repeat, we will no longer sit for the physical. On behalf of Mike Doig, on behalf of Y, on behalf of V, and on behalf of myself Z, that we agree that from now on that this physical side of things is closed, and we wish to close it here and now.*

At the end of this he said he would hand it over to us in turn to say a few words, and came to me first. However, I was feeling almost physically sick hearing him speaking those words for me, so I declined. The others thanked spirit for all the lessons and knowledge they had gained over the last couple of years.

The next week was one of the worst in my life, I just could not come to terms with what had happened and it churned over and over in my mind during the day and at night. How I got anything done that week I don't know. It took me six days before I had the circle notes typed out. I had texted that I would be briefly at the next circle, and when Z phoned I explained that I wished to speak to everybody to explain my thoughts.

Going over things I knew that Z had every right to decide not to do physical mediumship, but I had never ever thought that there would be anything other than a voice box due to the feelings of Y in particular. I felt I had been railroaded into making a decision on the spur of the moment, and that the others had not sought spirit's advice, which is what I had asked for at the beginning of the circle. V had been suffering for a while with his medical condition, and he had not yet got it under his control, so to blame spirit was wrong. Z had been tired and also a bit under the weather, which was why he went on a holiday. But the holiday was a disaster, filling his lungs with cement dust, and he only returned home the day before going to see Jock McArthur. He was in no condition physically or mentally to be sitting. However, the decision had been made, but now I needed to speak for myself. Interestingly, the last note in my circle diary was written as if I was an observer:

Thursday 18/08/11: At about 7.40 all the four members of the circle went down to the room. Mike said he had two statements to read out, then he would explain them and answer any questions they might have.
Mike's statements were:

1. "I wish to annul, reverse, rescind and nullify Z's statement to spirit - where it concerns myself - that he gave last week. I will speak for myself, and I place no restriction on spirit.
2. "I agreed to sit with you all for mental mediumship; I cannot do that at present."

Mike was not happy with how the decision had been arrived at. He reminded them of his words spoken on 11/02/10, how long ago spirit had seen the possibilities of the circle that we were then engaged in. He had said, "We have to put our trust in spirit…and go with them." Later Ho-Lin had said, "We can but only now go forward. You cannot go backwards, for if you do you only go back to square one", and later had said, "Go with the flow". That was what he thought the circle should have done. As a consequence of this difference and the emotions that go with it he couldn't sit in circle, for the harmony wouldn't be there.

While Mike had intended to be calm, his emotions and anger got the better of him, so that he was shouting, mainly at Z, who also became slightly angry. Mike said that the circle would have been working towards direct voice, and that in circle David(the shepherd) had said this in September last year, "Patience, voice box will come in time". He also said that the Jock McArthur workshop was a bit of a flop, but due to his ill health generally and his experience on holiday Z should not have come. However, the arguments just went round in circles. X came down and joined the group asking Mike to listen, which didn't really help, but she did say she would maybe join the circle in his place. While Mike had said that both Z and V should not be sitting because of their health at this time, he wished everybody well for their circle, and that he wouldn't burn his boats, if he could get rid of any resentment and if spirit and the others wished him to come back in the future, he would do so. He thanked them all and left.

Later that night Mike wrote cards to Y and Z to apologise for his emotional display, and as he didn't have V's address he asked Z to convey his apologies.

It has been interesting to go over all this again three years later. In retrospect, it was easy to see that the circle was coming apart at the seams. However, at the time we were in it rather than looking from the outside. That week of endless 'mental gymnastics' that I went through only had the effect of ensuring that I would explode at the last meeting! But that is exactly what I needed to do – I got rid of everything in one mighty whoosh! I was then able to carry on at a normal level. But that last circle rant was very out of character. It was an uncanny experience, for at one point it was as if I was out of my body, hearing myself yelling at the top of my voice (yet the sound was muffled) and thinking that I shouldn't be doing this, and that had not been my intention. To date that has been my only conscious occurrence of such a state.

Postscript: I wrote a letter to Jock thanking him for his help and the trouble that he had gone to for us, and included a small donation for his circle. He phoned me sometime later asking how things were going and I related that our circle had broken up. Typically, Jock was practical, "just form your own circle then"!

It was sad, but not entirely unexpected, when I got a phone call about seven months later telling me that Jock had passed to spirit on the 21st February 2012. A tireless worker for spirit had returned home.

CHAPTER 15

A Different Focus

After the dust had settled, so to speak, I took a short holiday with family, and while there bought a Mac laptop. This would prove to be very useful – once I had gained a little knowledge on how to use it! Many opportunities soon appeared to test both my creativity and patience in getting my ideas in digital form. However, a few weeks later I was at the Lynwood Fellowship seminar in Cober Hill with tutors Helen Brown, Ronnie Williams, and Hugh and Margaret Davis. The main theme of the course seemed to be around healing and was just what I needed then. Two particular events were of interest. The first when fellow attendee Rowland Bowker kindly gave me a copy of his book "Pathway to Kwamroo". The second occurred during a workshop run by Hugh Davis, when he mentioned to Audrey about a book being written so that all the old knowledge would not be lost – exactly what I had said to her earlier that morning!

When I got home my main focus was now mostly on work and ideas connected to the Lynwood Fellowship. Having finished typing out Don Galloway's first booklet, I started on the second one, and worked on an idea for a leaflet.

In November I had my first opportunity to attend the annual weekend seminar held at the Lindum Hotel in Lytham St. Annes. This completed the entire Lynwood Fellowship meetings for the year, and the very first time that I had been able to attend all of them. The tutors were Ann J. B. Davies, Mark Foster and Jackie Wright. This was a very informative course, with Ann starting the event with a detailed lecture on part of her research "An Investigation into Paranormally Produced Automatic Art (1840 – 2011)". [Now titled 'Art from the Invisible: A Chronology of Spiritualist art and artists'] As well as workshops Ann gave a demonstration on the first evening that was absorbing, especially seeing how one drawing started out as a female nurse and then turned into a male character! Jackie also shared this demonstration, mainly using clairaudience and clairsentience to give excellent detail with street names and numbers etc. During her meditation session the next morning, I unexpectedly met a white robed figure, who I thought was Arabic, though I did not see the face, and in answer to what I should be doing got, "Be of service". Mark's talks and workshops were packed with information, concentrating on "2012 Enigma", energies in the home and dowsing, plus technical equipment, and his enthusiasm for it all was infectious – and I won his book in the raffle!

The last part of the year saw me writing 'bits' for Lynwood, as well as continuing with Don Galloway's second booklet, which I finished by the end of February 2012. Also, I starting in earnest to make up my 'Meditation Cards'. So by the start of April both of Don's booklets were ready to go on the website and I had 52 'Meditation Cards' completed.

The first Lynwood Fellowship seminar at the beginning of April was memorable for Shonagh Moore's workshop with the crystal bowls, and the one where we went outside to record sounds of flora and fauna. When the latter was played through her laptop the sound of the snail eating was fabulous! My word, they do sound as if they enjoy their food! I also had a sitting with Helen Sewell, who discussed my astrological chart, and got confirmation that maybe my time of birth was slightly out.

In May I continued with Lynwood work, and Shonagh came up with a good idea regarding the 'Meditation Cards'. Due to the difficulty of changing them every day or week if put on the website, Shonagh suggested that they be put on a disc and could be sold. So that was done, and I did some work for the July seminar, as I was co-organiser with Shonagh.

In July 2012 I went to Dumfries to see "Clairvoyance Evening with Stephen Holbrook and Psychic Artist Sandy Ingham" at the Easterbrook Hall. As always, Stephen's mediumship was excellent, giving real help to many, some of who were in obvious need. Sandy Ingham worked independently, taking about five minutes to complete brilliantly drawn portraits, and then when Stephen had finished usually linked in with the same person. I went down to talk to them at the interval, asking if they would consider coming to the Lynwood Fellowship. They gave a positive response, but both are very busy workers and as yet we have not coincided with their free time and Lynwood seminar dates.

A few days later I was back in Cober Hill for the next Lynwood seminar. That first evening had Leah Bond and Su Wood demonstrating their mediumship by working together. Usually Leah started and Su linked in with her drawings, using the overhead projector to show the image on the large screen while drawing with a pen on acetate sheets. Both gave very good evidence and all the portraits and links were accepted. It was a real bonus to find at the end that many in the audience had never seen a psychic artist work this way. Brian Lynch also gave an excellent example of his mediumship as well. Su had brought her 'aura camera' and many couldn't resist having a session with her.

Other noteworthy events were the talk and demonstration by Anthony Neeps on how his work on healing 'patterns' evolved; Brian's lecture on the "Life and Times of Andrew Jackson Davis"; Leah's inspirational talk "Trance can only Enhance", and I was lent another Don Galloway booklet to copy out.

At the end of the month I was down in Eastbourne for the 32nd International Spiritualist Federation Congress week. Choosing to do Spirit Art and Trance for my workshops, I also managed to sell a few of the 'Meditation Cards' discs and raised £42 for the Lynwood Fellowship! Ann Luck took the beginners trance, and at the third workshop we each in turn sat in the 'hot seat' to see how deep we could go. Marie-Louise managed to speak, and I definitely saw a very old woman overshadowing her. Next it was my turn, and can only explain it as feeling spirit as a plant, like a huge lavender bush/hedge – very strange! The next day I tried going down on my own and found myself in a heavy atmosphere surrounded by solid green. *As I went down further this receded and the feelings around my head increased and everything became lighter. Then I saw the sea - a bit choppy, and it got calmer and lighter in colour. Very interesting! A significant first step for me.* On the last day I had another chance in the 'hot seat'. *This time it was very different, I sensed myself going down rather than looking for 'physical' steps. The energy seemed a little different - and the visual aspect was different, but eventually got a calm violet sea. Encouraged by Ann to say the word violet, so I did several times and then "flame" followed - but that brought my mind in and wondered whether it was my own mind* [Shonagh at Lynwood seminar had talked about the 'violet flame'] *and the colour became a bit chaotic!*

As always I enjoyed doing the Spirit Art with Coral Ryder, and in the third workshop particularly liked doing auragraphs for several people. Unfortunately I did not take any photographs of them! There was also an excellent demonstration of mediumship by Jackie Wright, Karen Willis and Darren Brittain on the Wednesday evening. On the previous afternoon two sisters from Sweden, Ulla and Anne Marie Alvarsdotter, gave a fascinating talk and presentation on "Saving Lost Souls". I was struck by the thought they had put into it, even to the particular use of language and so on. Eventually I got round to sending them a disc with the transcript of what happened in circle regarding 'saving lost souls'. I would like to see more of this brought into the open and discussed.

The rest of August was taken up with lots more writing and typing. At the start of September I joined a new circle, fortnightly this time, and I found this much more manageable with all the other things with which I was involved.

By the next Lynwood Fellowship seminar, 9 -13 September 2012, I had the third Booklet by Don Galloway ready for the website. The first evening demonstration of mediumship by Ewan Irvine and Sheila Green was very good. Then Joe Wilcock used two Spirit Art drawings by a person he knew, but who is too shy to do it in public. Joe then narrowed it down with some facts he picked up and the first portrait was taken by Audrey, while Shonagh took the second – very fascinating! Joe also gave several lectures on physical and mental mediumsip that were packed full of detail. As always, Joe's talks were very thoroughly researched and he had a range of information on flip charts, photographs of spirit extras and ectoplasm in various forms, and suggested books and websites.

The next month I continued with doing more 'Meditation Cards' and became an associate member of "The Churches' Fellowship for Psychical and Spiritual Studies". This was a great 'find', though it has been in existence for quite some time, for they have a great library of recordings from people who gave talks at their conferences. I have bought quite a few CDs and tapes on a wide variety of subjects, all of which I've found informative and some enlightening.

In November, the weather and accidents on the M6 caused an extra two hours to my journey to the Lynwood weekend seminar in Lytham St. Annes. However, I still arrived in time to catch the first talk by Phil Medley "Returning to the New Frequencies of Light". Angela McInnes gave a good demonstration of mediumship on the first evening. She came to me, partly encouraged by others in the audience who, given most of the information that had been related, thought that it was for me. However, I knew it was not, and indeed after it finished the 'real' recipient spoke to me saying he could take all of the details that Angela had given. He had a private sitting with Angela the next day. Helen Brown gave several thought provoking workshops, an innovative one that explored a Native American folktale, and another using Soul Symbol cards. The last session of the seminar was "Healing with Sound" with Phil. After choosing an instrument (drum, tambourine, rattle) and an initial warm up, we split into groups of four. One group at a time, three intuitively gave healing to the fourth person, using whatever rhythm they felt appropriate. This proved to be immensely powerful, with some saying that they had seen Native Americans and/or had heard singing. I had noticed that at the start I had felt only energy around my head, mostly at the 3rd eye centre, but by the finish my heart centre was wide open, a very powerful exercise.

Then it was back home to the usual routine of making up more 'Meditation Cards' and working on doing a programme for the first Lynwood seminar next March. This was a frustrating experience at first, but ultimately very rewarding, as I learnt to be a bit more creative on my laptop! Meanwhile, although the new circle was concentrating on healing I did get advice from spirit to use pen and paper and see what would transpire, as several were waiting to come through.

At the beginning of 2013 the last two active members of the old Distant Healing Circle made their way home. First was Sheila Ireland, who decided on her own to stop eating (a person who always loved her food), and she died on 8th January, at the age of 92. I was more than happy to say just a few words of tribute at the service before the cremation. Then just over three weeks later Vera Middleton died on 2nd February. Vera was a dear friend, somehow we had just 'clicked' when we met, and we regularly had fun discussing everything under the sun, and trying to do the crossword! She always had discomfort with her leg and foot, and at the age of 86 had started to have real trouble. However, I am glad that at the end she died peacefully.

With two tutors having to cancel, our secretary had valiantly found replacements quickly enough so that I could change the programme before it went to the printers. Unfortunately, my area experienced an unusual dollop of snow, and so the Lynwood Fellowship seminar, 24th – 28th March 2013, began without one of the organisers and he had the programmes! Shonagh, the other organiser, soldiered on despite having a dreadful cold and 'death-rattle' cough! However, I managed it the next day, arriving just in time for lunch, and then the Board meeting.

The two 'original' tutors were Linda Bennett and the incomparable Gerard Smith. I had missed Linda's lecture on the first afternoon, which was a pity, because the second was excellent. Entitled "Finding our way – the Journey", it was a passionate talk with reference to mediums of the past as well as her own experience, to say how life is there to help us understand how to help others.

Gerard gave three lectures, "The Unforgiving Minute", "The Watcher on the Hill" and "Did You Hear That Bird Sing?" All were well put together, encompassing various pieces of music, poetry, lots of good quotes and a variety of stories to give a significant message.

The two helpful replacement tutors were Alan Stuttle and Helen Brown. As well as workshops, Alan gave an interesting demonstration of Spirit Art on the second evening, with all the portraits having very different characters and energies. Helen gave an informative talk on Emanuel Swedenborg (1688-1772), but I was particularly interested in her workshop "Walking the labyrinth – pathway to wholeness". This involved a **huge** canvas sheet with a multicolour painted labyrinth. After explaining what it was about, Helen started on it herself as an example and I followed.

I decided that my journey to the centre was the story of my life, with each 'turning' a significant part in my story. Quite interesting that some of the colours matched up - like when I was a teenager I was walking between orange lines, and that colour was my favourite at that time in my life. When I got to the centre, that was where I was now. I picked a card, but can't remember the exact words, but more or less saying that the journey was necessary to find balance. On the return circuit, I was facing a different view, and although unknown, the past 'events' would be met again, perhaps in different forms and different ways. When we finished we lit a small tealight. When everybody had finished, Helen brought us to the centre with our lights. She then asked us for a word that we thought important - mine was compassion - and as we all at the same time blew out the candles, thought of those qualities being given to the world. A very moving and emotional experience.

Having caught Shonagh's cold (but not the full cough thankfully) I didn't get much done for a bit. However, at the end of April I was back to full health and went down to Eastbourne for The Gordon Higginson Fellowship week of "Physical Mediumship and Trance", with Glyn Edwards, Eileen Davies, Scott Milligan, Mark Stone, and guest speakers Stewart Alexander, Susan Farrow and Eric Hatton.

The Editor of "Psychic News", Susan Farrow, introduced everybody and chaired the first talk by Stewart Alexander, "My Journey". It was an abridged account of how he got into various circles and also began his physical mediumship. I not only bought his book a bit later, but also got an opportunity at the end of his talk to go up to him and express a very emotional thank you for the experience that I'd had at Gatehouse of Fleet in 1995. Stewart gave another talk the next day, advising how to set up and run a physical circle, before answering any questions, which were many, and we ran out of time.

Later that afternoon, Eric Hatton gave a talk entitled "Off the cuff". A really excellent speaker with a mine of information – couldn't possibly remember it all! However, a few highlights stick out: the evidential mediumship of physical mediums Alec Harris, Helen Duncan and Jack Webber; the village witchdoctor in what is now Zimbabwe; Albert Best and the toilet seat, and the "Philadelphia Experiment". I could have listened to that for another few hours! Eric also took part in an open debate and discussion on "The Future of Mediumship, Teaching and Spiritualism" the following evening, and had much to say with his wealth of experience on various committees and as a president of the SNU (Spiritualist National Union). Afterwards, I also managed to have a conversation with him and a few others in the bar.

I had another 'mission' in coming to Eastbourne, and inadvertently Mark Stone made an indirect reference to it in one of his workshops on trance. He talked about Coral Polge and how she had 'scribbled' a portrait, and then later she saw this person in a gallery – it was Maurice de la Tour. I had seen Psychic portraits by Cedric Bagnall in the 'Psychic News' that looked to be of great quality. This artist, who had worked as an illustrator on the old 'Victor" and 'Eagle" comics, was reputed to have as a control Maurice de la Tour! I phoned Jean Funnell and got details of where the Eastbourne Christian Spiritualist Church was situated, and arranged to meet her on the Friday to view the pictures.

When I got there, Jean was very welcoming, showing me around the little church and then she let me peruse the portraits at my leisure. They were just as good as I had expected them to be, and there was another painting, executed by a local church member who had passed with cancer. It was a tree resplendent in cherry blossom, but over time the dark areas had got lighter and the pink blossom had increased. Unfortunately I was unable to get any good photographs due to the windows and brilliant sunshine giving so many reflections! However, it was well worth the effort to see them in the 'flesh'. Generously, before I left, Jean had handed in a package for me to the hotel. In it was a book, 'Entwining Lives', channeled by Irene Bays, and the people mentioned in it served the Eastbourne Christian Spiritualist Church – how very nice of her.

Back at the course, Eileen Davies gave several interesting workshops, and also included handouts! One particular workshop was on trance healing, when after the initial talk, we were divided into pairs, and then Eileen talked us down, one sending the healing to the other. My partner Carol placed her hands on my neck, shoulders and chest, saying that I might be having problems with digestion, especially the stomach, and needed to watch what I ate. While she was doing this, I very clearly 'saw' detailed portraits of about five gentlemen. From their dress I would place them in the latter half of the nineteenth century and early half of the twentieth century. I sensed as soon as I had seen that sequence of images that these were her 'healing team'.

Then we swapped places. I felt drawn to her shoulders, neck, spine at the heart area and to her knees, and suggested that she should have fish oil. Carol acknowledged problems in those areas and said that she knew about the fish oil – but didn't do it. Then, relating when she had asked about who helped me, Carol had seen a monk, a priest, a nun and a healing nun – the ones with the 'flyaway' hats.

Scott Milligan gave two séances. The first was a little disorganized at the start, when we were requested to take from our person any metallic objects – like jewellery, belts and nail clippers and so on. At one point a woman said that I needed to remove my spectacles as they had metallic frames! Being the first experience for quite a few attendees, I think that a longer talk of explanation would have helped. Even though there was clearly a lack of energy, a trumpet did rise and several spirit people spoke through it. At the end Eileen suggested that we all practice our singing for the next one!

Two days later we had the second séance. Lots more and louder singing this time. Mouth organs played, drums were banged, bells rung, plus a ball was thrown, and two trumpets lifted and beat in time to the music. We were given a choice of more physical phenomena or letting a loved one through, but there didn't seem to be agreement! In the end 'Daniel' told us that there wasn't enough energy for the latter. Then 'Daniel', speaking from somewhere behind me and outside the circle, said he was getting a drink, and we heard the bottle being unscrewed and the cap dropped, and with a bit of difficulty (using Scott's hands) water was poured into a glass. Then, 'Eric' gave some nice philosophy before the séance was ended. When the red light was put on one could see that the cabinet had been turned so that the front was facing to the left. Behind me, some ten metres from the cabinet, Scott was still tied in his chair, which was surrounded by ordinary chairs that were in the Conference Hall. He was checked by those who had had done that job at the start, before subdued light was allowed. Incidentally, Eileen had said during proceedings, that the trumpet came to her and that against its light she had seen the fingers and hands of 'Daniel' and 'Scruff' (the name given by 'Daniel' for a little girl) as well as another. A very good séance indeed.

All too soon it was the end of the course. I had booked to stay the extra night, so that I could start my journey back early in the morning. During the evening I went down to the bar and joined up with two others – James and Yvonne from Cornwall – who were doing the same thing. We had a long and very interesting conversation, with James telling me about his many premonitions, which he recorded in a book. I remember him telling me that in his experience they usually occur on average about four hours or so before the event. James related – with an example of an England v Germany football match – that they might not be exactly as the actual event itself, but be close enough to predict the outcome.

When I got home it was onto the salads, to try and lose some of the weight that I had put on with all that lovely hotel food. Self-discipline, when related to food, is one lesson that I am still trying to master! During this time, almost exactly three weeks after the end of the seminar, I experienced my own premonition experience. I was having a bath around 2 o'clock in the afternoon on 24th May 2013. I tend to have baths in the mornings or afternoons as I find it difficult to go to sleep if they are taken in the evenings. They are nearly always leisurely affairs that last about two hours!

While I was relaxing in the warm water I had a daydream. I was visiting some sort of zoo. I put it like this, as it was not like the large organised zoos that one might find in a city, it was more like a small private one. A young woman was attending to some animal in an enclosure. I could not identify what kind of animal she was working with, but my attention was drawn to a large tiger that was watching her, and I knew that this tiger was dangerous and that the woman was in great danger. Riveted to the situation, when I thought that the tiger was about to attack her I started singing to distract the attention of the animal. Other people behind me who were also watching what was going on (I knew they were there though I never actually saw them) joined in with me, and we succeeded, as the woman came out of the enclosure safely. When I told her how dangerous the tiger was and that it had nearly attacked her she just laughed, telling me the tiger was ok with her. I knew that she would never believe me, and so I also knew that at some point the tiger would attack and kill her. Later that day while listening to the news on Radio Four, I heard that somebody had been attacked by a tiger in a zoo somewhere in Cumbria.

The next day I bought a newspaper, and in it there was a small paragraph saying that in the South Lakes Wild Animal Park, near Dalton-in-Furness, Cumbria, a zoo worker, 24 year old Sarah McClay, was mauled by a male Sumatran tiger while she was attending to jaguars. It was not known why she went through three security gates and into the enclosure. She later died of her injuries.

Two days later I was visiting with friends in another part of Cumbria. I told them of my premonition, and on checking reports of the incident on the Internet was told that it had occurred around 4pm, and that she had died about two hours later. Apparently the tigers were on a so-called starve day, when they are not fed to simulate conditions found in the wild.

Later in the following year, it was disclosed at the inquest into her death, that Miss McClay was killed by a Sumatran tiger as she cleaned out the dens in the Tiger House at the zoo. Apparently there was a defective bolt in one of the security doors. This enabled the tiger to get through and it was then able to gained access to her, with disastrous consequences.

To date I have not experienced any other event that could be classed as a premonition, apart from the usual ones that relate to knowing who it is when the phone rings, etc.

I continued with adding to the 'Meditation Cards', getting 78 onto disc before Lynwood's seminar starting on 7th July 2013. Levi Attias as usual had very engaging talks, the first even involving blowing a ram's horn! As for his pièce de résistance, that came at the social, with feats of 'magic' that left me in admiration – I had no idea of how he was able to do them! Irene Hartley gave a very productive workshop on inspirational writing, and a demonstration with flowers on the first evening with Jan Elliot. All contacts were taken and the details seemed to be correct, but it was interesting to see the difference in their approach.

Robert Puzey was an unusual tutor. He was a songwriter (for people like the 'Nolan Sisters'), a Hatha Yoga teacher, had written a book and talked about his 'Yoga-deage'. One workshop particularly stands out for me. We had to think of a 'nice' occasion when we were young and write about it or draw a picture. I chose the latter, and thought of the time when I was about six years old, sneaking a look at the wrapped Christmas presents very early in the morning, and being baffled by a long parcel with a 'bump' nearer one end. It turned out that they were stilts!

However, this exercise brought back many memories, and I started to remember the house and locality, and was surprised just how much detail came back to me. This led me on to think about my early childhood in general, and later I wrote a few pieces down that are incorporated in the first chapter of this book. So I must thank Robert for helping me to get my little grey cells working!

One of the most interesting conversations I had was with Rowland during a tea break on the first day of the seminar. He told me that he had gone to a funeral of a woman he knew, which took place in a church. During this he had done a Buddhist meditation and had asked her to appear. This she did, looking much younger, but only her head was visible. I then related the tale of my premonition, and Rowland said that he had actually visited that zoo a week before, but hadn't seen a tiger.

After the seminar I had a few days at home, and then went down to visit family for a week or so before returning. About two weeks later I had a sudden urge to check the keys of their front door that I had been given. Instead of two keys, now there was only one. I searched thoroughly for the other but in vain. [I will give a fuller account of this in Part 2 in Chapter 19] The next day I went to the usual circle meeting, and near the end, after a bit of discussion, the medium spoke to me about there being someone who had been before but was not family. He said about there being an Irish connection and the river Liffey, but I couldn't connect it with anyone. Then he said that the person was saying that I had a memory like a sieve, and gave me a clue – the word "spats". The circle closed shortly after that.

Well, I was not pleased about that at all, as the only connection with that word was with a 'Somersby' from the old circle, and who was a 'joker' that I did not trust! In fact, his name had come into my head as a possible candidate who could have taken the key. In the end my sister got another key cut for me, but the disappeared key did eventually turn up again, where it should have been, some months later.

As for Mr. Somersby being attached to the circle, well, I did think quite a bit on that subject. I remembered that I had been put 'in charge' of the circle at one point. Did I think that I was ready at that time to take on that role? No, but it had been a big opportunity to learn, and made me think more about the circle as a whole and the individuals in it. Spirits also have to learn, and maybe that is what is happening to our Mr. Somersby, perhaps he too is on a learning curve. So I decided to let things pan out by themselves for the time being and just 'go with the flow'.

Back to work on the 'Meditation Cards', though by now I had decided that they should be free to all, hopefully from the website. I managed to get 104 onto disc for the next Lynwood seminar, 8th – 12th September 2013. Here I attended all the workshops given by Jan Elliot. These were presenting the basics of numerology, but rather than the more common kind based on Pythagoras, this was Chaldean. The other tutors were Father Eric Fisher and Rita Flannigan, the latter being and radiating the greatest amount of energy and smiles that I've ever seen in a person!

On the second evening there was "Healing with Father Eric". We sat in a large circle with lots of pillows on the floor in the centre. Father Eric talked for a bit on healing and how he started this in America and it just continued. He invited Rita to come up, and then asked for a "catcher", so I volunteered. Father Eric held up his hand to her third eye centre and within a second or two Rita just fell backwards – and I just caught her – and gently lowered her onto the floor with a pillow under her head. Later Rita told me that she was aware of all that was being said, but she was just immobile.

Then Peter Hague was called up and the same was done to him, though luckily I had the help of John Campbell as a 'catcher'. Laying Peter on the cushions, I was assigned to give him healing, laying my hand on his abdomen to help with his back and also attending to his arm. Father Eric instructed me to think of a deep blue colour and to surround him with that. In fact I 'got' that colour a second or two before he said it, and then Marion came over and assisted also. Peter was quite relaxed, and said he felt as if he had been touched by the Holy Spirit – but 'inside'. He also commented that he felt tremendous heat, and eventually got up by himself. This was the first time I had ever seen this up close and only remember seeing something on television many years ago.

The next morning Rita gave a talk "Hypnotherapy and Past Life Regression Therapy". Near the end it went into healing, and Shonagh became the volunteer 'victim', being put under by Father Eric, with John and myself catching and placing her on the pillows. Rita then did her bit of healing, helping with knee and back troubles. When Shonagh came back, she described what she had felt, and said that at the knee it was like a flower unfolding and the pain vanished, and the back area was helped but was more resistant. Interestingly Rita had not been told of her back problems. Lastly, Nick was put under by Father Eric, who stayed a while giving healing, and Rita went though the same procedure as before. When eventually Nick was back on his feet, he described his experience as if he was slightly out of his body in a way.

So it was a really fascinating seminar, and at the social on the last night, Robert Puzey played his guitar and sang a few songs that we could join in with. Sally Winslade-Rafter gave an absolutely hilarious account of her experience of travelling to Lytham St. Annes on a bus last November. I give her full name, as it is expected that at some time in the near future she will publish a book of her 'stories', or maybe a CD/DVD. If you see it – buy it, as you certainly won't be disappointed.

Now for a neat bit of synchronicity! At the next circle meeting (16/09/2013), when linking to spirit I got an image on my right hand side of a hand holding a quill – it was all very dark with the quill looking like a black feather, about which in my notes I wrote: later I realised the significance of this – it has yet to come to pass. When I came to write the first draft of this book, I came to this point just a day after finding a black feather in the middle of the sitting room floor (24/01/2015)!

In the next meeting several members of the circle were given personal advice; I was told to continue to research the philosophy and go with my intuition, but that the healing would still be a prominent part of what I do. I was to keep doing the writing and painting, that I was to have patience as things will proceed and unfold as they should.

In August I got the chance to go to a weekend workshop in Lytham St. Anne's. Having looked into a number of areas over the years, I had not at any point intentionally decided to study trance, most probably because I doubted if I had much ability in that sphere. Now deciding to rectify this omission, I got the chance to work with Leah Bond, someone I both respected and trusted. At the end of the first session, Leah told me that I was holding back! That there were "lots of people" waiting to come through! In the second one I experienced much more visual imagery:

faces, then going along a path backwards, 'showers' of silver and gold dust, then 'rain' or ribbons of blue and silver, and I remember that my heart chakra was highly activated. However, I was not really settled and came back to normal awareness early as my teeth/mouth felt sore. I have a tendency to clench my teeth.

Later that day Leah decided to give us a trance demonstration, which was excellent, even though the Chinese gentleman said that although the energy was low he would proceed. He gave very good philosophy regarding life in general. He saw us like flowers in a garden – lots of different coloured lights; that the daisy was a great flower, no matter that you walk on it, it will spring back unbroken. He told us that we should give time to the spirit world, even if it was only ten minutes. Then he recited the last few lines of a poem that Leah had learnt when she was thirteen years old:

> I'll not willingly offend
> Nor be willing to be offended.
> What's wrong I'll try to mend
> And endure what cannot be mended.

At the subsequent session Leah gave a good talk, including the criteria of trance. Then 'working', this time I thought I was a bit calmer and a little deeper, but still lots of visual activity. In the next three sessions we concentrated on individuals in turn. When it was mine I tried to relax, but had to be reminded by Leah to relax my jaw! Observed lots of red and black colours with a young woman, then saw water at eye level and gradually was immersed in it. Just as the music was turned off I felt a surge of energy above and in front of my head, and near the end saw both male and female faces straight in front of me. Then the others gave me some feedback. Paul briefly saw a big saddleback pig behind me, then a Benedictine monk with a quill in his left hand, while Sarah saw me receiving healing. With Edith's turn it was lovely, even I saw energy to her right hand side. At least three or four of the others said that it was Gordon Higginson.

At the last session we had a review and then worked in groups of three, also choosing a card. When it was my turn I got lovely waves of green, lavender and purple and near the end a white bush type plant. Then I remembered that I had got that when the whole group had been sending me energy in the morning. The card that I had selected was 'Patience'! All in all I felt that it was not a bad first step, and that I would try to continue my exploration when I could, but needed to work on relaxing fully.

A couple of weeks later I was back at Lytham St Anne's for the Lynwood Fellowship weekend. Tutors were Ankha Laan-Ra, who gave a talk on "The Four Pillars Of Ascension", with workshops on light work, inner child and unity consciousness; Alan Stuttle who gave a demonstration and workshops on psychic and inspired art; lastly Andrew Wright, who gave a very evidential demonstration of mental mediumship. Andrew's last workshop was quite interesting. After talking on the basics of circle work and some of the forms of phenomena that one might expect, he selected two people and asked them to give their watch to another two people of his choice – one being myself, so that we could do some psychometry. Unlike the first person, I didn't get any information other than colour for 'C'. Firstly a large circle of violet, then a pale blue, and after that there was a long horizontal stripe of green on top with light 'whitey' brown and earthy colours below.

We then went onto table work, with 'C', 'L', Shonagh and myself. After a short time I felt a 'tingle' in the table, and then 'C's right hand started to shake slightly, and next her left one also. As this got more pronounced and 'aggressive' I didn't think it was right and wanted to take my hands off, but waited for instruction. Then I noticed that Shonagh's right hand was also shaking very slightly, at which point Andrew stopped it. He said that there was a clash of energies and that 'C' should not sit for anything physical at all. I wondered if the colours that I had perceived from the psychometry were now relevant, violet for philosophy to be spoken (blue throat chakra) when she had a solid foundation and 'earthed'. It was a good exercise in that it taught people to be aware and think about things!

Later that month, 21st -24th November 2013, I was back in Cober Hill for the International Spiritualist Federation "Mind, Body and Spirit" weekend. I spoke to the President Ann Luck, and offered the ISF the 104 'Meditation Cards' for their website if they wanted, giving her enough copies for the committee to look at individually.

Opting to do trance workshops in the morning and spirit/psychic art in the afternoons, all of us first went to the Flag Ceremony. It is a lovely tradition of the ISF, where a representative of each nationality present carries a small version of their national flag to be placed together with the others. Then at the end of the course, the procedure will be reversed. There were at least ten nationalities there, some from as far as Australia, Iceland, Canada and the USA.

On the first evening Steve Vogel led the 'Shamanic Wheel', which gave me a message that was very pertinent. The next evening there was a demonstration of Spirit Art with Matthias Güldenstein and Coral Ryder. They decided to make it experimental, so both worked at the same time, while a volunteer did mediumship. It turned out to be an excellent evening, and I think that most of the pieces fell into place, like a jigsaw.

In the morning Stewart Alexander gave a passionate and hugely informative talk about his start in being a physical medium. In the afternoon he gave a tutorial, on physical circles that was comprehensive and instructive, and he answered lots of questions from the participants.

Each morning Ann Luck set me up for the day with her Tai Chi, and on the last evening Bill Coller gave the best example of mediumship that I have seen to date, incorporating exercises to show his tutorial group what he had been explaining in his workshops. Wonderful!

Bill Parkins took the Trance group that I was in. At the start he gave us all a small booklet of notes, and talked about various states of 'low' trance, one being premonition. Then he gave us a breathing exercise to do, along with music that had been specifically made for him – it was lovely. At the next session we found a piece of paper on our chair that had a word on it. Taken down with the music, we had to speak about our particular word; needless to say the word I got was 'Patience'. Then, after asking for spirit to come near, we concentrated on one person at a time. During my turn I saw lovely deep blue/lavender with gold 'bits' in it, and felt energy around my head, beard and even my fingers, but no word came to me. Bill said I was questioning – just like his wife Mary!

The following day when we used the music I got a lavender colour, and then lots of striation, horizontal bands of blue/grey, and when asked by Bill I said it felt like 'eternal horizons'. I then felt surrounded by this lavender colour, it was very peaceful and calm. However, Bill didn't think that the energies in the room were quite right, so we stopped, and after discussing this with an individual, we sent healing and cleared it. Next was a visualisation that was 60% successful by myself. On the last day all were told to give out, except Mary and I, who were to stay in our 'deep' state. When Bill got to us, Mary sensed the people with her, while I got lots of the lavender again, and quite quickly I got a glimpse of a female face and later a male, but didn't recognise them. Bill told me that I had two people with me, one male who was behind me and a female who was situated to my left. I had lots of lavender again and got 'cotton wool' (think they were treating me like that!). Then quite a few changes of view occurred: a placid lake with only a few ripples on it, a barren grassy hillside that seemed bleak. Then it was back to nice colours of lavender and blue with gold at the centre right. Next there were disturbances and with time marching on, we had to finish. Nothing spectacular – but I did feel that it was another little step forward!

Coral Ryder started with an illustrated talk on Pariedolia – the imagined perception of a pattern or meaning where it does not actually exist, like seeing the moon with human features. A wide variety of images were shown, from clouds to rock formations etc. Then we got to make 'a mess' and looked to change some of it into faces or animals and so forth. At the workshop Coral gave a talk on spirit/psychic art in all its aspects, after which we worked with a partner to draw pictures with spirit guidance for each other. Then a little exercise to give an example of the difficulties that spirit has in this kind of communication.

Next day we tried again with several new partners, before starting on an auragraph (a symbolic picture or pattern). At the last workshop Coral conned us into doing an auragraph for ourselves before working again with another partner.

Great fun, but quite a hectic work rate to get it all in. In fact when I got home I found I had an auragraph unfinished, so did finish it and posted it to the person concerned. I thoroughly enjoyed the ISF weekend, and had a great time with friends old and new, and was energized for the winter ahead.

CHAPTER 16

The Work Really Begins

After a pleasant holiday with family, I got home and started to do a bit more writing. Then I noticed an advert in the local newspaper that a Spiritualist Group was having clairvoyant evenings every fortnight. Deciding to have a look at how it was doing, I went along on 11th January 2014 to see a medium that I had not heard before. At first it seemed to be run much the same as many others, but then the 'medium' was introduced. I've heard tales of some mediums doing strange things, but now I was about to witness it for myself!

He just asked people whom they wanted from spirit and preceded to give them 'information' from that spirit. Once or twice, judging by the responses of people in the audience, he may have had some kind of spirit link, but most of it seemed to be purely psychic. Then he came to me – "Who do you want?" I told him that I'd be delighted to receive a message from any of three friends who had passed over last year. He first asked me if it was one woman and two men, but I informed him it was the other way around. He then commented on my beard and said that one of the women had teased me about it [No]. He continued with that she had been ill for quite some time but deteriorated [Could apply to both of them] and I had sent out thoughts that God could take her, and that had led to some guilty feelings on my part [No]. However, she wanted to go as she had no fight left, while in life was a fighter and had great determination [Could apply to both women].

Then he turned his attention to the male, saying that he was a tall gentleman, [No] well "that was the way he felt inside"!! By this time I was getting fed up, but let him ramble on without giving me a single piece of evidence. He gave vague generalisations and any specific points, like a ring, I could not take. He did mention about a clock and its tick, which he could have picked up psychically, but otherwise nothing. Then just as he was about to leave me, he said that he had a gent like me, could be my dad. He informed me that this man just says, "I'm sorry son", and then told me that he didn't think he was an easy man to get on with. [No!]

Not really wanting to believe that things were really as bad as it looked, I went along to the next meeting. This time the medium was a woman, apparently with long experience. When asked to do the philosophy, she told the audience that she would be 'taken over' and that spirit would give her the words. Her voice changed slightly and she said that we are here to progress; that we are given choices, so it is up to us; we must nurture our light; not to forget the power of prayer; nor forget the angels; we are never alone; we should help each other. Not sure why she needed to be 'taken over' to relay such things. Then when it came to her mediumship **not one** relationship was identified. After her first contact she then said, "Who wants a message?" and she went to the first person that had put their hand up! After about the sixth 'message' she repeated that and then immediately asked, "Who do you want to speak to?" It was not an encouraging evening. Afterwards I had a cup of tea and was invited over for a chat. The medium said that nowadays people need to change and so does Spiritualism. There was another woman sitting beside the medium who agreed, saying we should work with the angels, and then came out with "that one doesn't even have to be in a trance now to deliver a trance message"! I was not entirely sure if that was said in earnest or because of what she had seen in this evening's philosophy – I do hope it was the latter.

On the 22nd February 2014 I went for the third time. Thankfully, this time the medium was the genuine article, though at the beginning of her life of service. After her introduction, 'L' used her mediumship to deliver about half a dozen 'messages' to recipients. Although there were long pauses at times in her delivery, all were accepted bar one. Each time she knew who to go to, and the one that wasn't taken was when she opened it out to the audience. That evening was encouraging, but overall one cannot be overly optimistic at what is presented to the generally uninformed public.

Meanwhile I had started my book, deleted it and started again. The second time I knew the format that I wanted to present, and the first few chapters were written quickly. During this time I had an experience while sitting at home during my distant healing session. As I was going through the names on the list, I moved my right hand slightly and at once felt a touch on my left hand. It is the first time that this has happened during distant healing. As co-organiser with Shonagh for the first Lynwood Fellowship seminar, I was also doing bits and bobs for that. However, before then, I was on another trance weekend course.

On the 4th April 2014, I was back at the Chadwick Hotel, St Anne's-on-Sea, with the tutor being Mark Webb. He gave us a talk first and then we tried to go as deep as possible and connect to our spirit helpers. Felt a bit of energy but was not impressed with anything. Mark said later that he saw philosophy with me, but the energy was not close enough, also there was a person similar to myself but his beard was shorter and trimmed. It was during this workshop that I got a big twitch in my right thumb. This thumb had been painful for a few weeks, but after the twitch the pain left completely, and only returned at 8.10pm on the Sunday evening as I was writing up my notes, after the seminar had officially ended!

At the evening workshop 'S' gave a demonstration of trance healing. It was fascinating to watch her face twitch and vibrate as her spirit helper came in close to her. I vaguely saw some energy above her hair, about 15 to 20 cm high. 'S' started at the patient's head and then went down to the mid section and lastly to the legs. As she was nearing the finish, I saw about 4 or 5 'sparkles' around her head, above, side and below. There were also differences in temperature; my ankles were quite cool, though it got warm at the end. 'S' again gave trance healing to another patient. Then Mark gave a good talk (how I wish I could have recorded it all), saying how trance was now on the increase. In addition he talked about doorkeepers, how that it is through the doorkeeper's aura that other spirits can come forward to work. So somebody might hear and see a Native American, although the medium would know that it was their Chinese doorkeeper!

The next morning I had difficulty due to a pain in my jaw and some of the teeth, and really tried to relax them during the tea break. Back with the group work, Mark reminded us that clairvoyance can sometimes come because trance goes through all the other states. I used a pillow to sit on and found that it was much more comfortable. This time I went down more easily and two or three times my mouth opened, but no words came out and none came into my mind. Others had success, especially Edith, with both Gordon Higginson and Winston Churchill coming through. At the end another person gave trance healing.

At the session after lunch the power seemed to build up strongly, but half way it went pear-shaped and I didn't get it back again. 'S' gave trance healing to another on the couch, and eventually did see the etheric around her.

Then in the later afternoon session I was asked to sit at the head end of the couch and a volunteer came as a patient. Asked to link in with spirit, I did some deep breathing that seemed to go on for a long time.

Then as the power built up I felt the need to stand - and spoke "I need to stand", not quite my own voice. Lots of violet colour that spread out in front to cover the whole body of the patient, and my hands were placed either side of her head. My lips parted and the lower one just kept quivering up and down for what seemed like ages, but it eventually went. Then I felt impelled to put my right hand on her forehead for a while, and then back to the side of the head. Saw some lime green 'splodges', more on the right side. Then felt the need to withdraw and sat down.

Then, just as I was about to move my chair back to its place in the circle, Mark said, "Where do you think you are going?" So 'P' came up and lay on the couch and I had to renew my connection. This time it was very different - lots of blue and green mixed up - all very calm and peaceful. Didn't feel the urge to get up at all for ages and then got a quick spasm in my left arm and in my mind was thinking of holding her shoulders. So got up and did just that, concentrating on giving out the colours. Briefly moved up to her head and the thought came into my head that maybe she should drink a little more water. BUT - made the classic mistake, thinking that it was just

207

me - so didn't say it. Then I sat down. However, I did own
up about it afterwards and got the telling off, that could
have just been me, but what might have followed could
have been quite important from spirit!

In the evening session Sarah was asked to give trance healing to another person. I saw the energy at the top of Sarah's head, a bit like a punk haircut! Quite fascinating, but I couldn't see all the different colours that many others did.

Then another person had the opportunity to try, before we opened as a circle to spirit. Various people spoke, but I got a picture of a rolling piece of writing, a bit like film credits.

The following day we continued that last exercise, and I was bold enough to speak! I started with the word 'water', how it is important to the earth, connected to energy, and then it was related to Jesus washing the feet of the Apostles – symbolic of service. After the tea break I again spoke, first with the word 'work', that is what we have to do here and in spirit, so if we are in a difficult situation it is up to us to try to change the energies.

By the end the atmosphere got very heavy so I was glad when we broke for lunch.

Mark started with a talk at the next workshop, and then asked Edith to get on the couch and for me to sit near her head and go into trance. *The energies started in a similar way to the very first time, with my lower lip quivering, but not quite so strongly and not for as long. Then the energies changed to a much more gentle kind, with blues etc., and I got up and placed my hands either side of her head. I didn't get any indication to speak, but at one stage got the idea of going around to her feet, but it didn't come back again so left it. Eventually I felt that spirit had probably withdrawn a few minutes before and ended. [About a third of the way through the healing Edith gave a kind of 'jump' and I felt that she was 'going off on her own', Mark spotted it and called her back.] Edith said she loved the healing, lots of heat at her back and her heart rate had slowed down.*

Another person gave trance healing before Sarah gave a demonstration of trance. Again I saw a little bit of energy around her and after a bit saw a thin layer of lilac very close to her hair and forehead. Next 'R' was asked. She got her main guide come through, but I could see that Mark wasn't very happy. He brought her back and asked her to bring somebody else. Again Mark brought her back, saying she had a Native American Indian with her with a very powerful energy, but that it was a different energy entirely that he was looking for. So she went back again and this time succeeded. Later Mark told 'R' that she was inclined to take control instead of leaving it to spirit. **They** should decide who should come through at any given time, not her, and that there were possibilities with physical mediumship if she let it happen.

After the tea break it was the last session, sitting in circle and giving out, and at some point Edith gave a talk. *I was busy trying to get in the power when suddenly and unexpectedly I got a sudden burst of colour - rose red - in an oval shape. This turned to pink and expanded until that was all there was, and then changed again to a white with pink edging. Next sequences came where it was like watching a film, with moving scenes passing quickly, sometimes horizontally, sometimes vertically. Got masses of snowdrops, then bluebells, got images of wet pavements, then rivers, a brick architectural structure that turned to indigo and then violet. Lots of whites at intervals, but all different, white with drifts of silver through it, etc., scenes at evening, at night and the dawn, then in daytime with green fields. It just went on and on until it stopped about five minutes before we closed!* This had been an incredible weekend and I felt I had moved forward a step or two. I wondered just how far I could have got if it had been a week in length!

Back home, I just managed to get in a circle meeting, where Don Galloway relayed through the medium some comments that showed he still took a keen interest on what was going on, and then it was the Lynwood Fellowship seminar at Cober Hill, 13th – 17th April 2014. This time we had a new tutor, Glennyce Eckersley, a lovely soul who radiated peace, and who is an internationally acclaimed writer and broadcaster. Glennyce had been inspired by Swedenborg's writing relating to angels, and that subject came up in her talks and workshops, and prompted many questions and discussions. Linda Bennett returned again, and with no snow this time to delay me, I was able to see her excellent demonstration of mediumship on the first evening. Linda organised well-constructed workshops and talks, the latter a good blend of the historical and the personal. The third tutor was the energetic Mark Foster, who seems to get more passionate and knowledgeable every time I see him. He gave us a chance to use dowsing rods and pendulums, and nearly got me to the point of understanding quantum consciousness. His contribution was highly popular and excellent as always, jam-packed with information and references. All too soon it was over, and back to working in my garden and on my 'book'.

Within a few weeks I found myself visiting several people in different hospitals, and picked up what I thought was a mild infection. It gave me an irritation in my throat, but I presumed that it would disappear in time. This condition was sensed when I went to a circle meeting in May, and was told that I had someone with me, what is called 'an attachment'. Apparently this spirit, a woman, had been attracted to my light and decided to stay with me for the time being. The medium's spirit helpers then got the woman, clothed in a long dressing gown, to pass over into the light where she should be. I was warned to watch my protection, especially when going into these sorts of places. Almost immediately I felt the difference and my throat condition just 'melted away'. Later in July, a certain spirit came through in circle giving me various bits of information from the draft of the 'book', just letting me know that they knew what I was up to!

In July, Father Eric Fisher returned for the second Lynwood seminar, and on the Tuesday he led a Healing Service. Again I was a 'catcher' and fairly busy as people were going down quickly. Then after Father Eric had attended to one individual he asked me, as a healing medium, to stay with her. When she 'came back', her friend asked me if I had a monk with me when healing, and she then confirmed that he had a piece of rope as a belt. Another tutor, Peter Halley, was new to me. His "Singing Bowl Sound-Bath Experience" started with a talk and then he gave us an improvised demonstration, with our eyes closed, for about 30 minutes. It was really good; I didn't get any visual, physical or psychic experiences, but just enjoyed the relaxation. Peter had brought two crystal bowls and umpteen metal ones with him, and poor Shonagh was like a child in a sweetie shop and couldn't resist buying one of the large metal bowls. The third tutor was Jennifer Jones who gave the mediumship on the first evening. However, I was particularly taken with her workshops, where she used the voice to do overtoning and also healing. In the latter one we divided into pairs, but being the odd one out I got individual attention from the teacher! Jennifer did experimental trance – a repeat of one that happened five years ago, and was kind enough to sing several songs at the social on the last evening.

Just two weeks later, I went down to Eastbourne for the ISF Congress and 'Mind, Body and Spirit' week. Arriving a few days early allowed me to indulge in one of my passions – searching in second hand bookshops – and there is a lovely one near the centre of town. I think I bought fifteen books! On the Sunday there was the Congress meeting that went very smoothly and finished at noon, which gave plenty of time to catch up with the news from old friends and start to meet a few new ones.

As before, I opted to take both the trance and spirit art workshops. Two of the trance groups combined, so we had the benefit of two tutors, Dianne Parker and Ann Luck. Ann also helped to start each day with a little gentle exercise before breakfast, doing Tai Chi – on the roof, as the weather was sunny. The first trance workshop was a bit poor – on my part! For some reason I found it very difficult to follow the instructions and felt I would fall asleep; that session was totally wasted on me (sorry!).

That evening Steve Vogel had a 'Shamanic Medicine Wheel'. We all got drummed in and then went up to the 'altar' and asked a question or for healing, and then chose the seat to sit in. Then, when all were seated Steve explained the procedure, rattled us in, and talked about the symbolism of the four compass points. After that he drummed a monotonous beat for about twenty minutes. I had often been warned by spirit of having 'too many fingers in pies', so my question was whether I should continue with exploring trance or just focus on healing, going to circle and writing the 'book'. I found that I had chosen to sit on the east area, connected to the air element, dawn, inspiration, new beginnings, communication and speaking. The new beginning was definitely the 'book', but that didn't negate the trance, as that would be inspiration and communication as well. So I thought that I had not framed the question properly, and decided to just continue with what I was already doing!

The next day Dianne talked about the various stages of trance, before we explored the sensing of our own energy and that of another. After the tea break, we were split into two groups, and each individual, bar one in each group, were given a slip of paper with a saying written on it. Then we had to go into trance and each in turn gave a talk on their 'saying', while the one without any 'saying' was to have spirit come through and mention the 'sayings' of all the others. I had decided that I would speak! So thought of a first sentence and then just said what came to me, it seemed to be all right. Near the end we had an exercise to recognise the different levels, and then in pairs one decided to go to a level and the other had to say which it was. Needless to say this was out of my depth.

There was an interesting experiment at the subsequent workshop. First going into pairs, we had to put our energy into the chair we were sitting on, then – still remaining in contact with the chair at all times – gradually get up and move around to stand behind it. Then we had to invite our guide to sit on our chair, and after a while move round to sit on it again, sitting in our guide's energy. We had to become aware of their presence, were they taller or smaller, male or female, slimmer or broader, where do you put your feet, arms, hands, do you sit up straight or relax? At the blending stage I sensed the ocean and tried to be part of it. Then we had to let our guide speak through us – for five minutes! I felt as deep as I had ever been, so decided I would start with "good morning". This I did and then followed it with bits about 'service' and taking the time to speak to people and so on. Mostly me, but maybe only 90%!

My partner though did very well. He became very straight in his seat, with broad shoulders and looked authoritative, as if his guide was much broader and taller than himself. Then he gradually leaned forward, head down, with his hands near each other between his knees, so that when he started to speak it was difficult to hear clearly. He talked about having courage, to focus on that, you have the ability, be focused, have confidence, to believe in what I am doing, be brave, don't move away from the line, he believes in me. Then he mentioned that it was so hot, and the perspiration was literally dripping of his head. Ann Luck came and asked the guide to move back a bit. He continued speaking, it will happen, do and believe, believe and do, and then he said, "I think that is all you need to know". Very interesting indeed!

After the tea break we did the exercise with slips of paper, mine was the same as last time, "Many hands make light work". I managed to start with cooperation, and added planning for mercy missions and remember that bees came into it, a little bit better this time. After this we formed a circle with the cabinet. With the first person in the 'hot seat' I saw changes in her face, especially at her cheekbones, and she talked for a bit. An Icelander was next, who talked powerfully – the need to trust each other more, to work through the past, give it light and healing and even come to love the past, we can learn from it, respect is needed, then, "I really love you all and bless you". I noticed that his feet were also twitching a little. Very deep and powerful.

The first workshop on the last day had another interesting experiment. Sitting in groups of three, one is a 'client', and the other two are the client's parents or grandparents. The client chooses who will be male and who female (irrespective of the sex of the people involved) and then describes the physical features and personality of each, without disclosing any other information. The mediums are taken down into trance, with the client then talking to each 'parent/grandparent', asking questions, like what was their favourite pastime, food, etc.

I chose to be the client first. 'R' as dad got at least 90% right, only saying the wrong name for a friend, and getting the name of a whisky half right! 'Mother' got best day as Sunday, liked baking, etc., and both thought I was very quiet when young (correct) and encouraged me to continue my pathway. Then 'B' became the client, and I was 'mother' and 'R' father again. 'R' actually brought through her grandfather and gave very good evidence concerning the death of a son at a very young age, places, etc. I got a sense of part of the kitchen (very brief flash of clairvoyance) and felt she liked sewing, as it was quite meditative, but found it difficult after that.

After the tea break 'R' was the client, who asked me to be his maternal grandfather and 'B' to be the grandmother. I struggled more this time, but did get an image of walking along the sand near the sea with a very young child of about two or three years of age. 'B' had lots of evidence, with knitting and so forth. Next we used the cabinet again. After two others had been, I got to go in the 'hot seat'. Managed to get down a little further, to the area of calm water, only little ripples on the surface – such peace and tranquility, surrounded by love – it was lovely. I was urged to speak by Dianne, just to describe what I was feeling, and then brought back. I found it very emotional, even talking about it, and was very near to tears. Later in the evening, one of the trance participants stopped me and said that when I was in the cabinet he had seen a light go into me from my left hand side.

The spirit art afternoon group was taken by Coral Ryder, who started going over the basics with a nice small group of six. She let Merja and myself start on our own. I asked my helpers in spirit to bring forward someone who this Finnish woman would know. I got a brief flash of clairvoyance that gave me an idea of how the hair went, but no other details. So I started on the hair and let the other details gradually develop. The face was a little distorted, but I just went with it, put in a little background and then concentrated on trying to get some information to go with it.

When I asked Merja if she could place the image she said no. So we did some of the group exercises, and then I gave her the information that I had written down. She then exclaimed, "Oh, I had thought it was a boy!" Merja said the name of the person and could take most of the particulars that I'd written. A very positive start!

The next day I finished one for another person in the group, but this time neither the image nor the information could be taken. Coral, with the aid of images and physical examples, talked about auragraphs, especially those by Harold Sharp. We then paired up with a different person and tried doing these for each other. After the tea break Coral gave us a hard exercise, trying to link in with a photograph inside a sealed envelope! Then Merja got up, and coming to the front gave a mini demonstration, drawing a portrait with symbols and giving mediumship, that Coral could take. I also got up, but found it very difficult. However, with lots of help from Coral, did get a portrait that Merja could take.

The next workshop was experimental. We were joined by tutor Karen Willis and her mental mediumship group, and split into three groups of around five people in each. Our wee group had to link in to get someone for Kris. I got a portrait of a woman, and felt some of the feelings that the mediums were saying. With a scarf/blanket over the mouth and throat, thought there was a problem there, plus a fascinator in her hair, so maybe a wedding, felt that there were great swings of mood with this person, and that there was a strong Native American influence.

Most of this was taken. Then we tried to do the same for Hildur. I got a woman at first (mentioned by Kris) but soon it changed into a young man, though I felt there was a link with the original woman. However, I was not very successful this time in getting details to go with the image, so perhaps I was tiring a little.

Next Karen asked Suse from her group to come up to the front to do mediumship, while Coral chose me to do the art! I selected a brown pastel, and worked on a large scale. Felt it was a strong male character, but didn't get much else – thankfully Suse filled in all those details. Yet again it was Merja who could take it!

We said goodbye to Karen and her group. Then Coral gave us a numbered ticket each, and we had to draw something for another person – the number representing somebody in another group! When we had just about finished, Ann Robson brought in her group and we paired up with the appropriate 'number'.

I felt that the drawing was quite positive, but yet again I only had a limited amount of background information. My partner thought that she could take it, but would have to check with her mother on the details. Then we paired off again, as that group had also been given tickets representing individuals in our group. They had gone about it in two stages, firstly on a psychic level and later with a spirit connection.

On the last workshop, one of our group was absent due to illness, but an elderly gentleman, who was a day visitor, took his place. Again we had tickets, but without knowing who exactly it was, we had to do an auragraph. My ticket was for the new visitor, and I went over to join him and discuss what I'd drawn. The discussion led to the subject of art in general, and soon we were deep in conversation on all manner of topics. It turned out that Philip Brown had taught art both in England and Spain, and had indeed published books on it. With his Swedish wife (now deceased), they had set up a successful stained glass business, and he had not long ago published a book on their last incarnation in the 16th century.

There were other interesting items in the course of the week: a talk by Isabelle Duchene on "Spirit Photography"; "Tea Leaf Readings" by Dianne Parker; the "Healing Service"; demonstrations of mental mediumship by Darren Brittain, Karen Willis and Jackie Wright, and the last one by Richard Schoeller. It had been a fabulous week and the tutors were brilliant.

When I got back home, it was back to the garden, and making preparations for the next Lynwood seminar. At this time I also made the commitment to try to sit for spirit art, even if it was sitting just by myself. I started this on the 3rd September 2014, and in the end decided to try to do it roughly once a week, except for courses and holidays etc. Some of the results are shown in Part 2, at the end of Chapter 19. If anyone can identify a portrait, please do get in touch, as I would love to hear from you.

The Lynwood Fellowship seminar ran from 7th to 11th September, with Peter Hague getting our energies going each morning before breakfast with Qigong. One of the tutors was Helen da Vita, with whom I had a 'private sitting'. Because of my poor memory I had brought my tape recorder, but had forgotten that it picked up interference when spirit energies were around. On playing it back I could hear only roughly the first minute of it! Helen gave an illustrated talk on Helen Duncan and on another evening gave a trance demonstration. However, it was during her Trance Healing workshop that I experienced an interesting sequence of images. We were divided into pairs, one the 'patient' and the other being the healing medium or 'giver'.

> *I was surprised how well I relaxed and quietened my mind. Having selected to be the 'giver', I asked spirit to use me, and got down to a quiet level. But soon the atmosphere changed and I suddenly saw an oval shape that was filled with a colour (can't remember the first colour), but it then cleared and the oval was calm water. This happened a second time, the colour being green, and again it cleared to show water. Also got an image of part of a garden with high hedges and two figures. Both were bright beings, but felt the one on the right was brighter - angelic. Again I got an oval with a colour that cleared to show water and then the oval gradually increased in size until it disappeared and all that I could see was a lake.*

The second tutor was Marion Hamilton, also a member of the Lynwood Fellowship Board, who gave a talk on the first night on "Stress Management" and continued on this subject at the workshop on the following morning (which I missed due to the private sitting with Helen). Marion also gave a talk on "The Seven Principles of Spiritualism" and two workshops that involved colour.

Phil Medley was our third tutor, giving three fascinating talks that were jam-packed with information; I couldn't keep up with my note taking! He also gave three workshops, "Healing with Sound". The third one started with only using the voice. Sally was asked to be the patient, while Phil, Peter and I toned together her name, Sa-Lee. She said that she found it quite nice but had got a fit of the giggles! Other 'patients' had a turn, with the second saying it was very powerful, and the third became very emotional, as he saw all his dead relations there.

So, a variety of subjects for the course participants, and in no time at all the seminar was finished.

A month later I was back at the Chadwick Hotel, St Annes-on-Sea, with tutor Stephen Smith advising us on 'Trance Healing'. I very much took to his philosophy and down to earth approach, also with his constant encouragement to learn to work with the mind and not to stand still, but always seek to move forward. He started with exercises on concentration and attuning to the 3rd eye centre (where one visualises the still flame of a candle), after which we worked in pairs, one the 'patient', and then we swapped.

As the patient at the start, I felt lots of dark blue energy around me. Johanna put her hands on my shoulders and sensed the energy as both soothing and warm. After a short time she then placed her hands on the small of my back – the first touch was like an electric shock! However, it immediately settled back to normal, though the colour faded and became slightly grey. Next Johanna placed her hands on each side of the heart chakra and I experienced lots of heat, but it was not uncomfortable. Then we swapped. I got a sequence of change in the colours, first green, then turquoise getting more and more blue, before the blue deepened in tone and became purple. Then it changed to reds for a short time, before going to a yellow/orange. During this I was aware of the flickering of my eyes – like REMs – and the colour changed back to blue. Johanna related that she had felt the colours travel down her body; right to her feet, and near the end had become almost unbearably hot. Stephen mentioned that breath and mind are connected, and that the chakra points are doorways to and from the inner world.

The next day Stephen emphasised the importance of attunement to the candle and still flame, it was an exercise in one-pointedness, a focus, concentration, then a link to the spirit helper. We did another exercise; this time our body became the candle and our head the flame. It took about thirty minutes, but ego is very clever at distracting you! Eventually I ended up repeating a mantra to myself, "I am the flame".

After the tea break, Stephen demonstrated trance healing, with several of his 'team' speaking to us. Then after talking about increasing the power through a way of breathing, Stephen divided us into pairs again. As the patient I felt an energy that was gentle and light, together with a light blue colour. Natalie told me that her healing guide was a nun, so it usually is very gentle. Then we swapped. Instead of the candle I saw a spot of purple light that gradually increased in size. When doing the 'power breathing' I felt as if I should be using my voice, maybe even just an 'Om'. Natalie said that she got a glimpse of a young Tibetan man with embroidered robes, displaying different colours.

After dinner I was again partnered with Natalie. As the patient, what I noticed right from the start was energy at the left of my head, and this proceeded to expand even before Natalie put her hands on my shoulders. There was lovely heat from her hands, which she moved from the forehead and lower back to cover both my ears. At this stage I got a red colour with a blue at the bottom (afterwards she confirmed she had this also). It was a lovely gentle healing with beautiful heat – I could have stayed like that for ages! After swapping positions, I felt that spirit was around me and at one point 'something' touched the thumb of my right hand. Also my feet got really hot!

On the last day Stephen gave a general talk on the true situation regarding life and the law of return, as taught to him by his teacher and others like the Dalai Lama. We then did trance, going down as usual and when 'into it' to do the Om on the outbreath – but mentally only. I got to where everything was getting lighter, and then I suddenly saw a white circle that looked like a planet. This disappeared and returned briefly, partly obscured by 'cloud'. Then instead of the planet there was black with dark blue 'clouds' around it, as seen in the illustration below.

It was like I was looking at a part of space. Stephen told me that this was the void, and that I should just go into it the next time I saw it. In addition he mentioned that if one has a problem with seeing the candle at the 3rd eye, one could imagine that you are holding it in front of you, to light your way.

Following the tea break, we had a short discussion on health and diet, before having an exercise of breathing and relaxing and then turning our eyes up 'into our heads', as this helps put you into an Alpha state but still have awareness. I wasn't successful at this. Then we divided into pairs for trance healing. Once more I was with Johanna and again I was the patient first. She put her hands on the heart area, and I saw an egg shaped void that was grey before waves of lavender colour came. At that point Johanna started to shake violently, and Stephen came to tell her to ask her guide to take a step back. At the end she said that she was very cold and held her hands out for me to feel, and they indeed were icy cold. Then we swapped. I put my hands close to her neck, partially around, with the thumbs upwards at the back. Johanna felt lots of heat and her hands were warm at the end of it!

After lunch Stephen mentioned meditation, saying that we should have a goal, either to invoke a spirit guide to help us in some way or to try to achieve something – it needed intention. Then we had an exercise to go into a trance state to meet a guide. After reaching a relaxed state, I saw a few bright colours and then lavender, especially when Stephen asked us to move our consciousness behind us. I felt lots of energy and invited my guide to come as close as possible. Above my head I 'saw' a sort of blue hemisphere and later white water. Then Stephen said that we should see some large double doors with specific handles, and on opening them be in bright sunshine and on a path. The path passed by water and came to a hill, over which would come a guide who would greet us and place something in our hands. I came to the large wooden doors with twisted round metal rings as handles, and when I opened the doors I was in an ordinary house! This totally threw me, and although I tried to go back and try again I didn't succeed. In reviewing it afterwards, Stephen said that I should have gone into the house, as it was my subconscious.

In the next workshop Stephen commented on guides and healing, and included 'psychic surgery', both here and abroad. At the end of it he said that the important thing is "to attune each and every day, and be dedicated". Then put into pairs, we had an exercise where we would allow our guides to put their hands in ours, letting them take our hands where they will – but working on the etheric only. Even before my partner did anything, I felt energy going around me, starting it seemed with my hands. Then when putting her hands lightly on my shoulders, I saw both blue and lavender colours. Next the touch of her right hand disappeared, and I never felt it again until at the end, but I did think of a point at my back. She confirmed this when finished.

We changed positions. Later she remarked that it had felt as if she was in a bubble of energy. I got hotter and hotter as it went on! My right hand was placed at the base of her neck, and then with just the forefinger and thumb about 3 cm apart, went up and down near the spine. This changed after a while to using the whole hand flat, held horizontally. At the finish she said that she could understand why it was that area, and that she had received a sequence of images.

Following dinner we had our last session, starting with a talk on what we had done and the opportunity to ask questions. Then we did some distant healing, and lastly a group healing for one of the participants. A very good seminar and many well deserved expressions of thanks given to Stephen.

Less than three weeks later I was back again in the same place, but in the Lindum Hotel, for the last Lynwood seminar of the year. Christopher (Darren) Deojee was back with us again, giving a talk "A change in State" and two workshops, "Insight or Energy" and "Embodiment". It is hard to briefly encapsulate all that he does, but he emphasises the need to empower ourselves, to get back our self worth. This requires a mental reprogramming to get a change; also the need to re-connect with Mother Earth and to use our voice, and the need to be more aware on the use of language. I would recommend you going to hear him if you ever get the chance.

Alan Stuttle gave a demonstration of Spirit Art on the first day, showing different ways of doing it, and also on the next evening. His first workshop was stimulating, asking one woman to sit at the front; he quickly did a drawing of her head and shoulders. Then he asked us to come up, one at a time, choosing a colour to put on the portrait where we felt it appropriate.

After which we were then to tell the person what the colour represented to us and how it related to her. Next Alan put us in groups of two, and asked us to roughly draw the head of our partner, putting in the colours we felt or saw. We then explained to our partner what the colours represented and anything else that we might think about. My partner drew a tree and gave me information that I could take, and I'm glad to say that she could relate to what I told her.

My partner was the third tutor for the seminar, Moira Hawkins. Moira gave a brilliant Trance Demonstration on the first evening. The lighting was turned down slightly, but she was perfectly clear to see by all in the room. I could feel the energy building after a minute and then her breathing became slower and deeper, and within another minute a voice with a cultured accent was heard (later identified as 'Charles'). He talked about the positive and negative aspects of people's thoughts; that even those who are called 'spiritual' can send out negativity and it has a negative effect.

First, the positive aspect of Absent Healing - it works - even if not for a particular condition, then it will be for something else, perhaps even to help a passing. Prayers are positive and are done with love.

The negativity in your world has exactly the same effect. Much of the newspapers and other media, give out a poor attitude that breeds that negativity. We need more compassion, more empathy, to see behind the actions of people. Love is the same as healing, and it can have a great impact on their thinking. ("Love thy enemy" came to mind.) Also - your negativity has an impact on yourselves. You can only be offended if you allow that comment, for example, to have an impact on you. Do not judge; think how you might have upset other people by the comments you have made. Be more positive; positivity can change your life.

Then 'Charles' talked about the tree, how a mighty oak came from a tiny acorn, and the time it has taken. You choose the life you are living - you have done so before you came. Next there was the story of a medium and her son, who was born with a disability. The mother one day cried, "Why has it happened to me? Why is my son disabled, could I not have had a normal child?" Her mother was there and was shocked - and told her that it was disgraceful what she was saying. But think about how she was chosen to give this boy a good life and giving her an opportunity to show what her love could do! And the mother changed her attitude. We must send love to all.

Then it was open for any questions. 'L' asked about someone who had abused and hurt a child - could one really forgive? The answer was that it may indeed be difficult to forgive - but send the love so that person can change; that in itself may protect other children. Carol asked a long question, involving our ancestor's genes. It was answered by saying that we choose about this life - not about choosing other generations. This material life is for our and others experience in our own lifetime. Then he mentioned soul mates and reincarnation, and explained it by using an orange on a tree, in an orange grove with lots of other trees and oranges. There is No Family as such in spirit. [We are all one.]

'A' then brought up a past family incident. 'Charles' acknowledged how desperate a parent would feel; but still, that soul is now fine, in spirit it will have no pain. So negative thinking will only harm oneself. Then right at the end, "It isn't difficult to become aware of spirit around you - but only if you make it difficult! Open your heart". Lastly he said that simplicity is the key.

We all sat for trance in Moira's first workshop. I was relaxed and knew that spirit was there, but nothing came to me so I didn't speak. Apparently Moira did say my name quietly, hoping to prompt me, but I didn't hear her. She said that she also saw my lips move as if I was going to speak, but I wasn't aware of that either!

In the second workshop, with Christopher helping, Moira placed us in threes. The 'trance medium' sat in the middle while the other two sat on each side, but facing the other direction. Then Christopher led us in voicing six 'AUMs', the mediums only doing five and then speaking in trance or letting spirit inspire them. This time, when it was my turn to be the medium, I had decided to say "hello" or "good morning". This I did and went on to talk about humanity being spirit as well, but because of the material 'overcoat' we were all 'disabled', as we needed to work to learn our lessons and shine our 'diamond', etc. I'm sure there was some inspiration there from spirit.

It was another good weekend seminar, and that basically brings me up to the end of 2014, and where I wish to end of this part of the book.

Well, dear reader, if you have managed to plough your way through all these experiences, I congratulate you on your patience and perseverance, as I'm sure that you would have found areas that may not have been of great interest to you at the moment. However, it was important to try and give a 'rounded' idea of what has happened through the years. My focus is now on finishing this book, on continuing with the spiritual healing, on trying to develop the spirit art and getting closer links with those who help me, and to seek opportunities to develop any trance potential that I might have.

I hope it has set you thinking back on situations and experiences in your own life, and wondering if you yourself have had similar or more vivid incidents in your personal history. With an open mind, a desire and courage to find your own truth, I do hope you start to seek, and wish you well on your journey.

PART 2

INTERPRETATIONS

CHAPTER 17

A Few Basic Concepts

For some people, and it seems as if their numbers are increasing, the material world is all that there is. They believe that when they die, that is the total end to their existence. They see the diversity on this planet and in the rest of the universe as just a matter of luck, a unique combination of factors dependent on chemicals, heat, water, and so forth, which came about because of the 'Big Bang'. Humans have up to five senses, but at death these cease to function, just as the organs of the body cease – and that's it.

Because of my personal experiences – most of which you may have read about in 'Part 1' – I can **never** subscribe to that view because I **know** that it is not true. At death the body does die, the brain, lungs, heart and all else that is material stop functioning and will start to decay. However, our minds still exist and will continue to exist for eternity. I remind you of what I wrote in Chapter 1, when as a young child I felt surrounded with love and was, without sound, told that I had a guardian and was loved. That was not childish imagination; it was my first known and natural contact with 'spirit'. Spirit communicated with me through my mind, and despite what some traditional scientists might say, the mind is a spirit 'vehicle' that interacts with the material body. At death, it returns to its proper place – from whence it came – in the vast realm of spirit.

However, at this point I don't want to belabour that fact, but rather give certain basic concepts. You don't have to believe in these, but in order to understand what I see as factual and to make sense of what I write about my experiences and their interpretation, I ask you to take them on-board for the moment. Later you may come to your own ideas about these, accepting or rejecting as you see fit.

1. The spiritual universe (or universes) is eternal, where we came from and where we will return. From this spiritual universe the material universe (or universes) was created; this is in constant change, with death and birth of planets, stars and galaxies. So too humanity, which has its origins in the spiritual universe and where it will return, as it is eternal.
   Not so the body, which is only a vehicle for use in the material universe, and like the material universe is subject to death and decay.

2. Spirit (spiritual universe/sphere etc.) is everywhere. Even in this material body that we use on planet Earth spirit is present. The physical body is 'denser' and has a lower 'vibration' than anything in spirit, which means that spirit interpenetrates the material. I'm not a scientist, so can only interpret things in my own way, so I hope you will excuse any wrong use of terminology, just as long as you get an understanding of what I'm trying to explain.

These two basic concepts are the heart of the matter and all else follows from them. Some of you at this stage may be asking yourselves what exactly does he mean by 'spirit'? To start to answer that question one first must realise that it is not personalised, i.e. it is not **a** or **the** spirit, but just spirit. This in itself suggests a collective principle of some kind. If one looks up the word 'spirit' in any dictionary, thesaurus or encyclopedia etc., one will come across very similar words and ideas in all of them. The list will include: **vital principle**, the **soul**, the **non physical part** of a person, psyche, the principle of **thought**, **mind**, inner self, the area of the emotions, character, phantom, ghost, apparition, disembodied soul, supernatural being, etc.

For the moment we shall leave aside all to do with 'ghosts', and concentrate on what I've put in bold type. We can see that in addition to being something that is essential for life, spirit is related to thought and the soul, **and** it is regarded to survive death of the body. This last point needs a little comment. Is your nose **you**? Is your toe **you**? Is your backside **you**? Is your body **you** or are **you** just using it for the purpose of this material life? I would hold to the latter. At what we call death the material body dies but the **you** continues in a different world of vibration. We have the body in order that we can fully function in this world, to learn the lessons that we need to learn in order to progress and evolve in our true universes of the spirit. Our bodies are like robots, programmed to follow the instructions from our mind. They are like machines, even though highly specialised and intricate, and can only function here on the material world and in the material universe.

So what about thought and the soul? The brain is part of our material body so cannot function after death. This is what causes the most difficulty with many people, who cannot then believe that you can survive death. But as I said before, you are NOT your body. The mind uses the brain, not the other way around! Your mind gives you awareness of yourself and the world around you, but it also is a channel for information to and from spirit. After death it continues as – like spirit – it is immortal.

Similarly, the soul is regarded as immortal, as the non-material part of **you**, associated with the emotional and moral nature, that which gives **you** a sense of identity. One can see that mind and soul are basically the same, though some would argue that the soul is an individualisation of spirit that creates individual personality. Whatever the differences (though I don't believe there are any), the fact is that both mind or/and soul are the parts of **you** that survive death.

So if spirit involves the mind and the soul, then it must be present both in the material world and in what comes after the death of the material body. People talk about 'passing over' to the spirit world. Essentially what is happening is that the spirit part of **you** is released from the material body to return to its natural environment – that is the world of spirit. It is the breaking of the silver cord, which has held the link between the material body and the spirit body – sometimes referred to as the etheric body. In fact there are said to be other bodies of the spirit, such as emotional and mental, which along with the etheric are called subtle bodies and help make up the aura that totally surrounds the human body. These subtle bodies are interconnected with each other and the material body until released by the death of the latter.

It is reputed that the silver cord enables the real **you** to travel during the sleep state to different parts of the material world, as well as going to the astral plane where **you** can meet family and friends who have already 'died', thus demonstrating that death is merely a transformation from one vibration to another. There is also a connection here with OBEs (out of body experiences) and NDEs (near death experiences). I have never had a NDE, but an OBE would explain the incident that I reported in Chapter 4, where my girlfriend at the time saw a naked image of me standing at the bottom of my bed. Although I had no awareness at the time of being out of my body, it could answer why it unnerved her so much.

Incidentally, that energy field around us called the aura (shaped similar to an egg) picks up sensations that we receive subconsciously, that is where we can enter a room and immediately get a positive or negative reaction to it. The same can happen when we meet people, as I described on the second page of Chapter 4; the vibration that I picked up from the boy somehow did not harmonise with mine, but I was able to overcome that.

Going back to where I started to write about spirit, spirit is present everywhere, in every part of the material and non-material universes. Wherever there is life, it is only life because of spirit. Wherever we think there is no life or nothing, even there too is spirit. Spirit is infinite and eternal and encompasses everything and everybody. Therefore all of humanity is linked by being a part of spirit – **we are all one**. [That also includes all animal, vegetable and mineral matter.]

If you think that is quite a bit to take in, I can add another bit for you to think about! All the phrases and words that can be used to describe God can also be used to describe spirit. Spirit is love, love is God, God is spirit and spirit is life. Spirit expresses itself throughout every universe and every facet of creation – and that also includes you. Through the natural law of spirit you (and I) progress and evolve ever closer towards that light of perfection, slowly shredding the dross of imperfections by service to others and increasing our knowledge of spirit.

Those who have already experienced an Earth existence may try to help or communicate with those still in their material life. This is natural – after all both are spirit – but there are various factors that help or hinder the ability to do this. The most important factor is that we have an independent life to lead on this planet and so 'the other side' cannot intrude to any huge extent. Our lives would serve no purpose if we were constantly told what to think and what decisions to make. In the next few chapters I wish to touch on some of the ways spirit do link in with us, though ultimately what we do is our own responsibility, we can't blame anybody else!

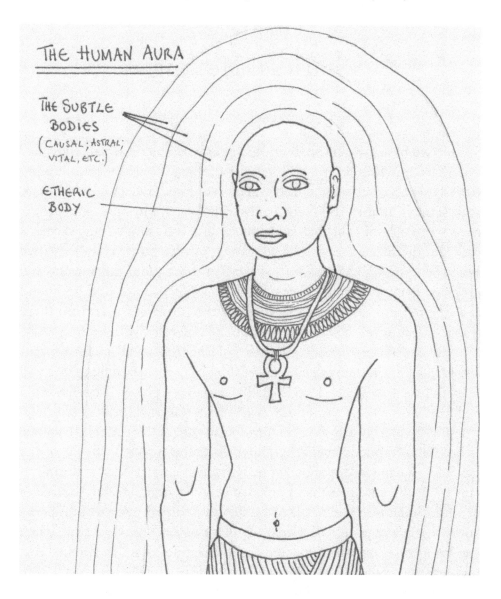

THE HUMAN AURA

THE SUBTLE
BODIES
(CAUSAL; ASTRAL;
VITAL, ETC.)

ETHERIC
BODY

CHAPTER 18

Spiritual Healing

Spirit have basic rules in their engagement with the incarnate, they may not interfere with our free will. However, they can give aid and healing where it is necessary, where it has been requested, where it does not go against our plan for this life, or against our karma. I'm sure some people have written books on that last subject, but very simply put, karma is basically the balance as it were, between all the positive and negative actions and thoughts that we have accrued throughout this life and any previous lives. It may be necessary in this life that we have to attend to some negative aspect and so increase the positive. Apart from these restrictions, spirit is always willing to help, especially with healing work.

Just as we have someone – a spirit 'guide' or 'guardian' – who oversees our life, so do those involved with healing have their healing guides and helpers in spirit. When I say that, I mean every person who has truly dedicated themselves to healing work of any kind will have spirit help, whether they are aware of it or not, and many are not! I would love to hear an account of someone with the ability to see spirit, saying what he or she saw while having an out of body experience in a surgical theatre during an operation. I'm sure that the number of people (incarnate and discarnate) involved would be high, at least double the normal material number! I know that many people have told me that I have a monk with me when I'm being a healing medium, and various mediums have mentioned that my maternal grandfather helps me in that respect. This latter disclosure does not surprise me at all, knowing that he was interested in Spiritualism in his material life, it would be more than natural that he would want to act and help others here.

Spiritual healing is not necessarily an alternative to allopathic medicine; indeed, in my life I owe much to conventional surgery and drugs that have enabled me to live – without them I would have died. Spiritual healing is complementary to any other form of healing, and certainly has no negative side effects, so is completely safe to use. It is particularly useful to use in conjunction with 'ordinary' medicine. A friend of mine, who did her final spiritual healing training course with me in 1996, developed cancer later in her life. At that time the particular cancer gave a life expectancy of about three years, and my friend was very sensitive to drugs and their side effects. With the help of spiritual healing and homeopathy, she was able to withstand the various drug treatments and survived at least another twelve or thirteen years, long enough to see and come to know her first grandchildren.

I often liken a healing medium to an electric cable, with the 'patient' being the appliance (toaster, kettle or iron, etc.!). The healing energy from spirit is the electricity, which enables the appliance to function with the help of the cable. When I've been asked by someone to help them with a problem, usually an illness or an injury, I first explain to them what I'll be doing and see if that is agreeable. Then I tune in to my healing helpers in spirit and also with the person, and ask that I may be used as an instrument to help the person receive healing from spirit that is right for them at this time. Using my hands away from the body, I next check the main chakras and 'scan' the rest of the person, concentrating on specific areas that I'm drawn to or sense are lacking vitality.

There are many chakras around the body, but the major ones are seven in number, as shown in the diagram below. The word chakra comes from the Sanskrit cakra meaning wheel or circle, and is used to describe these spinning vortexes of energy. These main chakras are related to the body's endocrine system and major organs, as well as having different colours associated with them, as in the table given below. (Main source of information from the NFSH, The Healing Trust.)

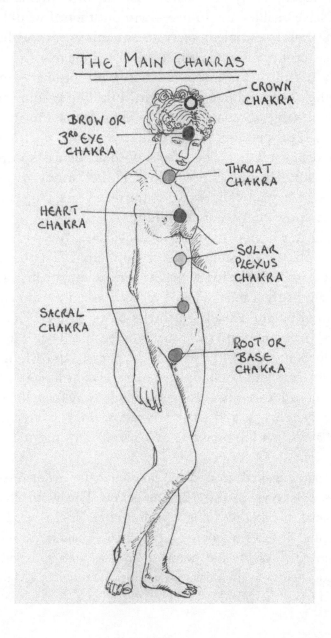

Chakra	Location	Colour	Linked to	Concerned with
Base or root	Bottom of spine.	Red	Adrenal glands, kidneys, spinal column, hips, legs, rectum.	Courage, security, confidence, individuality.
Sacral or abdominal	Just below the navel.	Orange	Ovaries, uterus, testes, prostate and lower back	Creativity, intimacy, pleasure and sexuality.
Solar plexus	Below where the ribs meet.	Yellow	Pancreas, liver, gallbladder, stomach, small intestine.	Strong emotions, self worth, personal power.
Heart	Centre of breastbone	Green	Thymus, heart, chest, lungs, arms, upper back, circulatory system.	Love, harmony, compassion, trust, hope, forgiveness and acceptance.
Throat	Throat	Blue	Thyroid and parathyroid, neck, throat, mouth, teeth and gums.	Communication and all creative self-expression.
3rd Eye or brow	Middle of forehead, between the eyebrows	Indigo	Hypothalamus and pituitary glands, brain, eyes, ears, face.	Intuition, insight, wisdom and innate knowledge.
Crown	Top of head	Violet	Pineal gland, cerebral cortex.	Spirituality, enlightenment, link with higher self and spirit.

It is helpful if the person is comfortable and relaxed during the healing session, which may last from twenty to forty minutes, or more, depending on the circumstances. During this time the person may experience a wide range of feelings and/or images etc., there is no particular set pattern, but often they report feeling changes in temperature, pins and needles, sensations on the skin or specific areas in the body, or seeing in their mind pleasant images or colours.

What follows are selections taken from my notes on the healing sessions that involved one person over a period of five years, until shortly before she passed back to spirit. My observations are in normal type; hers are in italics:

Felt a 'burning' sensation in my left hand when it was at her left shoulder – at the back, midway between spine and arm… also a sort of pulse or wave sensation at her solar plexus. *Said it was a lovely session. She had 'gone off' and went swimming.*

A slight 'rippling' effect on my hands at her left shoulder. *She had felt as if somebody had clasped her arm, but she knew I was working at her right leg at the time.*

Said that she was very relaxed – had felt she was levitating at one point. She also saw a nun – from long ago, maybe 16th century or earlier. Had pins and needles in her left hand and upper arm.

As I was working on the 3rd eye chakra I felt as if somebody was right behind me. I again felt a physical presence – this time with my hand – my left thumb for a moment felt it had met something solid, but nothing was there.

Felt something similar to magnets of the same poles being forced together – a lot of force and 'slipping and sliding' quickly interspersed. *Said it felt good.*

Felt some new and unusual energies this time. The energy reached 4 to 5 inches up my lower left arm from the wrist. It sort of tickled a bit! It was there for most of the session.

Liked it and had been very 'floaty'. Odd things came to her – her father's shirt that she sometimes ironed, and she saw golden rings/vortex coming towards her, plus a blue pulse, a bit like a jellyfish!

Said she usually sees a golden/orangey ball of light surrounded by purple – then lots of other things came.

She had got so much she couldn't remember it all. Several images to do with pyramids, bushmen, girl cycling etc. Had felt a cool breeze on her right side.

Got an 'odd' feeling at the ends of my fingers. Suddenly got a burst of feeling in my left hand at the lower back. *Said it was very different, as instead of 'going away' all her senses were heightened. She could hear everything quite clearly, the music, clock, birds in garden, my stomach, but at the same time very relaxed and calm. She got golden purple, and a voice saying that she needed to do meditation. She also saw a small image of the goddess Hathor in the golden purple, and an Egyptian head. Also saw a person she hasn't seen for over 40 years.*

Felt as if I had touched her leg with my right hand – but saw my hand was well away! *Said she felt quite relaxed and had felt there had been somebody with her.*

Felt a 'dullness' across her upper back/shoulders, and got a sensation in my left thumb at her right elbow. Also got a reaction at her left foot… I got a funny sensation in my left neck, so went to that position on her and felt a sensation in my left fingers – a bit like coldness when a wind is blowing – but just in the area between the fingers! Strange! *Had some pins and needles down her left shoulder and side – but said that she couldn't feel her arm at all, as if it wasn't there! She also said that she felt a rubbing on her left thumb. She thought that it might be me, in fact she had a quick look, but I was over the other side! Said she felt this rubbing quite a few times and it was quite strong.*

Said she had experienced a lot of light, also thought that I had put my hand on her upper chest/lower neck area, when she looked I was down at her feet.

Said she felt that someone had hold of her left elbow and was supporting it during most of the session, and even asked if I had tried contact healing. Also felt that there was someone with her and that she saw/sensed a face.

I got a little sharp pain on my right side, just at the bottom of the rib cage, when I stepped up behind her to begin the session. *She saw an Elizabethan lady's collar, and had a burning sensation all over her face.*

Picked up a sensation at the throat chakra as I was opening up. *Said she feels that she needs to let go of a lot of emotion.*

I got a sore 'dull' ache in my back, below the shoulder on my right. *She said that earlier in the week she had a sore point in that area, but it had diminished now.*

Got a bit of tingling in the fingers of my left hand at her left elbow, and a sensation a little like pins and needles in both hands when at her left ankle and knee. But lots of energy – lots of healing helpers. *Said she was very relaxed, 'floaty', and had seen a v shape of white light at the start (into her 3rd eye) with turquoise 'bombs' coming down it!*

I got a strange feeling in my left fingers – just at the ends, going into and under the fingernails. This stayed for some time. *She said she felt quite relaxed.*

At the last healing session that I had with her she said she had felt her mother with her, also spirit S.A. was there and held her hands, also her guardian spirit and other guides. It is more often the case that near the time of death spirits will come to reassure and help the person, and I'm sure that spiritual healing can bring aid and assistance to this process of 'rebirth' into spirit.

It is interesting to note the wide variation in her experience during the healing sessions; each one can be very different. Also, it can be pointed out that the healing medium can have different sensations; some will indicate where on the person to give special attention, but other feelings I have been unable to interpret. It should also be stated here that 99% of the time I work with a hands-off procedure. The only time I touch the person is at the start where I 'tune in' (attunement), by placing my hands lightly on their shoulders, or where a hands-on approach has been prompted by the person, or rarely, by spirit; on **all** these occasions it has been with the permission of the person concerned. In the above notes on some healing sessions, it will be seen that the person had occasionally thought that I had placed my hands on her, only to see that it had not been me as I was on her other side etc. However, that does not necessarily mean that her feelings were false, indeed healing spirits may well make themselves known to give comfort and encouragement. Equally, I also felt on quite a few sessions (and sessions involving many other people) that I had touched somebody – they had felt that solid – but it was not through any mistake of mine in touching the person. So I can only conclude that some spirit was closer to the person than my hands, at times even with their hands in front of mine. Additionally that may have been a reassurance to me that spirit were there working beside me – or even in front of me!

The form of spiritual healing is a personal choice, and I don't think it makes a significant difference in the actual healing energies as to whether one uses the hands-on or hands-off approach. Through the millennia, from Jesus to Harry Edwards and some modern spiritual healers today, the hands-on approach has been the natural choice. Indeed, many people find it much more reassuring and comforting. However, I was taught the hands-off method, and in our present culture and society where litigation is often the order of the day, I consciously chose to work that way, so that the healing energies are directed through the etheric layer to the physical body.

Not all healing mediums can physically get to the people who ask for help, nor may the people themselves be able to travel to the medium, or be able to travel at all in some cases. Under these circumstances what is called Distant Healing (or absent healing) is used. Those of you of a religious nature will understand this form of healing as very similar to what is called prayer. I have a 'Healing Book' into which I put the names of those persons who require healing (of whatever nature), and twice a week I specifically sit quietly and ask spirit to help them in their need. It is the 'thought' that matters. I think it was Ramadahn, the spirit that spoke through the mediumship of Ursula Roberts, who said that the healers in spirit followed the thought to the person. So it doesn't matter where the person may be or how far away in distance these people are, the appropriate healing will be given.

Before I finish this section, I have to comment on the results of spiritual healing. There is no guarantee at all that any physical recovery from injury or disease will happen, as that depends whether the healing is 'allowed' by those in spirit (remembering the bit I wrote about karma and the life plan). Unfortunately, there are some rare cases where the person requesting healing actually doesn't want any recovery! They may feel that they like the attention and concern of others over getting better. There are occasions when the healing may be dramatic in character, but more often it is steady progress. It can happen that spiritual healing can bring improvements to psychological conditions, or for those suffering pain, and can have a beneficial effect by improving the attitude of the person. I think that this last point is a most important one. Many come with a depressed or negative attitude to their problem, and it is wonderful when one sees a change to a positive and optimistic outlook. The body is an amazing instrument, usually capable of healing itself in time, but at a low point spiritual healing can give that little extra boost to help the body's own natural healing ability. However, the **true** benefit of spiritual healing is when it changes people's minds. Healing of the material body is an added bonus, but when the mind or soul has been touched then that person has begun a new journey. For the cynic, all I can say is that at the very least it gives a good night's sleep!

CHAPTER 19
Spirit Influence

When I was learning history and science at school, I was struck how similar events or ideas could be found close in time to each other in different countries, some quite far from each other. I can recollect being among a small group of boys as they argued about which person first invented the steam locomotive. One said that it had been George Stephenson; another suggested it had been somebody in France, while a third said it had been Richard Trevithick. I wondered if there had been some sort of knowledge 'in the air', that could only be picked up by certain individuals.

Many, many years later, a friend let me borrow a book written by an archeologist called T.C. Lethbridge, in which he put forward ideas about fields of electro-magnetic energy that I found interesting. Today modern scientists are conducting experiments that are pushing at the frontiers of knowledge, though they face fierce opposition from those closed minds who refuse to deviate from the traditional materialistic dogmas. [I think you might pick up a little bit of prejudice from me here, due to the history of prejudice from much of the scientific community over the last 150 plus years] However, *real* scientists who investigate with **open minds** are beginning to capture the attention of ordinary people. Dr. Rupert Sheldrake is one example in the UK, who has written about 'morphic fields', and many others, especially in the USA and Europe, are exploring quantum theories that seem to have resonance with ideas about spirit. Notwithstanding these exciting developments, I am not a scientist and have difficulty understanding them fully, so can only put forward my own very simple and perhaps limited explanations. [For those with a more scientific interest in these matters, I suggest a look at "**Spirit of the New Millennium**: The Ultimate Theory" by Frank Newman, ISBN: 0-9532053-1-2.]

Spirit has gently helped and guided humanity, 'dropping' little nuggets of inspiration and knowledge in every sphere of life. I dare say that Archimedes, as he relaxed in his bath, suddenly had an unexpected idea 'pop' into his mind; result 'eureka' – and as they say, the rest is history. Many of the 'greats' in our history have acknowledged inspiration after a daydream or nights sleep, including famous poets. I do not in any way class myself as 'great', certainly not in connection to poetry, but the incident that I mention in the first chapter is one trivial example. Spirit, though my subconscious, 'fed' that poem to me, and I think back to how pleased I was with myself for coming up with it! In this case it was to help me understand the ability of spirit much later in life, but with others it can result with helping the whole of humanity.

The bereaved can sometimes get a sense of the presence of a loved one through a scent (perfume, flowers, tobacco etc.), through something having moved (picture, photograph, object), through a sign (white feather, etc.), through the lights flashing, through radio or television being suddenly switched on, or just sensing a physical presence. There is no limit to what some will and can do to let us know that they are still alive. However, for most of us, we need the services of another person to make a connection, those who are able to link in with spirit, the people that we call mediums (or sensitives).

They will normally have ability in two or three of the following areas: clairaudience (clear hearing), clairvoyant (clear seeing) and clairsentience (clear feeling). I have never experienced clairaudience, but have at times had occurrences of clairvoyance, but usually it has been of limited duration, as you will have read in several instances in Part 1. In chapter eleven I've written about being at the Arthur Findlay College, and in a particular exercise saw branches of a tree, an image that I saw for only a second or so. Another person, with far greater attunement to spirit, may have held that image for longer and been able to recognise the particular type of tree involved and even seen other things in the background. That is the difference between a beginner like myself and one who has a greater rapport with spirit. That person will have worked out feelings, colours, symbolic images and so forth with spirit helpers to enable them to give out correct details. I remember being told by Doris that one medium, who had been a postman, got his guide to present him with the picture of a letter, so that the name of the relation in spirit and where they had lived was written on the envelope!

What can be seen here is that the whole exercise of mediumship is a team effort. It starts with the friend or relative in spirit who works with the spirit 'guide', who works with the material 'medium', who delivers the 'message' to the incarnate recipient. One can appreciate that through that 'chain of command' errors can creep in. Some people seem to think that the whole process is straightforward and easy – it is not! Many 'things' can go wrong, or are misinterpreted, or the harmony or energy could be lacking. That is why spirit informs us that every exchange between spirit and those on Earth is an experiment. The fact that it can work at all is marvelous.

Most of my interactions with spirit come through clairsentience. This is best described by the words 'sensing' or 'feeling', and can be very ephemeral or nebulous. One senses a person or setting, but in a mediumship situation it is important not to think about it, rather just say it, just give it out. If one does this then other feelings will follow on. However, if you stop to think about it, maybe asking yourself if that is from you rather than from spirit, then you interrupt the flow and will very likely come to a halt. We have to come to trust those in spirit that work with us, or who try to do so!

Another form of interaction is called physical mediumship. This can give incredible evidence of life after death. However, it is often viewed with great scepticism by many, despite most mediums submitting themselves to certain uncomfortable measures to prove that they are immobile. Indeed, one has to remember that this form of mediumship is potentially dangerous for the medium. In the past many have suffered great injury and have even died as a result, usually through the ignorant actions of unbelievers and those wishing to 'expose' what they can only think of as fraudulent behaviour. Alec Harris is one such medium that suffered from such an 'attack' and so did Helen Duncan, who finally died from her injuries. As a consequence of this, the numbers of physical circles are very limited and some are extremely cautious in letting those outside the circle temporarily into their group.

The physical medium is more capable than most in being able to allow spirit to form 'ectoplasm'. This is a substance that spirit is able to manufacture from the medium, others in the circle, and even from clothing or fabrics in the room. It is a viscous substance that is extruded usually from the medium's mouth, solar plexus or ear, and can be fashioned by spirit to form rods of great strength and hardness to sheets of soft 'cloth'. It is extremely sensitive to bright light, and herein lies the danger. Any sudden unexpected exposure to such light will result in the immediate and rapid withdrawal of the ectoplasm back into the medium's body and certain injury.

Because of that sensitivity, most physical circles usually start with complete darkness, allowing red or other light only at the command of spirit, who oversee the progress. Physical mediumship has occurred in natural light, and some physical circles today are working towards having greater light so that all participants can see everyone taking part. However, the last word must be with the medium and what his or her spirit helpers are agreed on.

Through the use of ectoplasm, spirit can give a full or partial materialization of a relative or friend. They can also move objects in the room, like the fantastic display of the trumpets that I saw through Stewart Alexander's mediumship in 1995. They can play musical instruments, levitate people, and among other things introduce apports. An apport is where an object (such as crystals, old coins, worthless jewellery, flowers etc.) are deposited in the circle or to a person from somewhere outside the room. Some other aspects of physical mediumship are table work or table tilting, that I referred to in Chapter 10 with Jean Duncan in Hafan-y-Coed, where Jean Skinner also demonstrated transfiguration.

Going back to apports, which I've written about in the reverse – where spirit has taken away an object, such as the key that I mentioned in Chapter 15. In cases like this one always first thinks of a logical explanation. People often forget where they put things, and this is not unusual as one gets older and maybe a little more forgetful. I fully admit that I sometimes can't find items, especially if they are important as I put them in a 'safe' place, and then forget where that safe place is! However, in case of these keys there was only ever one place where I kept them, and they were together on one key ring. I looked carefully, several times, where it should have been, so I am certain that it was not there. When it did eventually return, it was to that same place but not on the key ring with the other key. So if anybody has had an apport of a key around the end of July 2013, that then disappeared later – it could have been mine! Incidentally, this is often a feature of apports; the object does not always stay with the new 'owner' but can go back, sometimes very quickly but also maybe after many years.

When all the conditions are 'suitable' physical mediumship can be stunning, but then so can mental mediumship. If you go for a private sitting with a medium whose information is over 70% correct, then things have gone very well, but don't expect perfection every time. It should be remembered that the greater the trance state, or the better that the medium is attuned to spirit, the less of the medium's own personality will affect the evidence.

There are other examples of mental mediumship. One is Automatic Writing, where the medium is inspired by spirit to write philosophy or poetry. With excellent attunement and conditions, this can give different languages and information outside the natural knowledge of the medium, and even borders on the physical with spirit in complete control of the writing implement.

In the same way, another is Spirit or Psychic Art. The main exponents of this in the past were Coral Polge (died 2001) and perhaps the greatest in this field, Frank Leah (died 1972). My experiences in this area are very much as a beginner, as related in Chapter 13, where I was attending the ISF week in St Andrews, and the subsequent message in the circle from my spirit helper Ramos. In addition, at another ISF week (this time in Eastbourne, as written about in Chapter 16) where I also added a few photographs of the artwork. After that latter event, I started sitting about once a week on my own to try to bring through spirit inspired artwork. The following pages show 25 examples. If any of them makes some connection with you please get in touch, but do remember that I am a beginner and find sensing the information regarding the image particularly difficult, so do allow for that.

Eventually it emerged as a RAF mechanic that died of an illness in his late 20s. Got the date 1982, but not sure if that was the year that he died or was when he was born.

Thought somebody of Scandinavian background, possibly Finnish. Nice personality, sociable, generous nature and happy, optimistic outlook. Died with a relatively 'sudden' illness maybe connected to the pancreas and died within six months. Would only have been about 20 or even slightly younger.

Neatly dressed pensioner, probably born in the late 1930s and died around the age of 70. Liked order, the big band music of the 1940s and 1950s and had a collection of old vinyl records, tidy, spent a lot of time in his garden. There may have been some connection with the Civil Service.

Possibly wore spectacles for reading, was a family orientated person, who was kind and caring. Passed in her late 40s or her 50s. Feel she died through a drawn out illness over several years, maybe involving liver or kidneys. Felt that July would be a significant month, either for a birthday or for her passing.

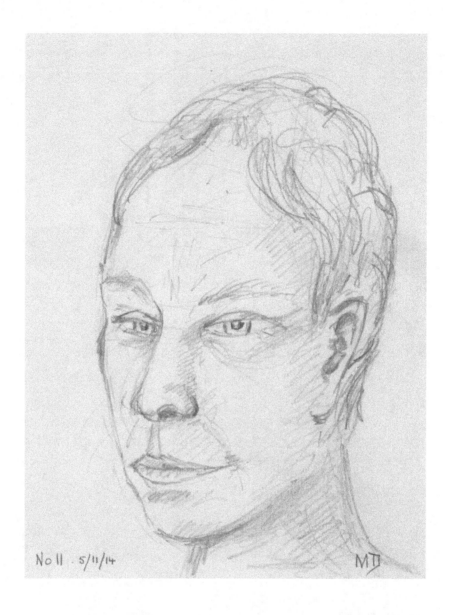

No 11 . 5/11/14   MD

Creative, could have done art, maybe an actor but his passion was for dance. Expressive, emotional with a quick tongue, not afraid to voice his opinions. Intellectual, perceptive, slightly aloof at times, but could be affectionate, caring and helpful. Feel he died in his 50s, possibly though HIV. There is a Spanish connection and he would have had at least one sister. At the end the name 'Kenneth' came to me.

He would have died in his early 20s, very quickly, maybe in an explosion and I had an idea that it was in Afghanistan. Felt he was in 'special forces' or a special job like reconnaissance or a sniper. Face much younger, so feel that the face would be very similar to a photograph that someone in the family would have. Last thought I had was to put in a poppy.

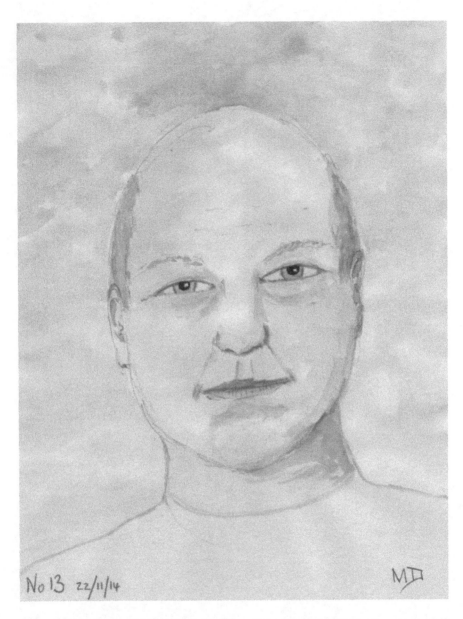

No 13 22/11/14   MD

Immediately thought he was English, well built, around 6' 3" or even taller. He loved the outdoors, would have played sports like golf, and maybe rugby when younger. Confident and easy-going, sociable and helpful, but determined once his mind was made up. Good family man with a wife, two children and a pet dog, and may have driven a 4x4. Thought that he died from a heart attack around the age of 60, earlier in 2014 or in 2013.

No 14
25/11/14

May have wandered on the wrong side of the law occasionally. Neatly dressed, had many acquaintances but very few close friends. Loved horse racing, intelligent, sharp-eyed, he took everything in. Could keep a secret and his mouth closed, never gave much away, but quite charming when he wanted to be. Feel he died in, or as a result of a car accident around the late fifties age range.

No 16
8/12/14

A young woman who took part in a ceremony, like a 'Festival of Light' around Christmas/New Year period. Candle indicates this, but would have worn a delicate 'cap' structure with 'gems' that sparkled in the light. Profile shows distinctive ear shape and a star earring, latter connected to 'festival' and/or suggestive of her 'spiritual' name. The pale turquoise blue background may have been her favourite colour, and I sensed that it could connect with her death, that may have been by drowning.

Sensitive individual who thought quite a bit about religion/philosophy and 'life' in general. Would have died at a much older age than image suggests. He 'dropped-out', isolating himself from family and friends by moving elsewhere, around the 1980s; the image would reflect how he looked at that time. A peaceful and compassionate man who felt himself out of place in the increasingly materialistic world.

Got the word 'Ty' and thought it was her name, but could be her nationality – Thai. Background water is the sea or a very wide river. Felt she was poor and had a simple life, and that she died shortly after giving birth to her child, perhaps due to blood poisoning. Sensed that her death was around 2008/2009.

No 19
10/1/2015
MD

Felt this woman died about 67 to 70 years old, but shows herself at her 'best time in life', 1960s or early 1970s. Wearing chic camel hair coat, enjoyed motor racing and the style at that time – Mary Quant, Op art, Biba Boutique, films with Audrey Hepburn, etc. Her interest in fashion could have led to modeling and involvement with clothing later on. Lastly, felt there was a French connection somewhere, or it could be in her name – like Frances?

The very large woollen hat (mixed colours) came first. My thoughts were going to Tibet or Nepal and that could be where he died, but not recently. A mountaineer, so could have died through an accident, but I did feel that there was some underlying health problem with him at the time. This could have contributed to his death – maybe he pushed himself further than was sensible.

Long faced gentleman with large nose, wore bifocals, taller than average, unkempt hair – would have a mannerism of running his hand though it when concentrating. Intelligent, well read and worked in the literary area, writer, editor or reporter; took his work seriously. Also sociable, very witty and humorous. Felt that he died very recently indeed, within 3 weeks maybe, and it was connected to his leg or legs. Got the letter Q to his name, maybe like Quinten, Quincy or Quinn.

Nordic woman, perhaps Danish, with her son. An artist, teacher, interested in her clothing and colours, also worked with stained glass. Brought up her son by herself so worked hard, instilled in him a love of nature and the outdoors. Could have died in the early part of this century maybe through illness. Lastly I was impressed to colour a small triangle piece silver directly above the boy's head. I see this as symbolic of her keeping a close contact with him from spirit.

The spectacles came first, but after colouring them pink felt I didn't need to add any more colour. Jewish, bright and intellectual, had a good memory. Died very suddenly, would be in the last 10 years, at a young age, in early 20s while still studying at university, where he may have been interested in astronomy and/or physics. The colour in the spectacles could signify eye problems, and maybe reading problems in his youth. Got John Lennon in my head, maybe he liked his music.

Got the word Tyrol so thought of Austria. Died in her 70s, would have been a keen walker and liked nature, enjoyed where she lived. Would have been very active, especially in her 20s/30s, with skiing etc. Felt she would have had only one offspring, have been a loving mother, but also quite a disciplinarian when she thought it necessary. At the end got the idea that this image would be for a grandchild or other family member rather than for her child to connect with.

Old man with a misshapen but favourite hat, would have spent as much time outdoors as he could, walking, fishing and enjoying wildlife and nature. Died in his 70s or 80s. Would have worked with his hands, maybe engineer or mechanic, liked to fix things himself. Could have carved wood or made small models for grandchildren. Self-effacing and a quiet man of great integrity. Possibly linked to the USA.

Definite Edwardian feeling, around late 1800s or early 1900s. I had the sensation of being confined by the clothing, lots of starch and few frills. Smart but plain clothing, practical, especially for her job as a governess to three children. Intelligent individual, the name 'Bowen' came to me, and thought her first name began with 'E'. Had brown hair and a light complexion.

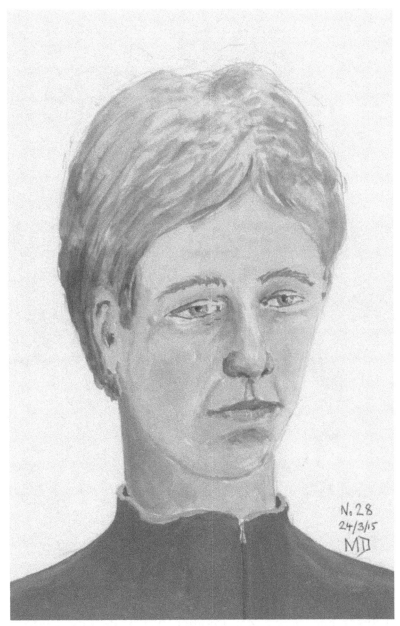

A tallish individual who had a serious side to his personality, concerned with what was happening in the world, yet convivial in social situations. Died very recently this year, in his late 20s or in his 30s. Athletic, may have pursued one or two sports, liked music and reading, and could have been a teacher. Didn't feel that he was British, but European, perhaps German.

Sensed this woman was a grandmother in her 70s, full of humour and laughter. Had learnt to look on the bright side of life due to difficult times when young. Had 3 or 4 children, but also at least one miscarriage. Possibly died of a heart condition. Generous with her love, liked music, singing and dancing. Seemed to have loads of energy, would have been much loved by family and neighbours. Got the name 'Elsie' right at the end.

Clergyman, probably Anglican, intellectual type who delved into aspects of history and theology fairly deeply, but may have also had an interest in healing. Good company with a very good sense of humour. Had prominent hairy eyebrows, wearing bifocals and a tweed jacket. Died in his 60s, possibly 70s; the yellow in his face suggests jaundice, and may indicate the medical problems that led to his passing.

No 31
14/4/15
MD

Sociable person who was a tomboy when young and remained active in her adult life. Lively and engaging personality, full of laughter, but this could also mask a sensitive side, especially on the emotional level. The close-cropped hair indicated that she joined the armed services, probably the army. Born in the 1970s, I sensed she died in the first decade of this century in her 30s – very unexpectedly and sudden.

Started with black pen and got the profile of a youthful farmer. He would often push his cap back up his head so that his dark hair would stick out. A hill farmer, who is happy and full of optimism and his plans for the future.

Then I stopped, and felt I should turn the page over. Uncertain about this I changed to pencil, and turned the page over…

... and a face emerged looking directly at me. The same person much older, more careworn, though still able to smile on occasions. Gradually he became disillusioned by the lack of understanding by society and officialdom, despite being hard working and dedicated. Sensed he died in late 60s/early 70s. He became ill, but it was as if he just gave up and didn't fight it, just very tired and ready to go.

A very youthful looking gentleman who probably passed in his early 60s. Businessman, who worked in a management role. Didn't have many outside interests as work his main preoccupation. Family man with a sense of humour, may have liked to watch cricket, usually on TV. Got the letter 'P', either first name or surname. Would have had a wide circle of acquaintances and I felt that he was probably English.

CHAPTER 20

Bits and Pieces

This is not a book where I am able, or it is appropriate, to include a comprehensive 'dictionary' to everything that might come under the terms Spiritualism, psychic phenomena, etc. Nevertheless, there are a few more items that I think need to be mentioned, if not fully explained in detail, or where I feel the need to expand on what has been touched on before.

First of all I would like to remind you of something I wrote in Chapter 10, when I saw a demonstration of trance by a couple of people while on a course at Hafan-y-Coed in July 2002. I wrote that, when several of the participants of this course were speaking while in trance, there was a light flashing on and off, just as if there was a light bulb inside their throat area. Now, often there are various pieces of evidence or phenomena that can be described as objective or subjective. In this particular case if what I'd seen had also been witnessed by the rest of the onlookers, then it would have been objective evidence, able to be confirmed by everybody. However, only I saw it, so it is subjective evidence. **Exactly** how spirit managed to do this I can't say, but would imagine it was carefully planned. That alone shows to what lengths spirit will go to help people who are genuinely interested in these matters. In addition, these sorts of occurrences usually happen when one least expects them, which makes the surprise even greater!

In Chapter 8 I touched on 'saving lost souls' or 'rescue circles', mainly when I attended day sessions with Doris. There are some (including a few mediums and tutors of repute) who say no soul is ever 'lost' and therefore they are in no need of 'rescue'. However, I would say to them that in my humble experience **it has always been spirit who has initiated such**

276

exercises. Why would spirit ask us to participate in this sort of assignment if it was unnecessary? From all that spirit has done for me I do not believe they would play such a silly prank. What I can say is that there must be a good reason for undertaking such a practice, and that rather than one reason I see it as at least twofold. Firstly, we can be of service in helping spirit get those who have physically died 'over' completely into their spirit plane of existence. This may or may not be an easy task, but also remember that 'all circles are healing circles', or put another way 'all circles are teaching circles'. There will be many who will be attracted by the light from the circle and who will then learn from what occurs. Secondly, it teaches those in the circle what the next plane of existence really is – that it is a plane of '**thought**'. Once that lesson is learned then they will have taken a big step forward. Going back to that day mentioned in Chapter 8, I wrote that the first took a long time, as the person did not believe that anyone would want to help him. The second, where 'Arbuthnot' was hung for stealing a sheep, he was resigned to being where he was because he thought that was what he deserved. These people, for a whole host of reasons such as fear or not realising that they have died, need to change their thinking. Once that has been achieved the rest is easy. Perhaps the words 'saving lost souls' are over emphasised, maybe Doris was nearer the truth when saying that is was more like them, "getting something off their chests".

Reincarnation is a subject that seems to spark much debate in any sort of spiritual group, with many people either very positive for it being true or equally positive in denying that such a thing can occur. When I first heard about it I had an inner feeling that it was true, and after reading many books and articles on the subject my feelings remain the same. Some believe that rather than the same spirit returning, it is one from the 'Group Soul' who incarnates and all can therefore benefit from that experience equally. However, I cannot see it just as an intellectual exercise, the 'experience' in the material world has to be experienced. Yet, I have still to come across any spirit helper or guide who gives a comprehensive and detailed account of its working. This leads me to speculate that spirit have decided to let us ponder this subject for ourselves!

A fascinating situation happened when the founder of Psychic News and Spiritualist publicist Maurice Barbanell (1902 – 1981) became the medium through whom the famous spirit 'Silver Birch' came to talk of spiritual truths and give guidance for humanity. Silver Birch did say that reincarnation exists, while his medium Barbanell held a contrary opinion, despite being told by another spirit, 'Red Cloud', that he had pledged to come back to help spread Spiritualism in a previous life. [There are a series of books on Silver Birch and his philosophy available. I have about ten of them now in my possession and highly recommend that you try to find at least one copy to read.]

This leads nicely on to mention more about a 'Life Plan'. Even when we go on a short holiday, we often have a reasonable idea of the main attractions that we want to see and the culinary, cultural and visual aspects that we wish to experience. It strikes me as crazy not to have some sort of plan for an incarnation that may last for threescore years and ten, or more! I'm sure that we have deep discussions with our guides and helpers in spirit to seek the most advantageous situations in the coming incarnation, so that the optimum benefit may be gained by oneself (and others). This would have nothing to do with material benefits, only spiritual ones. So for instance, we may decide that to advance spiritually we need to experience poverty, infirmity, rejection, or whatever will enhance our spirit light and consciousness. It may be a difficult concept for some to come to terms with, that they agreed to the real problems in their present life beforehand! However, the task is *how* they face up to these tests, and by overcoming them increase their God consciousness or spirit.

CHAPTER 21

God, Symbols and As I See It

I've mentioned that in my early life and up to the end of my teenage years God had been regularly in my thinking. Nearly twenty-five years went by without another thought, until I was 'shocked' into having to start doing it once again. This was just about the right time when many go through what is called a midlife crisis.

In 1897, on the island of Tahiti, the artist Paul Gauguin went through a crisis of his own. Disillusioned with religion, civilisation and also ill, he painted what he expected to be his last picture before attempting suicide (unsuccessfully). The title that he gave to what he believed would be his last masterpiece and artistic legacy was: *"Where do we come from? What are we? Where are we going to?"* It is a large painting full of symbols and references to the cycle of life, religion and with a central figure picking a mango that alludes to 'Eve' in the 'Garden of Eden'. Clearly Gauguin, like others before him and those alive today, was asking himself those same old questions, "What is life all about, what does my life really mean?"

When one gets to a certain age one tends to review life and often arrive at similar thoughts. Values start to change as the ageing process starts to knock at the door and the prospect of death becomes more apparent. As relatives and friends gradually begin to die and one finds oneself attending more funerals, the mind takes a more sober attitude and the material aspects to life may begin to seem less important. It is then that some people make a choice to think about death and what it may mean, while others retreat through fear into a more intense materialism.

Taking Gauguin's first question, many would state that as a species we are just evolving, natural selection being the mechanism by which this is accomplished. Others might argue that we have had a different genealogy, that at some point other beings (aliens or gods depending on your point of view) visited this planet and mixed with our ancestors. Religious fundamentalists might say that God created us in his own image. Perhaps the real answer is that at some level all these statements have a kernel of truth in them. It is obvious that human beings are evolving physically over the centuries. Personally, I have no doubt that there are other intelligent creatures on other planets in the universe, and that some of these beings from other worlds have and are visiting Earth. If God created humanity and the universe, that must include these aliens, who therefore are also made in God's own image.

The way different cultures have viewed the Gods/God throughout history is fascinating. Just taking the sheer number of names for a start: Allah; the Almighty; Alpha and Omega; Divine Principle; Brahma; Supreme Being; the Infinite; the Eternal; Creator; Preserver; Elohim; Yahweh, Jehovah; Adonai; Supreme Mind; Ra; Ptah; Amun; the Great Source; the Whole; the Ultimate; spirit; etc., etc. The multiplicity of names mirrors the difficulty of finding a word or series of words that could encompass the nature of such a deity. Humanity can only try to define God in an oblique way, like trying to describe a person from their shadow.

We 'create' God to a certain extent, at least we tend to portray 'Him' (and more often than not it has been seen as male) in such a way as to make the idea have power and a presence that we can relate to. The Ancient Egyptians seemed to have many Gods, often taking the form of an animal or bird, or partly this in combination with the human form, though in some cases they are entirely human in representation. [I suspect that all these were merely symbolic aspects of a one God to an inner core of the early priesthood and that this got lost over time – though I have no proof for this!] However the Greeks had their Gods with very human characteristics, not only with different sexes, but also with human emotions like love, anger and jealousy. I was brought up in the Christian tradition and was given the image of God as like a loving father, but with a stern side to His nature if I was not good! When I reconsidered religion after my 'awakening', I adopted the native North American term of 'Great Spirit' in order to remove the usual connotations associated with the word

'God', for many who use that term have a very different belief about God from myself.

We see the Gods as we want to see them, and as humanity has such a high opinion of itself that usually means just like us! Thankfully, I believe this is far from the reality. I remember attending a morning meditation at the Arthur Findlay College in July 2000. We were all asked to 'go into our own space' and then had to ask the question, "What am I?" I kept seeing totally clear images of children aged under two years of age, both boys and girls, some white, some black etc. The images began with just a single child and then after a short time two appeared together, then threes and fours, but at all times each and every child was smiling and clearly happy. Eventually the penny dropped and I got the message. I am a child of the universe – but just a *very* young child spiritually! Then we had to ask the question, "What are you doing here?" I saw lots of violet colour and got the answer: learning to grow.

Although humorous at the time, I knew from the clearness and the detail of those images that there was more to it than simply the obvious message about myself. Now I can comprehend that it related to the many billions of humans on this planet. Spiritually, we are but infants taking our first hesitant steps on the long, long road to enlightenment. To think that some people believe they can incarnate for less than 100 years, and then be advanced enough to spend eternity with God in Heaven! They imagine that God is human, even if superhuman. I think that Star Wars was closer to the truth, with Obi-Wan Kenobi's "May the Force be with you". With all our 'deadly sins', fears and frailties, how could God be just like us? Spirit is the ultimate creative force that is beyond one tiny aspect of It's material creation. Just for one moment think of the vast range of diversity among humans, among animals, among nature. Spirit encompasses all this and the entire material universe – and then there is the spiritual universe! Spiritually, humanity are infants taking their first faltering steps and trying to walk – with a great deal of encouragement from spirit helpers. When these guides and helpers address us as 'children' they do so because that is exactly what we are, spirit are telling us the absolute truth.

In order to get 'closer' to spirit, many groups and religions recommend the practice of meditation. It has often been explained that spirit are at a higher vibration of energy than ourselves on the material plane.

Therefore to work with us they have to lower their vibrations, and we should aim to try and raise ours; one way is through meditation. Indeed, spirit continually ask us to try this procedure. I am still working at trying to master this discipline, and the fact that it needs **discipline** is also of prime importance. Part of our learning in this material world is to use our mind to control the body rather than the other way around. Drink, sex, power, greed, drugs and even food can entrap the unwary so that the body becomes the master and the mind the slave. As discipline has less and less emphasis in children's education so comes the general increase in problems in teenage years and beyond to the detriment of them and to the wider society. Discipline of both mind and body are part of the tasks we are here to learn.

Initially meditation often starts to relax the body and brain, which, in this increasingly stressful world, is of real benefit medically. Some will use this time to contemplate on an important issue, while at other times people will carefully focus their minds on one thing – perhaps an object such as a flower or lit candle – or concentrate on their breathing. It is an exercise in looking 'into' oneself, as spirit is within as well as outside. To quote from the Bible, (St. Luke 17, 20-21):

20 And when he was demanded of the Pharisees, 'when the kingdom of God should come, he answered them and said, The kingdom of God cometh not 'with 'observation:
21 Neither 'shall they say, Lo here! Or, lo there! For, behold, the kingdom of God is 'within you.

Thus one of the symbols that was given to me early in 2007, when I had just started sitting with a circle of friends (see the first page of Chapter 12) eventually had an explanation over seven years later. That happened when I read an article in a magazine or newspaper (I have been unable to trace it) that coincided with reading a book. The title of the book is "Divine Healing of Mind and Body", and gives transcriptions of lectures that came through the trance mediumship of Murdo MacDonald-Bayne in South Africa in 1948. It is thoroughly Christian in outlook, though I have never ever heard any Christian refer to it, which is regrettable for it is a powerful illumination of many truths. It explains 'Satan', consciousness and exhorts us to become aware of the voice of God **within**. When I also read an article about a tennis ball being turned inside out in the presence of a certain medium, then the symbolic meaning of that giant mushroom became clear. We need to find the balance, find the spirit inside the material body and the spirit outside in the material world. Easier said than done you might say. Yes, indeed, but who said this life was going to be easy and what would we learn if it was? No, it is important that we apply effort and perseverance to achieve our goals. Each little victory leads us a step further on our pathway and makes us better prepared to face the next challenge ahead.

There have been many books written concerning meditation, but if you have never tried it before I suggest you try a simple example first. In a quiet place, sit comfortably with your feet flat on the ground, your back straight and your hands on your thighs or in your lap. Relax as much as you can. Close your eyes and inhale deeply, so that not only your chest but also your stomach area expands. Try to do this in a count of about five seconds, if you find this too hard reduce the number. Hold the breath briefly and then fully exhale to the same count. Repeat the process. The aim is to concentrate on the breathing – nothing else. So if your hear distracting noises, or your mind starts to wander, just bring your attention back to your breathing, remaining relaxed and calm at all times. Five minutes can be enough at the beginning, but once you get used to that, lengthen the time to ten minutes and then maybe twenty. Within a short time the breathing will become a natural rhythm and there will no longer be a need to count. It is important to perform this regularly, every day, and at the same time if this is at all possible. Gradually you will be conscious of your ability to discipline yourself and your body.

This world is our school, where we learn through experience of meeting different ideas, different people, different environments and so on. Eventually we may get to 'Primary School' level and then beyond that, but first we have to learn the very basics. The first thing we should learn is that life is better when we live in harmony together and help one another. Most of us have yet to fully understand that, look at the continual conflicts that occur year on year, century on century. We have to learn to be of service to one another and be less selfish and not so materialistic. Our ego may be necessary to live on this planet, but we must learn to have mastery over it and not inflate it. In all things we need discipline.

This is also true for the next stage, when our body dies and our mind/soul goes back to the first spirit level. Here we will still think of ourselves as human, so will still have 'our bodies' when we are welcomed by friends and relations and those we loved. For those who had lost limbs or were disfigured or diseased on earth, they will be taught to release those memories and become whole. Then we will be drawn together with those of like minds and as we gradually progress we will discover that we don't need the things of earth, not even our 'bodies' – after all we left those behind to be buried or cremated. Thought is king here; one merely has to think oneself somewhere and there one will be. However, we will all have work to do, much of it helping those who pass over into spirit, as well as some helping those still on the earth plane. After a time we may be given the choice of reincarnating back to earth or progressing to a higher spiritual level or plane of existence.

Our world now is in an ever deepening crisis, with over population, destruction of the environment, pollution of both land and sea, global warming, increasing shifts in population, less access to natural resources, increasing threats of global disease, war and terrorism, etc. All this we bring upon ourselves through ignorance, greed, and the pursuit of power. The continual search for and worship of Mammon is not just killing people physically, it is killing them spiritually as well. Only when humanity comes to understand the basic truths of life will we be able to reverse this stupidity and suicidal pathway.

The sad fact is that most of the world's population are not yet ready to receive the real truth: that **we are all one**. Spirit expresses itself through all forms and all living things; so each of us is but a small facet of spirit adding to the whole. To celebrate this fact I wrote a little ditty:

> We are all one yet each seems free,
> You and me and the chimpanzee,
> Golden eagle and bumblebee,
> Natter jack toad and old oak tree,
> Humpback whale to the smallest flea,
> Are all the same and ever will be.

I remember being told that each of us is on a journey seeking to be reunited with the Godhead, rather like us climbing different paths on our way to the mountaintop. This was satisfying, for it suggested that we all got closer together the nearer we came towards the top. Nevertheless, that image indicates a conclusion, an ending that cannot square with eternity.

The answer for me lies with the symbol that I received at a workshop with Doris on 5th December 1999. I included it near the end of Chapter 8, but will show it again.

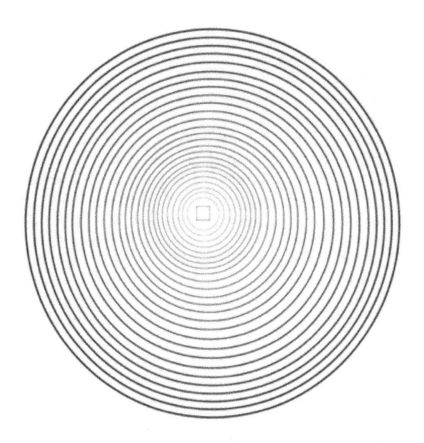

I now interpret this as the symbol of eternal progress. In the centre is the square of physical matter, where we are at present. As we evolve spiritually, so we enhance our ability to receive spirit consciousness. As we progress to higher and higher planes in spirit, so we more and more expand our consciousness and the more we emulate the Great Spirit – we become more Godlike. **That** will take eternity.

In the meantime we are undertaking a physical life to learn to bring out those qualities that will be the foundations on which we build in future incarnations as well as in the spirit realm. We learn that working together can create harmony with one another, not only individually, but also from group to group and country to country. We gradually learn the initial qualities of love through friendships, parents, grandparents, children and partnerships. We slowly find the courage to tell the truth, to stand up to injustice, to speak out against tyranny, discrimination, prejudice and corruption. We start to understand the importance of nature, and extend our love to both animals and the environment. No matter what our personal circumstances in this incarnation, it is our opportunity to try our best and do what we know to be right, without harming another aspect of spirit – another aspect of ourselves.

This learning is no easy matter and cannot be done in merely one incarnation! Just taking it in a material sense, think how long it takes one human being from birth before he or she is able to stand on their own two feet physically, emotionally and mentally, having complete command over their own life. How long does that take on average? Maybe 15/16 years perhaps, and what proportion of their life on earth is that? I would venture it was at least 1/6th of their earthly existence. Translate that in terms of spiritual existence where life is eternal – how long before we become adults spiritually? A little daunting and humbling is it not? Nevertheless, to become 'Godlike' must involve aeons from where we have started. That adventure will be thorough and extensive, but so worthwhile. For now, we have to learn as toddlers, often hurting ourselves when we fall over or blunder into something. Spirit is there to help us, to surround us with love and encouragement, guiding us gently forward.

I have tried in this book to show how much spirit has given to me despite having no ability or knowledge at the start; I was just an ordinary person. Spirit have helped and guided me because I had an **open mind** and was genuinely interested in seeking the 'truth'. You also have helpers around you who will gladly assist in your search; I earnestly press on you to do so if you have not yet started. I hope that you have found something of interest, something to think about in this book, and wish you all the best on this wonderful journey.

That only leaves me to thank all who have helped to bring this book into being, and especially in this context I would like to thank Brenda Dougall and Jim Cunningham. I could also mention others who have impinged on my life in both practical and philosophical ways, but there are too many. All I can do is to record my deep appreciation to those fellow travellers in life who have enriched my own.

Apart from adding a book list, the final words are not actually my own, but from spirit – from Ho-Lin:

"It is often said that a wise man listens rather than speaks. If, however, a wise man never spoke how would others share his knowledge? The knowledge he had been given and gained throughout his life. It is the duty of the wise man to share his knowledge with all who wish to listen. Not to share would be selfish and inconsiderate. It is the right of all to receive, if they so wish, the best advice and guidance that we can give them directly, or through one of our instruments of communication. It is therefore your duty my friend to share what we have given you. The advice and guidance was not for you alone, so is not yours to keep. You must remember though that it is not your duty, or our wish, for you to mould the mind of the receiver but simply to light the flame and allow the mind of the receivers to plan and follow their own pathway. We ask you to relay our words to those we bring together through you, so that they, when the time comes for them to pass on the knowledge they have acquired, will in turn relay these same words to others seeking knowledge. So it will continue. It is a very clear, simple request that we make. We now leave you with our blessing and seal on the service you endeavour to give, the pathway you endeavour to tread and the lessons you endeavour to learn."

BOOK LIST

For those new to this area, I thought it might be helpful to give a selection of books old and new, in no particular order, on a variety of subjects that I have found interesting.

"Spirit Healing" – Harry Edwards
"Life in Spirit" – Harry Edwards
"Abu Talks" Volumes 1 and 2
"A Journey of Psychic Discovery" – Alan E. Crossley
"A Lawyer Presents The Evidence For The Afterlife" – Victor & Wendy
    Zammit
"Alec Harris" – Louie Harris
"Ancient Egypt Speaks" – A.J.H. Hulme and F.H. Wood
"Autobiography Of A Yogi" – Paramhansa Yogananda
"Divine Healing Of Mind And Body" – Murdo MacDonald-Bayne
"Not I, Not other than I" The Life and Spiritual Teachings of Russel
    Williams; edited by Steve Taylor
"Faces Of The Living Dead" – Paul Miller (Psychic art of Frank Leah)
Silver Birch: "The Teachings of Silver Birch"
    "Guidance from Silver Birch"
    "Philosophy of Silver Birch"
    "More Philosophy of Silver Birch"
    "Light from Silver Birch"
    "Silver Birch Companion"
    "A Voice in the Wilderness"
    "The Seed of Truth"
    "The Spirit Speaks"
    "Lift up your Hearts"

"The Universe of Silver Birch"

"The Silver Birch Book of Questions and Answers"

"The Silver Birch Anthology"

"The Psychic Bridge" – Jane Sherwood

"Post-Mortem Journal" – Jane Sherwood

"The Country Beyond" – Jane Sherwood

"The Spirit Within" – 'Chan' through the trance mediumship of Ivy Northage

"Light Of The World" – as above

"Spiritual Realisation" – as above

"The Road to Immortality" – Geraldine Cummins

"Beyond Human Personality" – Geraldine Cummins

"They Survive" – Geraldine Cummins

"On the Edge Of The Etheric" – Arthur Findlay

"More Truth" – communicated by Arthur Findlay

"The Imprisoned Splendour" – Raynor C. Johnson

"Unfinished Symphonies" – Rosemary Brown

"Wisdom Of Ramadahn" – Ursula Roberts

"More Wisdom of Ramadahn" – Ursula Roberts

"Truths of the Spirit World", Volumes 1 to 7, through Ursula Roberts

"Your Healing Power" – Jack Angelo

"The Search" – Gertrude Clendenning

"Inevitable Journey" – Donald Galloway

"Voices In The Dark" the mediumship of Leslie Flint

"Steps To Eternity" – Elizabeth Baxandall

"Listen My Son" – Harry Emerson

"The Boy Who Saw True"

"The Dark Star" – Lord Dowding

"Many Mansions" – Gina Cerminara

"Life After Death – Living Proof" – Tom Harrison

"Memories of a Physical Medium" – Stewart Alexander

"Physical Séance Room Recollections" Double CD, from the Stewart Alexander Archives

"The Golden Thread" – Robert Goodwin

"Natural And Supernatural" – Brian Inglis (A History of the Paranormal from Earliest Times to 1914)

"Great Moments Of Modern Mediumship" Vol 1 – Maxine Meilleur

"What is Karma?" – Paul Brunton

"The Inner Reality" – Paul Brunton

"The Light Beyond" – Raymond A. Moody, JR, M.D.

"Many Lives, Many Masters" – Dr. Brian Weiss

"Same Soul, Many Bodies" – Dr. Brian Weiss

"Karma and Rebirth" – Christmas Humphreys

"Edgar Cayce's Story of the Origin and Destiny of Man" – Lytle W. Robinson

"A Forgotten Truth" – D.M.A. Leggett and M.G. Payne

"A Path Prepared" The Story of Isa Northage - Allan MacDonald